P9-DMD-276

Theories of the
CHAKRAS:

Cover Art: *Jane Evans*
Illustrations: *Marylou Draper*

Theories of the CHAKRAS:
Bridge to Higher Consciousness

By Hiroshi Motoyama

*This publication made possible
with the assistance of the Kern Foundation*

The Theosophical Publishing House
Wheaton, Ill. U.S.A.
Madras, India/London, England

© Copyright 1981 by Hiroshi Motoyama
Third printing 1988
A Quest original. All rights reserved
No part of this book may be reproduced in any
manner without written permission except for quota-
tions embodied in critical articles or reviews.

For additional information write to:
The Theosophical Publishing House
306 West Geneva Road
Wheaton, Illinois 60187

Published by the Theosophical Publishing House,
a department of the Theosophical Society in America.

Library of Congress Cataloging in Publication Data

Motoyama, Horoshi, 1925
  Theories of the Chakras

  "A Quest book."
  Includes index.
  1. Chakras. 2. Yoga. I. Title.
BL1215 . C45M67   294.5'43   81-51165
ISBN 0-8356-0551-5 (pbk.)   AACR2

Printed in the United States of America

Contents

Foreword

It gives me great pleasure to introduce the work of Dr. Hiroshi Motoyama to the scholars, scientists, and spiritual seekers of the English-speaking world. For those who are already acquainted with current investigations into yoga and the psychic and spiritual sciences, Dr. Motoyama will need no introduction. His preeminence and reputation as a scientist are well known, for he is foremost amongst researchers in this field at the present time. His pioneering discoveries during the last ten years have carried orthodox science to the threshold of the spiritual dimension, and will serve as a basis for future investigations into the greater potentials inherent within the framework of the human body-mind. The practices of yoga and tantra which will awaken those greater potentials will become the quest of scientists during this century.

This present book—*Theories of the Chakras: Bridge to Higher Consciousness*—is an outstanding document from both the scientific and spiritual points of view. In the first place, it presents a unique and authentic record of the spiritual experiences of an adept in whom the kundalini has been awakened by yogic practices. And second, it is the unique record of the pioneering experiments conducted at the In-

8

stitute for Religious Psychology, Tokyo, which presents clear, electro-physiological evidence of the existence of the network of chakras and nadis which form the infra-structure of the subtle energies existing in the pranic and psychic dimensions, which underlie and activate the physical, material body of man.

Dr. Motoyama's experiments successfully integrate the subjective and objective dimensions of knowledge, and will serve as guideposts and blueprints for experiments in the years ahead. If secrets of the universe are to be revealed, the spiritual dimension must first be breached and science must emerge from its present limitations of the material dimension.

In this respect, Dr. Motoyama's experiments are uniquely valuable. The awakening of kundalini is the most monumental experience an individual can undergo in life, which brings into operation another dimension of awareness. At the physical level, kundalini manifests as a higher voltage of energy conducted through the nervous system, resulting in a wider range of activity of the various systems of the physical body, and heightened awareness and capabilities.

The altered states of physiological functioning associated with awakening of each chakra are quite distinct from disease conditions, although they may produce a variety of physical and mental symptoms which may temporarily imitate them. This fact must become clear to physicians, scientists, and healers. Dr. Motoyama has himself experienced the awakening of kundalini and has presented an analytical record of that transition in the state of awareness. Furthermore, he has devised laboratory equipment so as to demonstrate the psycho-physiological parameters of an awakened kundalini in experimental subjects, thus paving the way for scientists of the future.

The awakening of kundalini is an experience which accelerates an individual toward the conscious fulfillment of his purpose and role in life. Through scientific means, Dr. Motoyama has clarified the knowledge and experience of kundalini so that others may be able to understand. His remarkable contribution elevates the status of kundalini from that of a religious or mystical myth into a psychological and electro-physiological event which can be demonstrated and recorded by scientific evaluation. Scientists, and humanity as a whole, are indeed fortunate that he has undertaken such a formidable task.

I believe this present work to be the most revolutionary scientific discovery since the relativity theory superseded Newton's model of the universe. Due to the genius of an enlightened mystic of science, Dr. Albert Einstein, the world has entered the nuclear era. Dr. Einstein projected his awareness into the subjective realms in order to conduct his famous "thought experiments" on the nature of light, and as a result, the orthodox model of the universe was modified and revised. At that time, as scientists strained to grasp the implications unlocked by the equation $E = mc^2$, a fantastic vision of the transformation of matter and the liberation of energy which underlies the manifested created world was awakened. Yet today the same concepts of nuclear fission and fusion are grasped by children of ten or twelve years of age in their elementary science classes at school. What better example can be cited as evidence of the evolving awareness or consciousness of man?

Man now stands at the doorway of the spiritual dimension. Within the next few years many scientists will validate the theory of kundalini and the chakras. Dr. Motoyama is a visionary scientist of Einstein's calibre. Just as Einstein unlocked the vision of the pranic dimension to reveal the energy underlying material creation, so too Dr. Motoyama's investigations have clarified the next step in the evolutionary transformation of the awareness of mankind as a whole. Insight into the dimension of spiritual energy is now only a step away from scientists who already can detect the activity of kundalini through their laboratory experiments and instruments, due to Dr. Motoyama's far-reaching contribution.

Entering the spiritual dimension

The kundalini is awakening in man and it is imperative that the scientists recognize and record this transformation in the structure and function of the human nervous system. The awakening of the higher human faculties and capacities can no longer be denied or disregarded by scientific orthodoxy. Man is standing in the upper echelon of the evolutionary pyramid. Those at the pinnacle possess an array of "supernormal" mental and psychic capacities of which the average man has little or no comprehension. They are devoting themselves to hastening the evolution of humanity which is suffering from physical, mental, and psychic ills. It is the destiny of mankind in the cosmic scheme to take the leap into the spiritual dimension, just as it was once the destiny of primitive life forms to emerge from the ocean onto the earth's surface. Our predecessors — animals — are similarly destined to rise up and assume an upright posture. Without that tremendous evolutionary step, man could never have become a cultivator or herdsman, he could have never mastered fire or language, and he would never have acquired color vision.

A similar situation exists today, and we have to reconsider human evolution in this light. Darwin's evolutionary theory is sound, but why aren't its logical conclusions recognized today? We have yet to become the 'supermen' of tomorrow, but unless we know how to speed up the process it can still take very many more lifetimes and maybe a few million more years. In the past, man's vision was clouded by the restrictive religious, cultural, and social concepts. Even today, this conditioning continues to influence our ideas of what we are and the role we play in hastening our evolutionary destiny.

Irrespective of their academic standing, scientists, psychologists, and physiologists have no more idea about their ultimate purpose or destiny, nor do they know how to realize it. As a whole, mankind as yet remains virtually unaware of its evolutionary potentials and possibilities.

Within each one of us there exists an animal, a human, and a divine being; these are the three dimensions of our existence. Our present state is not the ultimate one; we stand at an intermediate stage or platform. For centuries man has been living in one restricted frame of mind and because of this limitation evolution came virtually to a standstill. Only now are the Western cultures emerging from an extended period of darkness in which their men of vision and genius were executed or persecuted for heretical religious or political reasons, and in that climate of distrust, fear, and violence the spiritual knowledge was suppressed. Now the veil is lifting and man is once again exploring the possibilities of expanding his consciousness. The climate is changing, and mankind has become more receptive to new ideas.

Although at the present time we may not really know which way to go, as a whole, we are now definitely aware of something that is existing beyond the mind. Although we may not know how to realize or develop that perception, yet we have reached the conclusion that this mind cannot be the ultimate vehicle of knowledge. One thing is clear — man has to make a transition. We are not the first, nor are we the last expression in the evolutionary process. Perhaps we are standing at the crossroads. Perhaps this human life cycle can be made to serve as a springboard for the leap out of the evolutionary cycle. Today there are great scholars, but their statements are limited by their finite minds. There are brilliant philosophers, but their philosophy is subject to the limitations of their minds.

If man can jump over his mind, he will experience an absolutely new dimension of existence and his thinking about creation, the purpose of life, and so on. What appear to be true definitions today may be challenged in the future and fall in the light of newer discoveries. What is the assurance that we know the truth today? How can we know that our present concepts of man and creation are correct? If our vision is to be complete and truthful, we must have the requisite eyes — the eyes of intuition, of higher consciousness. There are faculties in man which he has not been able to express as yet; yet, these potentials lie dormant in every person. How can they be awakened? For an ignorant man, the mind is ultimate; but for a wise man, mind is a stage between and it is possible to transcend mind altogether and simultaneously give forth the finest expression of his creative energy. Man can exist without a mind, provided he has discovered another mind behind this mind.

Not only in this century, but for ages past man has been exploring the possibilities of expanding the frontiers of his consciousness. Not everyone is aware of the limitations of the personal mind, and there are millions of people even today who are not at all aware. Nevertheless, there have always been those who have tried to go beyond its confines. That process, that experience, has always been with man and is known in India as *tantra*.

In order to understand tantra, the concept of mind has to be defined. In everyday life, mind has come to mean the means by which man thinks and feels. Psychology has also similarly defined the mind. In tantra and yoga, however, mind means something quite different. Here, mind is termed as *chitta* which literally means awareness, and this term encompasses awareness on all the different levels of existence. The objective awareness is one of these levels; subjective awareness is another; absence of awareness is another.

Mind is not thought, emotion, or memory as is commonly believed. Individual mind is part of the universal mind, a part of what we know as total mind. What is this total mind? It is composed of a type of proto-matter and has two opposite poles known as time and space. Time and space are actually only categories of the mind. It is only in the orthodox or conventional way of thinking that time and space are considered to have a separate existence, different from the universal mind. Every form of matter has a nucleus, and so also has the mind.

On the material plane scientists have managed to liberate energy from the nucleus of matter by a process of fission. In the same way, yogis and spiritual adepts have been exploring ways similarly to liberate the energy from the nucleus of the mind and the material body. So long as time and space remain separated, nothing can emerge from the universal mind, but when time and space come close to each other, then the universal mind becomes a creative force. Although the individual mind is a part of the universal mind, nevertheless it still preserves its own nucleus. When this is exploded the individual attains enlightenment. Tantra and yoga have been practiced in India for aeons, in order to explode this nucleus and directly experience the universal mind.

The re-emergence of tantra

The subject matter of consciousness, its investigation and discovery, is known as tantra. It is a vast science in which every method of expanding the conscious experience has been explored. It has always been with man, ever since he began to probe the mysteries of his own existence. Tantra is not an Indian philosophy. There was a time when tantra was the spiritual practice of men and women of every continent. Evidence exists that prior to the Atlantean civilization, tantra was practiced in order to gain a greater vision and experience of reality. Tantra is the ancient spiritual heritage of mankind. Through accidents of history, civilization lost touch with the tantric tradition during the dark ages of the kali yuga. Now the Western civilizations are emerging from several hundred years of darkness, when a climate of distrust, fear, and hatred prevailed and during which tantra was suppressed. Now the religious and political climate is changing and tantra is re-emerging around the world.

Tantra has survived the tests of time and history because it is not a philosophy but a scientific system whereby man can improve the structure and quality of his body and mind, and through which he can transform his ailing personality. Although the system of tantra is most controversial and has been widely misrepresented, this great and sublime science has not been truly and accurately presented. It is necessary to explain how tantra brings about a metamorphosis in the entire structure of the personal consciousness.

What is expansion of consciousness? Expansion means the breaking down of the limitations of the individual mind. The senses provide the stimuli and the mind functions on the basis of their stimuli. This is the limitation of the ordinary human consciousness, because the sense perceptions are dependent on the quality of the sensory nervous system. Is cognition a quality of the mind or is it dependent on the stimuli that are sent to the brain? According to tantra, consciousness is considered a homogeneous entity. Even without the association of the senses it is possible to have knowledge, cognition, and perception. Normally, we don't possess this supersensory perception because our consciousness is not given the opportunity to experience its homogeneous nature. The mind, the consciousness, is homogeneous, but the whole consciousness is not functioning. If we know how to activate the silent areas of consciousness, the homogeneous state of the universal mind can be experienced and we can achieve total awareness.

Within this physical body there is a mundane source of energy through which the brain, the body, and mind function. In addition to this, there is a transcendental source of energy known as kundalini. In tantra, kundalini yoga is practiced in order to liberate this energy and illumine the entire consciousness. It is a system which activates the entire psychophysiological structure. Dr. Motoyama's experiments clearly define the existence of the chakras which act as switches for the higher centres in the brain.

Call to scientists

Today kundalini is being discussed in every society, language, and country in the world. Young scientists especially should dedicate themselves to recognizing and understanding the effects of kundalini — in themselves and in others. The scientists and medical men must form a bridge between the subjective inner dimension of spiritual awareness and the empirical dimension of science as Einstein, Itzhak Bentov, and Dr. Motoyama have done. Now it is time to step boldly forward and investigate scientifically the experience of kundalini. Its awakening is a psychophysiological event as well as a spiritual reality. Investigation into its vast potential is the newest frontier of science. Imagine the far-ranging benefits in the treatment of diseases when it is scientifically revealed that specific sounds and forms (mantras and yantras) can activate the physiological and physical body systems.

Scientific experiments to evaluate and determine the effects of the practices of tantra and yoga will vastly accelerate man's evolution. I have absolute conviction and faith in the far-ranging effects of yoga to heal man's sick body and refine his personality and transform his level of conscious awareness. Dr. Motoyama has bridged the gap and demonstrated the scientific reality of kundalini and the resulting boon for mankind.

Yoga will emerge as a mighty world power and will change the course of world events.

Hari Om Tat Sat.

Swami Satyananda Saraswati,
Founder, Bihar School of Yoga,
Monghyr (Bihar), India
30 June 1981

Acknowledgements

I am truly grateful that this book is now appearing in English, published by the Theosophical Publishing House.

In the United States, material civilization has reached a highly developed state, perhaps the most advanced in the world; now it is time for Americans to realize the importance of spiritual advancement, to cultivate true spiritual growth. It is my fervent wish that this book will help further this goal, in America and throughout the English-speaking world.

This book could not have been written without the work of my predecessors — Arthur Avalon, C. W. Leadbeater, and others who first presented the chakras to the reading public. I am especially grateful to Ganesh and Company of Madras, India for their kind permission to quote from Avalon's *The Serpent Power*, and to Swami Satyananda Saraswati, whose Bihar School of Yoga publications form the basis of the chapters of Yoga practice, and also Chapter VIII.

The manuscript was completed through the cooperation of many people. I would like to thank especially Dr. Toshiaki Harada, ex-staff researcher, and Miss Kiyomi Kuratani, the Head of the Translation Department at the Institute, for preparing the original translation, and also the latter for her diligent editorial help; Mr. Arthur H. Thornhill III of Har-

17

vard University, who delayed work on his doctoral disserta-
tion to rewrite the manuscript; and Mrs. Rande Brown
Ouchi, who assisted in the rewriting and made many
valuable suggestions. I would also like to express gratitude
for her efforts in presenting my work to Western readers in
Science and the Evolution of Consciousness, published by
Autumn Press, 1978. Finally, special thanks to Ms.
Rosemarie Stewart of the Theosophical Publishing House for
her editorial services and helpful advice.

Hiroshi Motoyama
Institute for Religious Psychology, Tokyo
July, 1981

Introduction

This introduction is intended primarily for those approaching the subject matter of this book for the first time, in the hope that it will help clarify the content of what follows.

In India, the techniques and practices of Tantra Yoga—an esoteric branch of yoga—have been handed down for thousands of years. Among them, there is a group of methods for awakening the Kundalinī and the chakras. Through this awakening, the practitioner is said to be able to transcend ordinary human limitations and to evolve into a free and immortal being fully aware of the world and of an existence where there is no death. In the course of Indian history, a number of great saints have appeared who have attained this highest stage of spirital enlightenment through the methods of Tantric Yoga or their equivalents (Shakyamuni Buddha, for instance). It is precisely these methods that this book attempts to describe and elucidate. This introduction will give a general description of what is meant by "exoteric" and "esoteric," by "chakra" and "nādī," and by "the body" and "the mind".

19

The Esoteric and the Exoteric: Yin and Yang

Everything has two aspects; a surface aspect, which is exposed to light, and an interior, hidden aspect which is not so exposed. A plant, for example, has above the ground a stem, branches, and leaves which are warmed and lit by the sun, whereas its roots are underground, untouched by any beam of sunlight. In winter, the portion above ground may appear to have died; but as spring brings its warmth, the branches burst with life, fresh green leaves appear, and buds open. None of this could happen were it not for the roots, the hidden part of the plant. It is the unexposed roots that supply the energy to sustain the portion that lives out in the snow, rain, wind, and sun, and it is thanks to the roots that this part returns from its wintry state to life. The latent, dark, unexposed aspect of things is known in Chinese philosophy as "yin", while "yang" is the name given to the patent, the bright, the exposed.

Similarly, all religions have both a yang aspect and a yin aspect. The yang aspect, that which is open, public, and generally known, is called the exoteric aspect. Yang/exoteric teachings speak of God, Buddha, or the Absolute in terms of their relationship to this world, the world of concrete forms. God, Buddha, and other deities are presented in ways comprehensible to the average man. Shakyamuni and Kannon (Avalokiteshvāra) in Buddhism, God the Father in Christianity, and Amaterasu Ōmikami in Shintoism are just such examples. These deities are all said to be at work for man's salvation and the maintenance of peace in the world. The exoteric part of religion, therefore, represents man's faith and devotion to deities working in close proximity to the physical world. It is religion centered on the world of human beings.

In contrast, the yin aspect of religion, that is, the inner, hidden part, is what we term the esoteric. This phase of religion is centered on the world of deities rather than ordinary humans. The ultimate goal of esoteric teachings is to elevate human beings to a state where they are no longer merely human, but have become transcendent beings themselves. In the esoteric branches of religion, methods designed specifically for the transformation of human beings into greater beings are taught and practiced under the strict supervision of qualified teachers.

In Christianity, then, it is possible to regard Protestantism as the exoteric teaching and the sacraments of Catholicism as the esoteric. In Japanese Buddhism, the Jōdo and Shin sects can be considered exoteric and Shingon Buddhism esoteric. In the yogic tradition, hatha yoga and kriyā yoga, both of which emphasize control of the physical body, are exoteric, and tantra yoga, the hidden core of all the different types of yoga, is esoteric.

The Three Bodies and The Three Minds of Tantra Yoga

The legend behind the existence of tantra yoga is that it was created and taught to mankind by the Lord Shiva. Lord Shiva, known as the Destroyer, ranks with Lord Brahma, the Creator, and Lord Vishnu, the Maintainer, as one of the three great Gods of Indian religious teaching. The tantra yoga given by Shiva provides the means whereby a man can transcend himself and attain a state of being unified with and equal to that of God, the Absolute, Himself.

According to the teachings of tantra yoga, man has three bodies and three associated minds, one in each of the three major dimensions of being. During spiritual growth, a man must ascend the evolutionary ladder through these dimensions step by step, gradually increasing his awareness of the higher realms. In this way man can liberate himself from the limitations of the three bodies and their corresponding minds, finally entering the kingdom of God.

Specifically, the three bodies and the three minds are:

a) the physical body and its mind, i.e., the consciousness that operates in association with the physical body;

b) the astral (subtle) body and its mind, i.e., the consciousness that we experience primarily as emotions and feelings; and

c) the causal body and its mind, i.e., the consciousness that is expressed mainly as intelligence and wisdom.

Of these three, the physical body and its mind exist and work in the tangible world. This set, then, might be termed yang in relation to the other two, those that cannot be known by either the physical senses or the thinking rooted in physical sensations. This yang part, however, is in fact sustained and kept alive by the hidden yin aspects—the astral and the causal.

The Chakras and Nādīs

The three body/mind sets exist and operate in different dimensions, each maintained by the type of prāna (vital energy) necessary for and appropriate to that dimension. This does not mean they are separate entities, but rather that they are parts of an organic whole. Each body-mind has within itself energy centers for controlling the flow of prāna and a system of energy channels. These channels are called nādīs, and the centers controlling them are known as "chakras". In the physical body, the channels are represented by the cardio-vascular, lymphatic, and acupuncture meridian systems,* and the centers are represented by the

---

* Acupuncture Meridian System: In acupuncture theory, developed in China, Ki or vital force is considered to circulate in the human body through a systematic network of energy channels. These channels are usually referred to as "meridians".

brain, the nervous plexuses, and the acupuncture points. The corresponding centers and channels of all three bodies are closely interrelated.

Besides being a control center in each dimension, a chakra works as a center of interchange between the physical and the astral, and between the astral and the causal dimensions. Through the chakras, subtle prana in the astral body can be transformed, for instance, into energy for the physical dimension, thereby providing the physical body with essential life energy. Some of the most spectacular examples of this particular transformation are seen in the cases of yogis who have been buried underground for incredible lengths of time and yet remained alive. This is thought to be possible through the action of the Vishuddhi (throat) chakra which, when activated, supposedly enables a person to subsist on astral energy in the form of "ambrosia". This energy comes into the physical body from the Bindu visarga (see Chap. VIII) of the astral body, and can be induced through a technique of halting respiration known as khechari-mudrā. The astral energy is then materialized as the oxygen, protein, fat, etc., necessary for the maintenance of life, enabling the person to survive even if buried.

It is further thought that physical energy can be transformed into astral energy through the work of the chakras, and that physical energy can be converted into psychological energy (ojas) within the physical dimension.

Thus, the chakra is seen to be an intermediary for energy transfer and conversion between two neighboring dimensions of being, as well as a center facilitating the energy conversion between a body and its corresponding mind.

As the chakras are activated and awakened, man not only becomes aware of the higher realms of existence, but also gains the power to enter those realms, and then, in turn, to support and give life to the lower dimensions.

The Location of the Chakras and Their Functions

There are seven chakras. In the early stages of awakening, the chakras are usually perceived as wheels of light, or local auras, of various colors. The locations, colors, and physical functions of the chakras may be summarized as follows.

Mūlādhāra chakra: In the area of the coccyx. Perceived as a disc of red light. Controls the genito-urinary system.

Svādhishthāna chakra: 3-5 centimeters below the navel, usually perceived as a disc of vermillion light. Also controls the genito-urinary system.

Manipūra chakra: Around the navel. Perceived as a disc of blue or green light.

As an aside, it is interesting to note that in acupuncture there is an important point located at the navel called the shinketsu point (shencheh, CV8).* This is thought to be the point where divine energy flows in and out of the body. The yoga teaching is similar to this. It claims that the prāna for the entire physical body enters from higher dimensions through the kandasthāna, a spherical region around the navel enclosing the manipūra chakra. The prāna is then converted into physiological energy and distributed throughout the body by way of physical nādīs for the maintenance of life.

---

* In this book the Japanese name, the Chinese name and the standardized number for each acupuncture point are given. For example, chukan (chung-wan, CV12) refers to the twelfth point on the conception vessel meridian, pronounced "chukan" in Japanese and "chung-wan" in Chinese. The exact location of the points may be found in any standard acupuncture reference work. The abbreviations for the meridians are as follows: LU, lung meridian; LI, large intestine meridian; ST, stomach meridian; SP, spleen meridian; HT, heart meridian, UB, urinary bladder meridian; KI, kidney meridian; HC, heart constrictor meridian; TH, triple heater meridian; GB, gall bladder meridian; LV, liver meridian; GV, governor vessel meridian; and CV, conception vessel meridian.

Anāhata chakra: Near the intersection of the median line and a line connecting the two nipples. Also called the heart chakra. Perceived as a disc of intense red or golden light. Controls the heart.

The corresponding acupuncture point is the danchū point (shanchung, CV 17) on the conception vessel meridian.

Vishuddhi chakra: In the throat. Perceived as a disc of violet light. Controls the respiratory organs.

Ajnā chakra: Between the eyebrows. Commonly known as the third eye. Perceived as a disc of white light of great intensity. This chakra controls the secretory functions of the pituitary gland as well as intellectual activities. It is said that when this chakra is awakened, one meets one's own divine self, i.e., the True Self.

Sahasrāra chakra: Located at the top of the head. This chakra is in overall control of every aspect of the body and mind. When the "Gate of Brahman" in this chakra is opened, one can leave the physical body and enter the realms of the astral or the causal. This chakra is perceived as a large disc of golden or rosy light.

The prāna absorbed at these seven chakras is distributed in the appropriate form and dimension throughout the three bodies and minds by the network of nādīs. Let us now turn to a discussion of these channels.

The Nādīs in the Physical Body

It has not yet been clearly determined just how many nādīs exist. Some teachings speak of a total of 72,000 while others say there are as many as 340,000. Nevertheless, all available teachings cite ten or fourteen nādīs as being more important than the rest. Of these, special importance is attached to the three major nādīs—the *Sushumnā,* the *Idā,* and the *Pingalā.* Among the modern researchers engaged in physiological or anatomical studies of yoga, there are many who contend that the nādīs are represented in the physical body by the nervous system. They theorize that the sushumnā corresponds to the spinal cord and the idā and pingalā to the sympathetic nerve trunks located on either side of the spinal cord. This interpretation sounds plausible at first, but a study of the ancient expositions of the nādīs in the Upanishads and other yoga classics makes the theory difficult to accept.

According to the Upanishads and other sources, the sushumnā lies in the central canal of the spinal cord, and has an opening at the Gate of Brahman. Anatomically speaking, the central canal of the spinal cord contains no nerve fibers, only cerebro-spinal fluid. It is also neurologically impossible for the spinal cord to have an opening at the top of the head for the inflow and outflow of the prāna.

The governor vessel meridian, as known in acupuncture, shows clearer correspondence within the sushumnā. The energy flow in this meridian starts at the tip of the coccyx, ascends the spine, reaches a point at the top of the head called hyakue (paihui, GV20), and then courses down along the median line to a point just below the navel. The energy flowing in this meridian is said to be of the yang type and to control the whole body—which is what is said about the sushumnā. Furthermore, in acupuncture theory, the Ki (Ch'i) energy of the cosmos is said to flow in and out through the hyakue point, which would seem to correspond to the Brahman gate. Thus, the sushumnā shows a closer correspondence with the governor vessel meridian than with the spinal cord.

As for the idā and pingalā, the ancient writings state that they start at either side of the Mūlādhara chakra (in the perineum) and terminate at either nostril. This clearly differs from the anatomical description of sympathetic nervous trunks, which do not start or end in these locations. On the other hand, the second lines of the urinary bladder meridian, which lie on either side of the spinal column, are known to course by the perineum and to terminate beside the root of the nose.

To summarize the similarities between the teachings about the nāḍīs of yoga and the meridians of Chinese medicine:

- They are both channels of vital energy, i.e., prāna or Ki.
- The courses of the energy flow in them bear a close mutual resemblance.
- Many of the functions they perform are the same. (This will be discussed in detail in later chapters.)

The nāḍīs of the physical body and the acupuncture meridians may therefore be considered essentially the same.

How, then, did anyone—ancient or modern—come to discover the nāḍīs and the meridians? First, the masters of acupuncture, moxibustion, and massage were able to discern intuitively the existence of meridians, or rather of energy flow, during treatment of patients. The color and condition of the body surface, changes of body temperature, etc., all probably served to give hints as to the existence of the energy flow.

Second, both yogis and acupuncturists became aware of the internal energy flow through a kind of extrasensory perception during meditation. Much is written in the literature to substantiate this view, specifically in *The Yellow Emperor's Treatise on Internal Medicine (Huang Ti Nei Ching)* and various sūtras of yoga.

Awakening of the Chakras

A detailed exposition of the changes that arise in the body and mind when a chakra is awakened will be given in later chapters. Here two brief examples will be offered as sample illustrations.

When the manipūra chakra is in the process of awakening, the area around the navel feels filled with energy and power, and any digestive malfunction shows improvement. There may also be a sensation of tremendous heat gathering around the navel or inside the abdomen. At such times, a disc of varicolored light (e.g., red, blue, and gold) is perceived inside the abdomen or in front of the center of the eyebrows. There are usually some psychological changes as well—the emotions are enriched, sensitivity is increased, and the capacity for sympathy with others and the ability to control the emotions develop.

Prior to the awakening of the anāhata chakra, as another instance, there may be frequent pain in the front of the chest or an irregular functioning of the heart, such as an accelerated pulse. During meditation, a disc of deep vermillion or golden light is perceived in front of the heart or at the point between the eyebrows. Further, voices or sounds coming from other worlds are heard. A buzzing sound like that of bees and a sound resembling that of a flute are common. An attitude of optimism becomes constant. No matter what kind of difficulty may be encountered, there is no feeling of disquiet, but one of ease and confidence and the knowledge that the situation will somehow improve. Also, the feeling of love for others becomes intensified. Psychokinetic (PK) ability—the ability of the mind to control matter directly or to achieve certain objectives pictured in the imagination—begins to manifest itself, thereby making healing the sick possible.

By activating and awakening the chakras through the right methods, a person can evolve into and enjoy the higher realms of being. Tantra yoga offers systematic methods of awakening these chakras properly without danger. Detailed results with explanation of physiological and physical experiments conducted on individuals who, through correct tantric yoga practice, have awakened chakras, undergone physical and psychological changes, and consequently developed certain paranormal abilities, will be given in the last chapter of this book.

These experimental results imply that man can uplift himself and evolve to a higher state of being.

It is my earnest wish that this book will enable readers to be correctly informed, to learn the proper methods of practice, and to awaken in themselves awareness of the existence of the higher dimensional worlds.

There are those who may claim that it is too grandiose a wish for us humans to become more than human. But it must be stated that this wish is neither impossible nor too dangerous, as long as the correct practices are performed without error. It should also be added that the guidance of a qualified teacher is essential in case difficulties are encountered along the way. In such cases, if no other qualified person is available to the reader, he should feel free to inquire without hesitation at this institute, The Institute for Religious Psychology, where instruction and guidance in the awakening of the chakras is given on a regular basis.

I
The Practice
of
Tantra Yoga

The Purpose of Yoga

The purpose of yogic disciplines has been described in a great variety of ways: as the discovery of Truth, as the realization of the Self, as the realization of the identity of Brahman and Atman, as the unification of man and God. These descriptions all point to the underlying concepts of yoga. For the purposes of this book, however, we will use the following definition: yoga is a means of achieving union with the inner True Self, the God within.

The Sanskrit word "yoga" has two meanings. The first of these, "union", implies harmony, unity, and stability. The second meaning, "yoke" (as used to link oxen drawing a wagon), signifies the unification of the individual self with the divine. This unification is possible through concentration upon a sacred symbol or entity, such as a chakra, mandala, or mantra, or simply upon the inner True Self. The realization of this goal necessitates the complete negation of the individual, discrete self which is an obstruction between the seeker and his goal of complete freedom. Only when the negation of individuality is attained can the aspirant begin to live in a higher dimension in which all things, including the individual self, are encompassed as one. From this union springs true life, and in it lies the gateway to spiritual liberation. Understood in this way, self-negation and self-realization are in no sense contradictory. As one continues to elevate his or her level of existence through continued practice, union with God—the ultimate goal of Yoga—can eventually be realized.

In our ordinary perception of reality, subject and object exist as distinct, discrete entities. Indeed, science is based upon the contradistinction of subject and object. A scientist attempts to observe phenomena in a precise fashion and formulate laws which explain what he has observed. The observing subject himself, however, is not considered; the knowledge obtained is therefore knowledge about the object only, and not the subject who has recognized and perceived the object. In this sense science does not examine the entire field of observation and its knowledge is thus incomplete.

In contrast, knowledge obtained through the unity of subject and object takes into account the reality of both, and the profound universal oneness from which they arise. This union of subject and object—present in the state called Samādhi—is a major goal of yogic practice. In scientific work, an object is perceived through the filter of the five sensory organs. However, when the subject, which confronts and stands in opposition to the object, is negated and transcended the essential nature of the object may be perceived directly by the superconscious, rather than through the sensory organs. This form of knowing may be called wisdom. It is the purpose of yoga to reach the state of oneness of subject and object in which true wisdom exists.

The activation of the chakras is an indispensable means to realize this goal. The techniques for chakra awakening, a part of tantra yoga, enhance the functions of both mind and body, and are the most effective way to develop "siddhis". Although commonly defined as "miraculous powers", siddhis are best understood as faculties bestowed upon the aspirant when he experiences the divine realm of existence.

Mere intellectual belief in the world of deities is empty theorization; we must actually experience the reality of this world in order to unify with the Absolute and obtain final liberation—Nirvana. The awakening of the chakras transports one to the divine world, the world of the True Self.

The Eight Disciplines of Yoga

Yogic practice is comprised of eight types or "limbs" of discipline. They were first codified by Patanjali, who compiled his *Yoga Sutras* in the fifth or sixth century B.C., based upon the teachings of various Yoga sects. The eight disciplines are:

(1) Yāma (abstention from evil conduct)
(2) Niyāma (virtuous conduct)
(3) Āsana (physical postures)
(4) Pranāyāma (regulation of the breath)
(5) Pratyāhāra (withdrawal of the senses)
(6) Dhārāna (concentration)
(7) Dhyāna (meditation)
(8) Samādhi (union of subject and object)

These disciplines may be classified into five groups:

(1) *Moral training:* Yāma, Niyāma. Purification and harmonization of the mind.
(2) *Physical training:* Āsana, Pranāyāma. Regulation of vital energy and blood circulation; regulation of nervous and muscle functions.
(3) *Mental training:* Pratyāhāra, Dhārāna. Breaking through the shell of the self through introversion and the control of consciousness.
(4) *Spiritual training:* Dhyāna. Attaining superconsciousness and contact with spiritual beings.
(5) *Samādhi: Oneness with the Divine,* the highest stage of spiritual development.

In actual practice, certain of these disciplines are practiced together in powerful configurations known as mudrās. The mudrās are very important practices which traditionally have been taught only to outstanding disciples. They are more effective than either isolated pranāyāma or āsana practice, and thus were considered potentially dangerous for those not adequately prepared. However, nowadays they are taught openly to earnest disciples by various gurus throughout the world, perhaps to fulfill the heightened spiritual needs of mankind in this age of crisis.

Mudrās are types of gestures which generate great psychic power and deeply "spiritual" emotions. Certain mudrās are used to control involuntary, normally subconscious physiological processes. They develop awareness of the flow of vital energy (prāna) in the astral body, and allow the practitioner to gain conscious control over it. Once this has been achieved, prāna may be sent to any part of the body, or even transmitted to others (this is what makes psychic healing possible). Many of the mudrās combine āsana, pranāyāma, and bandha (see Chapter III) practices into one. Since each of the constituent parts generates its own beneficial effects, the cumulative effect can be tremendous. The mudrās are important as preparation for pratyāhāra and dhārāna practices; in fact, they are the core of the techniques for awakening the chakras. At the same time, they promote physical and mental health.

A detailed explanation of the mudrās will be given in Chapter IV, following āsana (Chapter II) and pranāyāma (Chapter III) instruction. Let us complete this chapter with a discussion of the beginning practices of yogic discipline, yāma and niyāma.

Moral Training

The human mind is composed of both conscious and unconscious elements. Normally, the conscious mind exerts a certain amount of control over the unconscious. However, unconscious impulsive desires such as appetite, sexual desire, and emotional attachment are constantly at work, affecting the consciousness; when they come to dominate a person's mind, he becomes a selfish, antisocial individual who exerts a negative influence on all those around him.

Reckless motorcycle gangs are a typical example. Driven by the desire for speed and the need to show off, they feel no guilt over the annoyance they cause others. However, sooner or later they often suffer serious injuries or even kill themselves. Self-destruction is the fate of those who cannot control the blind, instinctive desires which originate in the unconscious.

I do not mean to imply that unconscious drives generate only negative effects or always cause misconduct. If controlled, this powerful energy can be rechanneled into a higher dimension and used to promote harmony. However, those without the requisite self-control often exhibit neurotic tendencies and unstable behavior. For example, attracted by mutually-shared weaknesses, such persons often join together to form groups which antagonize society, as in the case of the motorcycle gangs.

Disturbed or neurotic individuals often appear at our Institute, seeking help. Frequently we find two contributing factors present: deficient moral discipline during childhood, and a lack of religious worship at home. It is my belief that a child needs to be taught, both at home and at school, what is good behavior and what is not and to be praised or scolded accordingly. Children disciplined in this way tend to develop greater self-control than those who are not. Furthermore, if they are taught that God helps the good and punishes the bad, they tend to unconsciously refrain from bad conduct in adulthood.

Only those who can exercise self-control can achieve mental stability and maintain a proper balance between the conscious and unconscious realms of the mind. Without this balance, spiritual advancement through concentration and meditation practice is impossible. Thus, yāma and niyāma are indispensible prerequisites for advanced yoga practice.

Yāma

The *Yoga Sutras* state that yāma has five aspects: non-violence, truthfulness, non-stealing, continence, and non-greed.

Non-violence: Violent behavior usually arises when emotions such as hatred and the greed for power cannot be controlled. The self-accusation and guilt that remain in the unconscious as a result of violent behavior disturb the balance of the mind and inevitably impede spiritual advancement. Furthermore, non-violence is essential for the maintenance of peaceful co-existence within our society.

Truthfulness: Truthfulness and sincerity help generate a stable and tranquil mind, and contribute to harmonious social relations.

Non-stealing: Stealing naturally results in social censure, and also has deleterious effects on the mind and body of the perpetrator.

Continence: Next to the desire for food, sexual desire is the strongest human appetite. By abstaining from sexual relations for specified periods during spiritual practice, one may develop the ability to control instinctive desires. This fosters calmness.

Non-greed: Acquisitiveness is one of man's strongest instincts; its control contributes to both inner tranquility and a peaceful society.

The *Yoga Sutras* state the observance of yāma also generates certain siddhis (spiritual powers). For example, if a man practices non-violence, his enemies will disappear, evil men will abandon their weapons, and lions will pass by him without attacking. One who is established in truthfulness will find his wishes fulfilled spontaneously. Similarly, when the wholehearted observance of non-stealing is perfected, wealth will spontaneously accrue from unexpected sources. Continence generates energy. After five or ten years of meditation practice coupled with continence, the adept is able to transform sexual energy into spiritual energy (ojas). This in turn produces telepathic and psychokinetic powers, as well as enhanced mental and physical health. Finally, the complete extinction of greed is said to generate the ability to perceive one's past and future lives. Past, present, and future are clearly reflected on the mirror-like surface of a serene, immutable mind.

Niyāma

According to the *Yoga Sutras*, Niyāma also has five aspects: purification, contentment, mortification, recitation of sacred sounds, and worship of divine beings. These practices are related to one's personal conduct, in contrast to the social morality which is the basis of the yama observances.

Purification: Both mind and body should be made pure. Yogis bathe three times a day to maintain physical cleanliness; for mental purification, various means are employed. One method is to rejoice when others feel joyful and to feel their sorrow as one's own. This gradually expands the range of one's emotions and makes the mind pure and free. Regulating the breath through prāṇāyāma exercises is also important. The function of the heart consequently becomes quieter and more relaxed, and the mind is no longer easily excited by external stimuli. Concentration on the anāhata and ājna chakras is also a very effective method to purify the mind. This practice cultivates the quality of serenity (*sattva*). In yoga, three qualities of life (the "three gunas") are posited: *Tamas* (inactivity, inertia, indolence), *rajas* (activity, passion), and *sattva* (serenity, calmness, knowledge). When the *sattva guna* gains dominance over the other two, a shining white light is experienced extrasensorily, and peace ensues.

Contentment: This is satisfaction with the basic necessities of life—the absence of desire for superfluous things. Once a person realizes that everything he has—his body, his mind, life itself—is granted by God, that in effect he owns nothing, he experiences deep gratitude. This results in unequalled tranquillity of mind.

Mortification: The appetite, one of the strongest human instincts, may be overcome by fasting. A weak mind may be strengthened by various forms of asceticism. For example, in Japan water asceticism—dousing oneself with buckets of icy water in midwinter, or standing under a waterfall—is widely practiced. Fasting and water asceticism facilitate the emergence of the superconscious by slowing the body's metabolism and quieting the areas of consciousness related to bodily functions.

The Recitation of Sacred Sounds: Chanting scriptures, mantras, and other sacred sounds which reveal aspects of the Divine is an extremely powerful practice. At first the practitioner is conscious of sound as it arises in his throat; as the awareness deepens, his consciousness becomes increasingly clear and unifies to become the sound itself. The mind is purified and becomes tranquil.

Worship of Divine Beings: This refers not to the Ultimate Being, but rather to divine spirits who have their own individuality. The essence of these deities is *Purusha*, the universal consciousness of True Self. In this world of karmic ties, purusha can only exist in a stained, impure form, but divine beings dwell in its pure state, enjoying complete freedom beyond the confines of time and space. They are the spiritual guides of yogis and their gurus; through their visualization and worship, the seeker's mind becomes calm and clear. Superconsciousness and psychic powers are bestowed, and direct encounters with divine beings become possible.

The observance of niyāma has many benefits. Through purification of mind and body, sattva (tranquility, peace, wisdom) pervades the devotee's being. He acquires the ability to concentrate and control his sensory organs. Moreover, an intuitive power is bestowed upon him enabling him to distinguish between higher dimensions of the mind, which are still subject to the laws of karma, and purusha, which transcends karma. Through the practice of contentment (the absence of material desires), one experiences the higher world that supports our lives, enjoying peace of mind and superlative happiness. Through the practice of mortification, psychic abilities—both physical and mental—are bestowed. Through the recitation of sacred sounds one is able to encounter divinity. Through the worship of omnipotent, pure, divine beings, one can enter the peaceful, transcendent state known as non-differentiated samādhi.

The purpose of yāma and niyāma, then, is to prepare the mind for spiritual enlightenment. Yāma stabilizes the mind in the realm of social behavior, and niyāma purifies it by minimizing worldly, outer-directed activity. Although it may sound like conventional moralistic preaching to advocate good behavior and abstention from evil conduct, yāma and niyāma are actually practical necessities for one who engages in spiritual practice.

II

Yoga Āsanas

Many people associate āsanas with physical exercise and vigorous movement. This is a misunderstanding, however, for the actual meaning of āsana is "posture"—a stationary pose in which mind and body are relaxed and composed. Physical exercises generate physiological effects on the muscles and bones, while the purpose of yoga āsanas is to foster mental and spiritual—as well as physical—health.

Certain external differences are obvious. For example, physical exercises often include quick, sharp movement accompanied by rapid, even violent breathing. Āsanas, on the other hand, are practiced with gentle movement, deep respiration, and pointed concentration. They are maintained for several breaths before a slow return to the starting position. Undue strain is unnecessary. Through the āsanas the functions of the internal organs and muscular and nervous systems are toned and stabilized.

According to tradition Lord Shiva, who is worshipped by yogis as the deity who releases human beings from this world, created yoga and the āsanas. He is said to have devised 8,400,000 āsanas and taught them to the goddess Parvati, his first disciple. In the ancient tradition, the practice of āsanas is said to release one from the bonds of karma. Each person is thought to reincarnate 8,400,000 times, and the practice of each āsana supposedly releases him from one incarnation. However, in reality no more than a few hundred āsanas have come down to us after several thousand years, and only 84 of them are described in detail in the scriptures.

The word "tantra" is derived from "tonati" (expansion) and "trayati" (liberation). Tantra is thus an esoteric system of spiritual practice which aims at expanding the consciousness and liberating the mind. It is said to have originated from the secret body of knowledge, including the āsanas, transmitted from Shiva to Parvati and taught in turn to her offspring. In practice, tantra employs āsanas, prānāyāma bandhas, and mudrās to purify the mind and body.* Activation of the chakras is an integral part of this system.

Historically speaking, the first extant commentary of the āsanas was recorded by the great guru Goraknath, who lived in the tenth century A.D. Before this time, the secrets of yoga science seem to have been kept hidden from all but the most outstanding disciples. Now, however, anyone may practice yoga and study its wisdom. In fact, yoga has attracted a worldwide following in recent decades, a phenomenon perhaps attributable to an increasing need for mental and spiritual growth.

Traditionally the āsanas are classified into three levels of difficulty—beginning, intermediate, and advanced—which require progressively higher levels of physical suppleness and strength, muscular control, harmony of breathing, and mental concentration. Another traditional distinction is

---

* Many of the practices described in this book are also found in hatha yoga, mantra yoga, etc. However, they may be considered a part of tantric practice because our underlying aim is to activate the esoteric system of chakras and nādīs and consciously control its energy flow. The inner awareness and conscious utilization of this esoteric structure—in particular the controlled activation of shakti, the female creative cosmic force which generates all manifest form—is what distinguishes tantra from conventional yoga practice.

made between dynamic and static āsanas. The dynamic āsanas resemble physical exercises, acting to remove stiffness, strengthen the muscles and improve the skin, improve the functions of tho lungs, and enhance the activity of the digestive and excretory organs. These are suitable for beginners and include the "wind-release" āsanas (pawanmuktāsana), the "salutation to the sun", leg-stretches, forward-bends, the "cobra" pose, etc. The static āsanas are practiced by holding a fixed posture for several minutes or more while breathing quietly. They provide a mild massage for the internal organs, endocrine glands, and muscular and nervous systems, and are good preparatory exercise for meditation, due to their calming effect on the mind. These āsanas are practiced with mental concentration on one area of the body, and include the "lion" pose, the shoulder stand, the lotus posture, etc.

For this book, new groupings for the āsanas have been devised which classify them by their function as preparatory practices for chakra awakening. The first group consists of āsanas for increasing the absorption of prāna into the body and mind, and for balancing its flow. These may be called the prāna circulation āsanas, and include the beginners' āsanas and some of the dynamic āsanas. Āsanas of the second group strengthen the sushumnā, the central psychic channel which runs through the spine. They help correct a bent spine or displaced vertebrae, and facilitate the flow of prāna through the sushumnā. The third group is comprised of āsanas for concentration upon the chakras.

These three groups represent three progressive preparatory stages in the awakening of the chakras. First, the prāna flow throughout the body must be activated and normalized. Then the prāna flow throughout the sushumnā—the most important nādī—can be increased, and the passage purified. This facilitates the rising of kundalinī, the psychic power said to lie dormant at the base of the spine. Kundalinī awakening is indispensable for true chakra awakening.

Finally, direct concentration on the chakras provides the direct stimulation which enables their full awakening.

Before a detailed explanation of the āsanas is presented, some general precautions should be noted.

- Before starting āsana practice, empty the bladder and intestines.
- As the stomach must be empty, do not attempt āsanas until at least 3-4 hours after eating.
- Do not practice after prolonged sunbathing.
- In general, breathe through the nostrils, in harmony with the movement of the āsana (details given later).
- Do not practice on an air-filled or sponge mattress. A spread blanket may be used.
- Practice in a quiet room, well ventilated with fresh air. Strong breezes or cold or dirty air should be avoided. Also, make sure that you have ample space to stretch, free of furniture.
- Do not subject the muscles and joints to undue force or strain. The āsanas should be practiced within the comfortable limits of the student's ability.
- If you suffer from chronic illness such as an ulcer or hernia, practice only suitable āsanas or none at all, following the advice of a qualified teacher.
- The best time to practice is said to be from four to six o'clock in the morning.
- Perform the āsanas slowly with full awareness of the body. If slight pain or pleasure is experienced, do not react but simply be aware of the sensation. In this way, concentration and endurance will develop.
- Wear loose clothing which is simple and comfortable. Remove wrist watches, jewelry, and other ornaments.
- A cold shower before starting will greatly enhance the effects of āsana practice.
- Perform shavāsana (literally, the "corpse" pose, p. 44) at the beginning and end of āsana practice, and whenever

fatigue is experienced. This relaxes and energizes the body, filling it with prāna and balancing the flow.

- If you feel excessive pain in any part of the body, stop practicing immediately and seek a teacher's advice.
- If you have intestinal gas or excessively impure blood, do not practice the inverted āsanas. This is to prevent toxins from entering the brain and causing damage.
- A vegetarian diet is not essential. Eat enough food to satisfy your appetite, but not so much as to cause a heavy, lazy feeling.

Group 1:
Āsanas for Promoting Prāna Circulation

According to the Āyurvēda, a classic of ancient Indian medicine, the human body is controlled by three "humours": phlegm (kapha), wind (vāyu), and acid or bile (pitta). Irregularity in the function of any of these three upsets the body's metabolism, and disease will eventually develop.

Vāyu refers not only to gases of the gastro-intestinal tract, but also to a type of prāna, conceived as a subtle body fluid that flows through the nādīs. I consider the nādīs to be essentially equivalent to the meridians of Chinese acupuncture; from my research, it appears that these channels are formed of connective tissue and filled with body fluid. It is at the joints that the flow of ki energy (equivalent to the grosser form of prāna) is easily impeded. Poor flow here can cause rheumatic pains and result in deficient energy flow throughout the entire body, the root cause of many disorders. The main objective of the first group of āsanas, then—called pawanmuktāsana, the "wind-releasing" exercises—is to promote the unimpeded flow of prāna through the nādīs, primarily by releasing the blockages in the joints.

Before pawanmuktasana, or any āsana practice, shāvasana (the "corpse" pose) is recommended. This relaxes the body and allows prāna to be easily absorbed and distributed.

Shavāsana (corpse pose)

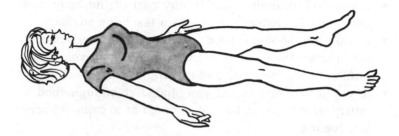

Lie flat on the back with the arms at the sides, palms facing upwards. Move the feet slightly apart to a comfortable position. Close the eyes. Relax the whole body. Do not move at all even if discomfort arises. The breath should be rhythmic and natural. Be aware of inhalation and exhalation. Count the breaths—1 in, 1 out, 2 in, 2 out, and so on—for five minutes. If the mind starts to wander, bring it back to the counting; if the number is forgotten, start from 1 again.

As awareness of the breathing process continues, you will experience increasing physical and mental relaxation.

Pawanmuktāsana (wind-releasing exercises)

Starting Position

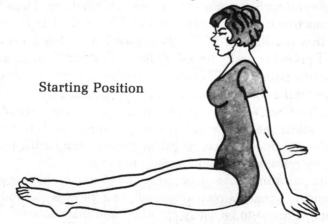

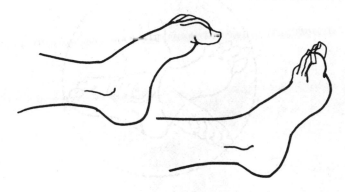

(1) *Toe Bending*

Sit erect on the floor with the legs fully extended. Place the hands palms down on the floor beside the hips and lean backwards, using the straight arms for support. Focus attention to the toes. Move the toes of both feet slowly backwards and forwards, without moving the legs or ankles. Repeat ten times.

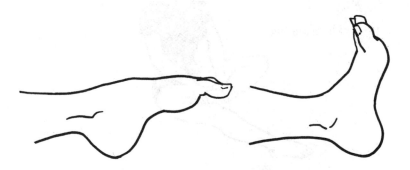

(2) *Ankle Bending*

Remain in the starting position described in (1). Move both feet backwards and forwards as far as possible, bending at the ankle joints. Repeat 10 times.

(3) *Ankle Rotation*

Remain in the starting position. Separate the legs slightly. Keeping the heels in contact with floor, rotate the right foot clockwise at the ankle ten times, and then counter-clockwise ten times. Repeat with the left foot. Then repeat the exercise, rotating both feet together.

(4) *Ankle cranking*

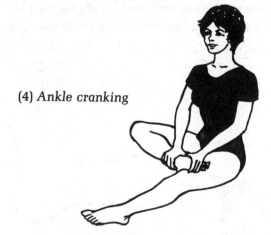

Sitting in the starting position, place the right ankle on the left thigh. While holding the right ankle with the right hand, rotate the right foot with the left hand clockwise ten times, then ten times counter-clockwise. Repeat the procedure with the left foot on the right thigh.

(5) *Knee bending*

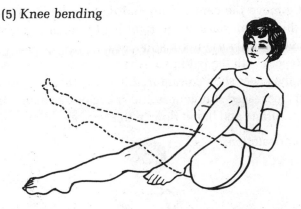

Sitting in the starting position, bend and raise the right knee, clasping the hands under the thigh. Straighten the leg without allowing the heel or toe to touch the ground, keeping the hands under the thigh. Return the leg to its previous position, bringing the heel near the right buttock. Repeat 10 times, then do the same with the left leg.

(6) *Knee rotation*

Sitting in the starting position, clasp the hands under the right thigh near the trunk and lift the left leg off the floor. Rotate the lower leg in a circular motion about the knee ten times clockwise, then ten times counter-clockwise. Repeat with the left leg.

(7) *Half butterfly*

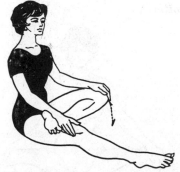

Place the right foot on the left thigh. Hold the left knee with the left hand and place the right hand on top of the bent right knee. Gently move the bent leg up and down with the right hand, relaxing the muscles of the right leg as much as possible. Continue until the right knee touches, or nearly touches the floor. Repeat with the left knee. After some days or weeks of practice, the knees should comfortably touch the floor. As a result of this increased suppleness and range of movement in the hip joints, prāna and blood flow in this area are improved.

(8) *Hip joint rotation*

Sitting in the same position as in (4), hold the right toes with the left hand and the right knee with the right hand. Rotate the knee around the hip joint ten times clockwise and then ten times counter-clockwise.

Repeat the same process with the left knee.

(9) *Full butterfly*

In the sitting position, place the soles of the feet together and bring the heels as close to the body as possible. Push the knees toward the ground with the hands, allowing them to bounce upwards again. Repeat twenty times.

(10) *Crow walking*

Squat on the floor, place the palms on the knees, and walk while maintaining the squatting position. You may walk either on the toes or on the soles of the feet, whichever is more difficult. Continue for a short time without strain. As a variation, you can touch the knee to the ground at each step.

Crow walking is a very good exercise to prepare the legs for meditation postures, and it is useful for those who have poor prāna and blood circulation in the legs. It is also recommended for constipation sufferers, who should drink two glasses of water before doing one minute of crow walking, followed by two more glasses of water and another minute's walk. If this is done three or four times, the constipation should be relieved.

(11) Hand clenching

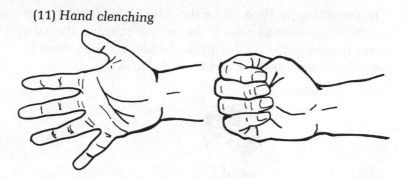

Sitting in the starting position, extend the arms forward at shoulder level. Alternately extend and clench the fingers of both hands. Close the fingers over the thumbs to make a tight fist. Repeat 10 times.

(12) Wrist bending

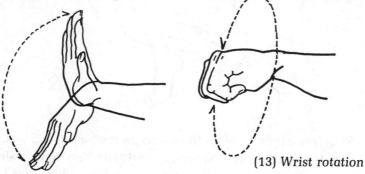

(13) Wrist rotation

Maintain the starting position with the arms extended forward at shoulder level and bend the hands back at the wrist, as if to press the palms against a wall with the fingers pointing upwards. Then bend the wrists to point the fingers down. Repeat alternately 10 times.

Starting from the same position as in No. 12, drop the left hand. Clench the right fist and rotate the wrist 10 times in each direction. Repeat with the left hand. Extend both arms in front of the body with the fists clenched. Rotate the fists together 10 times in each direction.

(14) *Elbow bending*

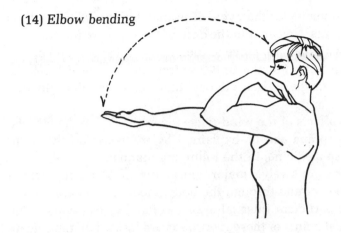

Assume the starting position and extend arms forward, palms turned upwards. Bend both arms at the elbows and touch the shoulders with the fingertips, then straighten the arms again. Repeat ten times. Next perform the same exercise, but with the arms extended sideways.

(15) *Shoulder rotation*

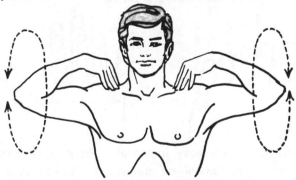

Maintaining the same position with the fingertips touching the shoulders, move the elbows in a circular pattern, rotating the shoulder joints. Do this 10 times in each direction. Make the circular motion as large as possible, bringing the two elbows together in front of the chest.

This completes the cycle of āsanas for stimulating all the limb joints. Note that in the case of the lower extremities you start with the toes, move to the ankles and knees, and end at the hip joint. For the upper extremities, proceed from the fingers to the wrists, elbows, and shoulder joints, in that order.

The effects of the wind-releasing āsanas upon the circulation of prāna can be explained by the meridian theory of Chinese medicine, in the following manner:

There are twelve major meridians of ki energy which course over and through the body; most of them are related to one particular internal organ which they transverse. The terminal points of these meridians are located on the fingers and toes, and are known as *sei* ("well") points. For example, the sei point of the lung meridian is located on the thumb; that of the large intestine meridian is at the tip of the second finger. The position of fourteen sei points (the twelve major plus the stomach-branch and diaphragm meridians) are indicated in the diagram below (the meridians are virtually identical for both left and right sides).

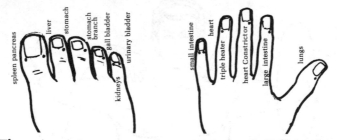

The sei points are very important, for it is here that ki energy enters and leaves the meridians. The energy level at these points is said to accurately reflect the condition of the entire meridian. In the case of acute illness, acupuncture or moxa treatment here is known to have an immediate effect. The hand-clenching and toe-bending exercises of pawan-muktāsana directly stimulate the sei points, and thus promote better ki-energy (prāna) circulation.

Chinese medicine also speaks of the gen ("source") points, located either in the wrist or ankle, or between the sei point and the joint. Diseases in the internal organs related to the specific meridians are often reflected at the gen points and treatment there is frequently prescribed. Therefore, the exercises which bend and rotate the ankles and wrists stimulate the gen points and help normalize the functions of the internal organs related to the twelve meridians.

The Yellow Emperor's Treatise on Internal Medicine—the oldest text of Chinese medicine, and the original source of the above information—further states that the knees and elbows are closely connected to the gen points, and that they too can have an effect upon diseases of the internal organs. Thus the rotation of the knees and elbows is beneficial; stimulation of the hips and shoulder joints has similar effects.

In terms of Western medicine, also, the joints are considered to be very vulnerable parts of the body. Fluid tends to accumulate and stagnate in these areas, and the whole body gradually becomes fatigued. This condition can lead to rheumatism and neuralgia, common complaints of the modern age. In this sense, too, the benefits of wind-releasing āsanas can be observed. In addition to improving the ki energy flow through the meridians, they promote the circulation of blood and body fluids through the joints, thus helping to cure illness and maintain good health.

Group 2:
Āsanas for Regulating the Sushumnā

As explained previously, the principle aim of these āsanas is to strengthen and adjust the central psychic channel which runs through the spinal cord, the sushumnā nādī. Displacement of the spinal vertabrae is detrimental to the flow of prāna through the sushumnā, and causes disorders in the nerves and internal organs—as well as the nādīs and chakras—controlled by them. The āsanas in this second group are designed to correct vertebral displacements, thus helping to purify the sushumnā. This is an indispensable preparatory step for arousing the kundalinī and awakening the chakras.

(1) *Tādāsana*

Stand erect with your feet four to six inches apart. Gaze at an object directly in front of your eyes. During inhalation raise the arms overhead with the palms facing upwards, and look up at the hands. Lift the heels and stretch the whole body as if it were being drawn upwards. Hold the breath for one or two seconds and then, during exhalation, return slowly to the starting position. Repeat 10 times.

Tādāsana   Hasta uttānāsana

Benefits: Tādāsana develops and stretches the rectus abdominis (stomach) muscles, and promotes proper spinal bone growth. It clears up congestion around the intervertebral foramina, and also protects the nerves emerging from these foramina from undue pressure by correcting vertebral displacements. Walking 100 steps in tādāsana after drinking six cups of water can clear non-chronic intestinal blockages.

(2) *Hasta uttānāsana*

Stand with the trunk erect and the arms at the sides. While inhaling, raise the arms above the head at shoulder width and bend the head and trunk backwards slightly. Concentrate on the vishuddhi chakra for one or two seconds, then go into pada hastāsana.

(3) *Pada hastāsana*

Exhaling, bend forward from the hips until the palms or fingers touch the toes, or grasp the backs of the ankles and, if possible, place the forehead against the knees. In the final

Pada hastāsana

pose, breathe out completely, drawing in the lower abdomen, and concentrate on the svādhishthāna chakra for one or two seconds. Raise the trunk slowly and move back into hasta uttānāsana. Keep the legs straight throughout the movement. Practice these two āsanas in alternating successions 10 times.

Benefits: Hasta uttānāsana stretches the abdominal viscera and improves the digestion. It also removes excess abdominal fat and exercises the arm and shoulder muscles. All the vertebral joints are stimulated and the spinal nerves toned. The functioning of the lungs is improved through the expansion of the alveoli (lung compartments).

Pada hastāsana benefits the digestion and the blood circulation, and is an effective treatment for constipation and gastro-intestinal disease. Surplus fat in the abdominal region is reduced. The spinal nerves are toned and the spine is made supple.

(4) *Yoga mudrā* (Psychic union pose)

Sit in the lotus position (padmāsana) and close the eyes. Hold one wrist behind the back with the other hand and relax. Slowly bend the trunk forward until the forehead touches or nearly touches the ground, relaxing the whole body as much as possible in the final position. Slowly return to the starting position. If necessary, beginners may place padding under the buttocks while performing this āsana.

Breathing: Breathe normally, relaxing the body. Inhale slowly and deeply in the starting position, and then exhale while bending forward. Breathe deeply and slowly in the final position for five or more minutes, and inhale as you return to the starting pose. Repeat the āsana a few times.

Concentration: On the manipūra chakra.

Caution: Do not strain the back, ankles, knees, or thighs by stretching more than their flexibility permits.

Benefits: This āsana massages the abdominal organs and helps to counteract malfunctions there, including constipation and indigestion. The individual vertebrae are separated from each other and the spinal autonomic nerve fibers passing through the intervertebral foramina are gently stretched and toned. These nerves connect the entire body with the brain and improvement of their condition contributes to overall health. This āsana is also very effective in awakening the manipūra chakra.

(5) *Paschimottānāsana* (Back-stretching pose)

Sit on the floor with the legs extended, arms on thighs, and relax the whole body, especially the back muscles. Slowly bend the upper torso forward, sliding the hands along the legs to grasp the big toes with the fingers and thumbs. If this is impossible, hold the feet. If even this is difficult, as is often the case with beginners, hold the ankles or the legs as near to the feet as possible. Again consciously relax the muscles of the back and legs. Keeping the legs straight, pull the trunk a little lower toward the legs, using the arms rather than the trunk muscles. This should be a gentle process without any sudden movements or excessive strain anywhere in the body.

If possible, touch the forehead to the knees. As this is usually difficult for beginners, bending forward as far as possible is sufficient. Do not use force under any circumstances. Some weeks or months of regular practice will enable the forehead and even the chin to touch the knees. Remain in the final pose for a comfortable length of time, relaxing the whole body, and then slowly return to the starting position.

Note: The knees must not bend, as one aim of this āsana is to stretch the posterior muscles of the leg. These will elongate in time.

Breathing: In the sitting position breathe normally; then exhale slowly, bending the trunk forward to grasp the toes. Inhale while holding the body motionless and exhale when pulling the trunk further forward with the arms. In the final pose breathe slowly and deeply, and inhale when returning to the starting position. If it is impossible to hold the final pose for long, simply hold the exhalation.

Duration: Adepts can comfortably maintain the final pose for five minutes or more. Beginners, however, should repeat the abbreviated āsana several times. The spiritual benefits are considerable if the final position is held with complete relaxation for extended lengths of time.

Concentration: On the svādhisthāna chakra.

Limitations: People who have displaced intervertebral discs should not attempt this āsana; nor should those suffering from sciatica, chronic arthritis, or sacral infections.

Benefits: The hamstring muscles are stretched and the hip, sacroiliac, and lumbar vertebral joints are loosened. Flatulence, constipation, backache, and also excess fat in the abdominal region are effectively removed. All the abdominal organs are toned and abdominal disorders, such as diabetes, may slowly improve. The kidneys, liver, pancreas, and adrenal glands are activated. As the pelvic organs are also toned, this āsana is especially useful for relieving gynecological complaints. It also improves the flow of fresh blood to the spinal nerves and muscles. Paschimottānāsana is traditionally regarded as a very powerful āsana for spiritual awakening and is highly praised in ancient yoga texts.

(6) *Pada Prasarita Paschimottānāsana* (leg-spread variation)

Sit with the legs spread as wide as possible (180° is ideal) and breathe normally, relaxing the whole body, especially the back muscles. Exhale slowly, bending forward, and place the hands on the floor with the fingertips touching. Try to touch the forehead to the back of the hands. Breathe slowly and deeply in the final pose for several minutes, then return to the starting position.

Concentration: On the svādhishthāna chakra.

Benefits: The same as paschimottānāsana, but this pose is more effective in loosening the lower back and the hip joints.

(7) *Bhujangāsana* (Cobra pose)

Lie on the stomach with the legs extended and place the palms on the floor underneath the shoulders. Rest the forehead on the ground. Relax the whole body. Slowly lift the head and shoulders off the floor, pulling the head back as far as possible. In performing this movement, raise the shoulders with the back muscles, not the arms. The whole back is slowly bent back as far as possible until the arms are straight. Keep the navel close to the floor.

Breathing: Inhale while raising the trunk. Breathe normally in the final pose, or, if the final pose is held for only a short time, the breath can be held inside.

Duration: Keep the final pose as long as is comfortable, and repeat five times.

Concentraton: On the vishuddhi chakra.

Limitations: People suffering from peptic ulcers, hernia, intestinal tuberculosis, or hyperthyroidism should not do this āsana.

Benefits: This āsana tones the ovaries and uterus, and is helpful in the cure of female disorders such as leukorrhea, dysmenorrhea, and amenorrhea. It is also beneficial for all the abdominal organs, especially the liver and kidneys. It stimulates the appetite and relieves constipation. The spine is kept supple and healthy, slipped intervertebral discs are corrected, and backache is relieved.

(8) *Dhanurāsana* (Bow pose)

Lie flat on the stomach and inhale fully. Bend the legs at the knees and grasp the ankles with the hands. Tensing the leg muscles, raise the head, chest, and thighs as high as possible off the ground, bending the back into a taut bow while keeping the arms straight.

Note: Do not repeat this āsana until the breath returns to normal. In the final pose, hold the breath in or breathe slowly and deeply. One may also rock back and forth in the final position. Exhale slowly while returning to the starting pose.

Duration: Keep the final pose as long as it can be comfortably maintained. Practice the āsana five times.

Concentration: On the vishuddhi chakra.

Limitations: Not to be practiced by people with hernia, peptic ulcers, intestinal tuberculosis, or twisted or bent spines.

Benefits: Because this āsana massages the abdominal organs and muscles, it helps to relieve gastro-intestinal disorders such as chronic constipation and dyspepsia. It is useful in cases of liver malfunction, and can also reduce excess fat in the abdominal area.

(9) *Halāsana* (Plough pose)

Lie flat on the back, arms straight at the sides and palms flat on the floor. Keeping the legs straight, slowly raise them to the vertical position and beyond. Use the abdominal muscles without pressing the arms against the floor. As the legs pass the vertical position bend the trunk upward, curling slowly so that the legs come down over the head and the toes touch the floor. Keeping the legs straight, bend the arms and support the back with the hands. Relax the body, and remain in this final pose for a comfortable period of time. Then return to the starting position, or perform the following:

(a) Walk the feet away from the head until the body is completely extended and the chin is locked tightly against the top of the chest. Maintain this pose for a comfortable length of time and then return to the final pose of basic halāsana.

(b) Walk the feet towards the head as far as possible with the legs straight and the toes on the floor directly above the head. Grasp the feet with the fingers. Maintain the pose for a comfortable length of time and then return to the final pose of basic halāsana.

Slowly return to the supine position.

Breathing: Breathe normally in the supine position, then inhale and hold the breath when assuming the pose. Breathe slowly and deeply in the final position.

Duration: Advanced practitioners can remain in the basic final pose for 10 or more minutes. Beginners should hold the pose for only fifteen seconds during the first week of practice, repeating it four times. The time can be increased by fifteen seconds each subsequent week until the posture is held for one minute.

Concentration: On the vishuddhi or manipūra chakra.

Precautions: Beginners, unless they have flexible backs, should do pūrwa halāsana — in which the student raises the legs over the head at a 45-degree angle — until their back muscles and joints become supple enough after several weeks of daily practice to assume the final pose.

Limitations: The old and infirm, and those who suffer from sciatica, other back ailments, or high blood pressure, should not practice this āsana.

Benefits: Halāsana regulates the functioning of the abdominal organs, especially the kidneys, liver, and pancreas, and activates digestion. It can alleviate constipation and also slim the waist area. It regulates the activity of the thyroid gland and thus stabilizes the metabolism. This āsana is also helpful in cases of diabetes and piles. It loosens the vertebrae and tones the spinal nerves, thereby contributing to the health of the whole body.

(10) *Matsyāsana* (Fish pose)

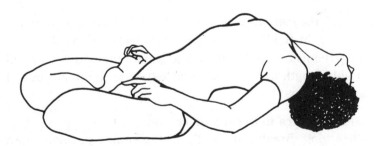

Sit in the lotus position (padmāsana) and breathe normally. Bend backwards, supporting the body with the arms and elbows until the top of the head touches the ground. Hold the big toes and place the elbows on the floor, arching the back as much as possible. Breathe in and retain the breath during this movement.

As a variation, interlock the fingers of both hands and place them behind the head.

Breathing: Breathe deeply and slowly in the final pose. (People with tonsillitis or sore throats can, if they wish, practice shitakārī prānāyāma.* Hold the breath inside when returning to padmāsana and then breathe normally.)

Duration: Remain in the final pose for five minutes if possible, but do not strain unnecessarily.

Concentration: On the manipūra or anāhata chakra.

Benefits: As the abdominal organs, especially the intestines, are stretched, this āsana is useful for abdominal illness. Constipation sufferers seeking relief should do this āsana after drinking three glasses of water. It is also useful for those who suffer from lung ailments such as asthma or bronchitis, as it encourages deep respiration, helps to recirculate stagnant blood in the back, and regulates the functioning of the thyroid gland.

The ten āsanas described above stretch the spine through forward and backward movement. The following āsanas adjust the spine by twisting.

---

* *Shitakārī Prānāyāma: The tongue is folded back so that its lower surface touches against the palate, as in khechari mudrā (see p. 101). The teeth are clenched and the lips drawn back as far as possible. Then yogic breathing (See p. 78) is practiced, inhaling through the teeth and exhaling through the nose. This is effective for cooling the whole body like the other prānāyāma it resembles, shitālī pranayama (in which the tongue is curled up to form a narrow tube and protrudes from the mouth).*

(a)

(11) *Trikonāsana* (Triangle pose)

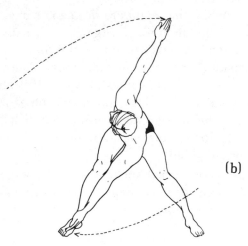

(b)

Stand erect with the feet 2½ to 3 feet apart and extend the arms to the sides. Bend the body at the hips to form a right angle as in Figure a and swivel the trunk, touching the right toes with the left hand as Figure b. Look up at the extended right arm, whose palm should face to the right. Then swivel the trunk in the opposite direction and assume a similar pose on the left side. Bring the trunk to the center, return to the starting position, and lower the arms.

Breathing: Inhale when raising the arms, exhale while bending the trunk, hold the breath out while swiveling, inhale when raising, and exhale while lowering the arms.

Duration: Practice five times in succession.

Benefits: Through trikonāsana, the spine and spinal nerves are massaged, the entire nervous system is gently stimulated, and the muscles of the lower back are stretched. Sufferers from nervous depression thus benefit. The āsana massages the abdominal organs and thereby improves the appetite and digestion, and is also helpful for removing constipation by stimulating the peristaltic contraction of the intestines.

(12) *Dynamic Spinal Twist*

Sit with the legs extended forward and separate them as much as is comfortable. Keeping the arms straight, stretch the left hand to the right big toe and the right arm behind the back, keeping both arms in one straight line. Turn the head and look backwards, directing the gaze to the right hand. Then turn the trunk in the opposite direction, reversing the arm positions. Repeat this cycle 15 to 20 times. At the beginning do the exercise slowly, then gradually increase the speed.

(13) *Ardha Matsyendrāsana* (Half spinal twist pose)

Sit with the left leg straight in front of the body and the right foot flat on the floor next to the outside of the left knee. Bend the left leg to the right and place the left heel against the right buttock. Place the left arm on the outside of the right leg, and grip the right foot or ankle with the left hand. The right knee should be as near as possible to the left arm-pit. Turn the body to the right, placing the right arm behind the back. Twist the back and then the neck as far as is comfortable without strain. Remain in the final pose for a short time and then slowly return to the starting position. Repeat on the other side of the body.

Note: This is a very important āsana and should be practiced at least once every day.

Breathing: Exhale while twisting the trunk, breathe as deeply as possible without strain in the final pose, and inhale while returning to the starting position.

Duration: When the spinal muscles are flexible enough, maintain the pose for at least 1 minute on each side of the body.

Concentration: On the ājnā chakra.

Benefits: The spinal nerves are toned, and the back muscles and intervertebral joints are made supple. Digestive ailments are removed through massage of the abdominal organs. The āsana regulates the secretion of adrenaline from the adrenal glands and also activates the pancreas, thus counteracting diabetic tendencies. Nerves originating in the back are toned, and lumbago and muscular rheumatism are relieved. The entire nervous system is stimulated by this āsana. Slipped intervertebral discs (including vertebral displacements) may also be corrected.

Simplified variation for beginners:

People with very stiff bodies who find ardha matsyendrāsana impossible to do should extend the leg normally folded under the buttocks straight in front of the body. Otherwise the technique is exactly the same as in standard ardha matsyendrāsana. When the body becomes supple enough, one should proceed to the full posture, as the effects are much greater.

(14) *Bhu Namanāsana* (Spinal twist prostration pose)

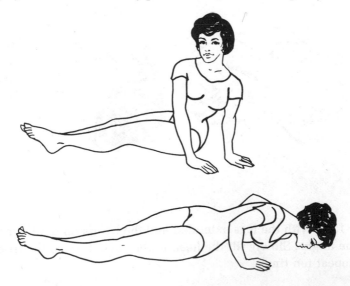

Sit with the spine erect and the legs extended forward. Place both hands by the side of the left hip. Twist the trunk 90° to the left. Bend the upper body and touch the nose to the ground. The buttocks should not rise. Raise the trunk and the head and return to the starting position.

Breathing: Inhale in the starting position; exhale while bending the trunk, and inhale on the return.

Duration: Practice up to ten times on each side.

Concentration: Either focus the mind on the breath, or else consciously relax the back muscles.

Benefits: The spine and lower back are stretched, loosening the muscles and stimulating the spinal nerves.

This concludes the description of the spine-twisting āsanas. The following is an āsana for adjusting the cervical area.

(15) *Neck Movement*

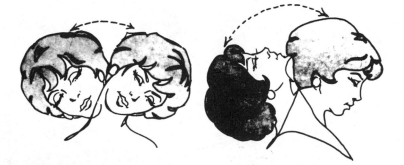

1. Sit with the legs extended and the hands on the floor by the thighs. Slowly tilt the head to the back, then to the front. Repeat ten times.

2. While facing forward, slowly tilt the head to the left, then to the right. Repeat ten times.

3. In the same position, tilt the head forward, at the same time turning it to the left and right. Or, keep the head erect while turning it to the left and right. Repeat either ten times.

4. Slowly rotate the head in as large a circle as possible without strain, ten times in each direction.

Benefits: The neck is a vital crossroads in the body. All the nerves connecting the different parts of the body with the brain must pass through it. Therefore, regular neck exercises help to maintain overall health by adjusting the cervical vertebrae, and normalizing the functioning of the systems in the cervical and cephalic region.

Group 3:
The āsanas for meditation

(1) *Padmāsana*
    (Lotus pose)

Sit with the legs extended forward. Bend one leg, placing the foot on top of the other thigh with the sole upward and the heel touching the pelvic bone. Fold the other leg so that the foot rests in a similar position on the opposite thigh.

Note: Practice padmāsana together with jnāna mudrā or chin mudrā (See p. 96 Chapter IV). In this āsana, the spine must be held straight and completely steady, as if fixed to the ground. A low cushion under the buttocks will make this āsana easier to perform. Practice padmāsana after the legs have become supple through practice of the preliminary āsanas described before.

Limitations: People with sciatica or sacral infections should not practice this āsana.

Benefits: Practitioners who have mastered padmāsana can hold the body completely steady for long periods of time. Steadiness of the body brings steadiness of mind, and this steadiness is the first step toward productive meditation. This āsana helps to direct the proper flow of prāna from the mūlādhāra chakra to the sahasrāra. In addition, the coccygeal and sacral nerves are toned by the infusion into the abdominal and back regions of large amounts of blood which normally flow into the legs. Physical, nervous, and emotional problems are effectively cleared up.

(2) *Siddhāsana* (Male accomplished pose)

Sit with the legs extended forward. Fold the right leg and place the sole flat against the inside of the left thigh. The heel should press against the perineum, the area between the genitals and the anus. Fold the left leg and place the foot on the right calf, pressing the pelvic bone just above the genitals with the left heel. Thrust the toes and outer side of the left sole into the groove between the right calf and the thigh muscles. It may be necessary to slightly shift the right leg for this; grasp the right toes and pull them upward, placing them between the left thigh and calf. The legs should now be locked with the knees on the ground and the left heel directly above the right heel. Hold the spine erect, as straight and firm as a tree rooted in the ground.

Note: Siddhāsana is only for men. It can be practiced with either leg on top, and always with jnāna or chin mudrā (see Chapter IV). Many people—especially beginners—find it easier to assume and maintain this āsana for long periods when a cushion is placed under the buttocks.

Limitations: Persons with sciatica or sacral infections should not practice this āsana.

Benefits: Siddhāsana is a meditation pose which facilitates spinal steadiness for long and deep meditation. It activates the two sexually-related psychomuscular locks, mūla bandha (See p. 90) and vajroli mudrā, which redirect sexual impulses back up the spinal cord to the brain. The practitioner can thus gain the control over sexual functions that is essential to the maintenance of celibacy and the sublimation of sexual energy for spiritual purposes, as well as control over sensory activity. The entire nervous system is also calmed.

(3) *Siddha yoni āsana* (Female accomplished pose)
Sit with the legs extended forward. Fold the right leg, placing the sole flat against the inside of the left thigh and the heel under the labia majora. Bend the left leg and pull the right toes up into the space between the left calf and thigh. Hold the spine fully erect as if it were rooted in the earth.

Notes: Siddha yoni āsana is a form of siddhāsana for women that has been handed down only by word of mouth.

Practice with either leg on top and with either jnāna or chin mudrā. It is most effective when underwear is not worn. Beginners will find this pose easier to maintain for long periods if a low cushion is used under the buttocks.

Limitations: Women with sciatica or sacral infections should not practice this āsana.

Benefits: Siddha yoni āsana is an excellent meditation pose in which the female aspirant can maintain the physical steadiness necessary for deep concentration. It may be used effectively by the yogini to aid spiritual meditation, and by the householder wishing to control sexual desire. It directly affects the nervous plexuses controlling the genital organs, and also serves to tone and balance the entire nervous system.

(4) Baddha yoni āsana

Sit in any meditation āsana and inhale slowly and deeply. Retain the breath and raise both hands to the face. Close the ears with the thumbs, the eyes with the index fingers, the nostrils with the middle fingers, and the mouth by placing the ring and small fingers above and below the lips. Concentrate on the bindū visargha at the back of the head (See Chapter VIII, p. 234), maintaining the breath retention, and try to perceive any ordinarily inaudible manifestation of sound. After holding the breath for as long as is comfortable, remove the middle fingers from the nostrils and exhale while keeping the other fingers in their respective positions. Inhale again and close the nostrils with the middle fingers. Repeat the process several times.

Concentration: On the bindū visargha.

Benefits: This is an excellent āsana for withdrawing the mind from the external world. Many different philosophies as well as the science of yoga teach that the source of the universe is a primordial, unceasing sound or vibration. This āsana makes possible awareness of the different manifestations of this sound through awareness of the psychic sounds which emanate from the bindū visargha in the back of the head. This is actually a technique of nāda (inner mystical sound) yoga, through which the yogi is trained to hear the full spectrum of sounds from the grossest to the most subtle. The physical benefits of padmāsana and siddhāsana are duplicated; in addition, this pose is useful in treating diseases of the eyes, ears and brain.

The āsanas, then are yogic methods for improving the circulation of prāna and blood, for correcting the spine, and for activating the nādīs and the nervous system: in short, for bringing the physical body into harmony. When a radio doesn't work properly, defective parts are repaired or adjusted until finally the entire mechanism is in working order. It is the same with the human body. However, no radio will function if it is not supplied with electric power. The yogic process for drawing energy into the body is called prānāyāma, which will be discussed in the following chapter.

III
Prānāyāma
and
Bandhas

Prāna means vital force. Yogic philosophy maintains that this vital force pervades the whole cosmos and permeates all things, both animate and inanimate. Furthermore, this fundamental force is said to be closely related to respiration, for it is primarily through breathing that prāna enters the human body. Air and the oxygen in it may be regarded as manifestations of prāna, but they are not prāna itself. Prāna is both more subtle and more fundamental than any gas. *Āyāma* means expansion, and has overtones of restraint and control. Thus prānāyāma means "techniques for controlling prāna."*

Many people consider prānāyāma to be mere breathing exercises for absorbing extra oxygen into the blood stream, but this is only one of its benefits. The aims of prānāyāma—to be detailed in later chapters—include: 1) the absorption of prāna into the subtle energy (astral) body through the visualization of the process; 2) the increase of prāna flow through the subtle nādīs; 3) the conversion of this subtle energy into vital energy of the physical dimension through

---

* The aim is not the control of universal prāna—only that which enters and flows through the body.

77

the functioning of the chakras, which connect the subtle nādīs with the physical body; 4) and the increased circulation of this energy through the blood vessels, nerves, and meridians. Therefore, prāṇāyāma is properly regarded as a group of methods to absorb and circulate prāṇa into the physical and astral bodies, invigorating both.

First we will present a description of "yogic breathing," which should be practiced daily as preparation for prānāyāma.

Yogic Breathing

Yogic breathing is a combination of abdominal breathing and chest breathing.

Abdominal Breathing: Expand the abdomen by contracting and lowering the diaphragm as you inhale a large amount of air into the lungs. Then contract the abdomen by relaxing the diaphragm and letting it rise so that the maximum amount of air is expelled from the lungs. During this process, do not move the chest or shoulders.

Chest Breathing: Inhale by expanding the chest and exhale by contracting it. It is important not to move the abdomen.

Yogic Breathing: Inhale deeply, expanding first the abdomen and then the chest to take the maximum amount of air into the lungs, smoothly and without a break. Exhale, relaxing the chest and abdomen, until the maximum amount of air has been expelled from the lungs. This sequence must be done in a wave-like motion, without any jerks.

Yogic breathing should be practiced before prānāyāma everyday so that it becomes a habit. At first the practice will require conscious effort, but later (within a matter of weeks) it will become natural and unconscious throughout the day. When this habituation has been achieved, the maximum inhalation and exhalation are no longer required.

Through the practice of yogic breathing, the student becomes less susceptible to colds, bronchitis, asthma, and related disorders. He or she is filled with energy, and looo easily tired; and the mind becomes calmer and free from anxiety. As already stated, this yogic breathing is not prānāyāma itself but a preliminary practice, and should be performed naturally throughout the day.

Before we discuss the details of prānāyāma practice, please note the following precautions:

* The bladder, stomach, and intestines should be empty, so practice prānāyāma not less than four hours after eating.
* Practice after āsanas but before meditation.
* During prānāyāma, relax the body as much as possible, avoiding strain or discomfort. Keep the spine, neck, and head erect and centered.
* Retain the breath as long as is comfortable. Excessive retention may cause lung damage or dysfunction.
* Practice in well-ventilated (not drafty), clean, and pleasant surroundings, not in a dusty, smoky, or foul-smelling place.
* When beginning prānāyāma, some constipation and decreased urinary output may be experienced. In the case of dry movements, intake of salt or spices should be avoided and, if a loose movement should result, prānāyāma practice should be suspended while a diet of cereals (rice), and yogurt is adopted for a few days.
* Siddhāsana and siddha yoni āsana are the best poses for prānāyāma, because they allow maximum expansion of the shoulders.
* In the advanced stages, prānāyāma should be practiced under the guidance of a teacher.
* Persons practicing intensive prānāyāma should not smoke tobacco, cannabis, etc.

Methods of Prānāyāma Practice

(1) Nādī Shodhan Prānāyāma

Sit in padmāsana or siddhāsana and place the hands on the knees, straightening the spine and holding the head upright. Relax the whole body and close the eyes. Be aware only of the body and the breath for a few minutes.

Stage 1: Basic technique

Keeping the left hand on the knees, raise the right hand and place the index and middle fingers between the eyebrows. They should remain in this position throughout the practice. The thumb should be placed by the right nostril and the ring finger by the left nostril.

Close the right nostril with the thumb. Inhale then exhale through the left nostril, five times at normal speed.

Release the pressure of the thumb on the right nostril and then, pressing the side of the left nostril with the ring finger, breathe in and out at normal speed five times. This should be repeated for 25 cycles, one cycle consisting of five full breaths through each nostril. The student should not breathe heavily and there should be no sound as the air moves in and out of the nostrils. After 15 days, move from Stage 1 to Stage 2.

Stage 2: Alternate nostril breathing.

Close the right nostril with the thumb and inhale through the left nostril. After completing the inhalation, close the left nostril with the ring finger and release the pressure of the thumb on the right nostril, breathing out through it. Then inhale through the right nostril and close it at the end of the inhalation. Open the left nostril and exhale. This is one cycle. The length of the inhalation and exhalation should be equal (for example, a count of five in and five out, or whatever rate you find comfortable). There should be no strain under any circumstances.

After a few days, the periods of inhalation and exhalation should be lengthened, but should not differ from each other (a 1:1 ratio). Care must be taken not to speed up the counting during exhalation to compensate for shortage of breath.

At the slightest sign of discomfort, reduce the time of each inhalation and exhalation. After 15 days or more, leave this stage and practice Stage 3.

Stage 3: Antaranga kumbhaka.

Close the right nostril and inhale through the left. At the end of the inhalation, close both nostrils, using thumb and ring finger, and retain the breath. Exhale through the right nostril and then inhale through it, keeping the left nostril closed. Again retain the breath with both nostrils closed as before. Open the left nostril and exhale, keeping the right nostril closed. Each action—inhalation, retention, and exhalation—should be performed to a count of five. This is one cycle: practice 25 cycles.

After several days of practice, alter the periods of inhalation, retention, and exhalation to the ratio 1:2:2. In other words, for an in-breath to a count of five, hold the breath inside for a count of ten and breathe out to a count of ten.

After a few days, increase the inhalation count by one (i.e. from 5 to 6), and the retention and exhalation counts by two. When these longer periods have been mastered to the point that there is not the slightest discomfort, again increase the length of each cycle, keeping the ratio the same.

After some weeks or months of practice, increase the ratio to 1:4:2. When this is mastered, change the ratio to 1:6:4; and upon mastery of this, to 1:8:6. This is the *final* ratio.

When the final ratio can be done for 25 cycles with complete relaxation and without the need for a rest, then proceed to the final stage, Stage 4.

Stage 4: Antaranga and bahiranga kumbhaka
(Internal and external retention)

Inhale through the left nostril and retain the breath. Exhale through the right nostril and hold the breath out. Breathe in through the right nostril and retain the breath. Exhale through the left nostril and hold the breath out. This is one cycle: repeat for 15 cycles. The ratio for this should start at 1:4:2:2 (inhalation: internal retention: exhalation: external retention).

You should slowly increase the respective durations, keeping the same ratio. Advanced practitioners can perform jālandhara or mūla bandha (see the section on bandha) during the internal and external retentions of Stage 4.

Precautions: Nādī shodhan should be practiced between āsanas and meditation. The breath should not be retained to the point of discomfort. Each new stage should be attempted only when perfection is achieved in the preceeding stage. Practice in a well-ventilated room, with great care and only under expert guidance.

Benefits: Because it induces calmness and tranquility of mind, Nādī shodhan is an indispensable prelude to advanced meditational practices. All the nādīs are cleared of blockages, the flow of prāna in the ida and pingalā nādīs is equalized, and the blood system is cleansed of toxins. The whole body is nourished by the extra supply of oxygen that is absorbed, and carbon dioxide is efficiently expelled. Stale air in the lungs is removed. The brain cells are purified, encouraging the centers of the brain to work nearer their optimum capacities.

(2) *Bhastrika prānāyāma* (bellows prānāyāma)

Sit in padmāsana or siddhāsana with the head and spine erect and the eyes closed. Relax the whole body.

Stage 1: Place the left hand on the left knee and rest the index and middle fingers of the right hand between the

eyebrows, with the thumb beside the right nostril and the ring finger beside the left nostril. Close the right nostril with the thumb. Breathe rapidly and rhythmically through the left nostril 20 times, expanding and contracting the abdomen. Then, close both nostrils with the thumb and ring finger, and do jālandhara or mūla bandha (See Chapter III pp. 89-92). Retain the breath for a comfortable period of time, then release the bandha and exhale. Close the left nostril and breathe 20 times, again with quick but rhythmical expansions and contractions of the abdominal muscles. Then inhale deeply, close both nostrils, and perform jālandhara or mūla bandha. Hold for some time and slowly exhale. This is one cycle; perform three cycles.

Stage 2: Sit in the same position placing both hands on the knees. Breathe rapidly 20 times through both nostrils simultaneously. Then inhale deeply, retain the breath, and perform jālandhara or mūla bandha. After a comfortable period, release the bandha and breathe out. This is one cycle; three should be performed.

The complete practice of bhastrika includes both stages.

Duration: Beginners should perform about 20 repetitions of rapid breathing. Advanced practitioners may increase gradually to 50, and the cycles can be increased from three to five.

Note: In this technique, the lungs are used like a blacksmith's bellows.

Precautions: A feeling of faintness or perspiration indicates that the practice is being done incorrectly. Avoid violent respiration, facial contortions, or excessive body shaking. If any of these symptoms are experienced despite correct performance of the method, the advice of a teacher should be sought.

Relax throughout the whole process and rest after each cycle. For the first few weeks, bhastrika should be done slowly. The speed of respiration should gradually be increased only as the lungs grow stronger.

Limitations: People with high blood pressure, vertigo, or any heart ailment, as well as beginners, should not do bhastrika without expert guidance.

Benefits: Harmful substances and germs in the lungs are expelled. Asthma, tuberculosis, pleurisy, as well as any inflammation of the throat involving phlegm should show improvement. Digestion and appetite are stimulated. This prānāyāma induces tranquility of mind and is very helpful in awakening kundalinī.

(3) *Ujjāyi prānāyāma* (Psychic breathing)

Ujjāyi prānāyāma is performed by contracting the glottis in the throat and forming khechari mudrā (in which the tongue is folded backwards so that the underside is pressed against either the back of the hard palate or, preferably, the soft palate). Breathe deeply and softly, like the gentle snoring of a sleeping baby. There should be no sensation of breathing through the nostrils, only through the throat.

Ujjāyi prānāyāma may be practiced in almost any pose—for example, in many of the mudrās and with meditational techniques such as ajapa japa (See Chapter IV, p. 123).

Duration: It can be performed for several hours.

Benefits: This prānāyāma is very simple to do, but has subtle influences on the whole body. It produces a calming effect on the nervous system, and a serene and pliable state of mind results.

Insomnia sufferers should practice ujjāyi prānāyāma in shavāsana but without khechari mudrā. It is also useful in cases of high blood pressure, for reducing the heart beat, and as an excellent aid to various meditational practices, due to its subtle effects on the psychic plane.

(4) *Sūrya Bhedana Prānāyāma* (Vitality stimulating technique)

Sit in padmāsana or siddhāsana with the hands on the knees and the spine and head erect. Close the eyes and relax the whole body. Raise the right hand, placing the middle and index fingers between the eyebrows and the thumb and ring finger gently on each side of the nose.

Close the left nostril with the ring finger and inhale deeply through the right. Close both nostrils, retain the breath and perform jālandhara and mūla bandhas. Maintain for as long as is comfortably possible. Then release mūla and jalāndhara bandhas. Open the right nostril and exhale through it, keeping the left nostril closed with the ring finger. This is one cycle.

Duration: Practice ten cycles and try to increase the retention period gradually over a period of a few weeks.

Precautions: Do not practice immediately before or after meals, as the energy is needed for digestion. It is said that if the idā nādī (connected to the left nostril) is blocked during or after a meal, indigestion will probably result. This prānāyāma also should be practiced with much care under expert guidance.

Benefits: As the pingalā nādī (connected to the right nostril) is activated, the practitioner becomes more dynamic and can perform physical activities with more efficiency.

Note: There are other prānāyāmas which activate the idā nādī by breathing through the left nostril. However according to ancient yoga texts, they must not be taught or practiced due to their powerful and unpredictable effect.

(5) *Murchā Prānāyāma* (Fainting prānāyāma)

This prānāyāma requires a stable sitting posture, such as padmāsana or siddhāsana.

Inhale deeply and slowly through both nostrils while bending the head backwards and performing ākāshī mudrā (See Chapter IV, p. 98). Retain the breath for as long as is comfortable and perform shāmbhavī mudrā (in which the eyes are focused upwards on any fixed point or on the point between the eyebrows. See Chapter IV, p. 97). Keep the arms straight by locking the elbows and pressing the hands to the knees. Then exhale, bending the arms, closing the eyes, and slowly

returning the head to the upright position. Relax the whole body for a few seconds with the eyes closed and experience a light, calm feeling spread throughout the mind and body.

This is one cycle. Repeat several cycles.

Note: Breathe only through the nostrils throughout the entire process.

Duration: Perform each cycle before meditation for as long as possible without strain, slowly increasing the duration. Continue for many cycles until a sensation of faintness is felt.

Limitations: This prānāyāma should not be performed by people with high blood pressure, vertigo, or high intracranial pressure. It should be practiced with great care under expert guidance.

Benefits: This is an excellent pre-meditation practice, because it enables one to draw the mind inwards and reach a spiritual state in which external sensations such as hearing and feeling disappear. Tranquility is induced throughout the body and mind, and tension, anxiety, and anger are effectively removed. It is also useful for people suffering from abnormal blood pressure, neurosis, or mental problems.

This concludes the description of prāṇāyāma practices. The next section will introduce the bandhas, practices which help focus the absorbed prāṇa and direct it to the chakras.

BANDHAS

The word *bandha* means to hold or tighten. This is an accurate description of the physical action required in these practices: various parts of the body are gently but firmly contracted and tightened. Bandhas help improve physical health through massage of the internal organs, stimulation and regulation of the nerves, and the removal of stagnant blood.

Though these bandhas are performed on the physical level, they subtly influence the chakras. Contraction of the body at the chakra points induces mental concentration upon the chakras themselves. Furthermore, the breath retention that always accompanies the bandhas causes prāṇa to accumulate in the areas of mental concentration.

The bandhas help to release the *granthis* (knots of spiritual energy—see Chapter IX), which impede the flow of prāṇa in the sushumnā, thus generating the increased circulation of spiritual energy. When the granthis are loosened to some extent, a tightening of the sushumnā is experienced, a sign that psychic energy has begun to flow. This tightening is experienced by advanced practitioners when the kundalinī starts to awaken and the chakras are about to open.

Bandhas should be practiced in isolation until mastered; later, they are performed in conjunction with prāṇāyāma and mudrā. This prevents prāṇa which has been absorbed through prāṇāyāma from dissipating. When these three forms of practice are combined, the psychic ability of an individual starts to awaken and advanced yoga begins. (This is detailed in the section on chakra awakening).

As explained above, bandhas are always accompanied by breath retention, and the duration of this retention should be gradually increased in time without undue strain. The retention may be internal or external.

Here we will present three fundamental bandhas, the jālandhara, mūla, and uddiyāna. The ancient *Yoga-chudāmani Upanishad* states that if a yogi masters nabho mudrā and uddiyāna, jālandhara and mūla bandhas, he will be liberated; and according to *Yoga-shikkā Upanishad*, constant practice of these three bandhas develops control over prāna.

Though there are descriptions of these bandhas in *Yoga-shikkā Upanishad* and *Yoga-kundalinī Upanishad*, the following accounts are based on Swami Satyananda Saraswati's more detailed, modern descriptions.

(1) *Jālandhara bandha* (Chin lock)

Sit in a meditation posture which allows the knees to rest firmly on the floor, such as padmāsana or siddhāsana. Relax the whole body with the palms on the knees and the eyes closed. Inhale deeply and hold the breath.

Bend the head forward and press the chin tightly against the top of the sternum. Straighten the arms, locking the elbows. Simultaneously hunch the shoulders upward and forward (this helps to ensure locking of the arms), keeping the palms on the knees. This is the final pose.

Jālandhara bandha should be maintained until the breath can no longer be held comfortably. Then, relax the shoulders, bend the arms, slowly release the lock, raise the head, and slowly exhale. Begin the process again when breathing returns to normal. The whole practice can also be performed with external breath retention.

This bandha closes the trachea and compresses the organs in the throat.

Duration: For as long as breath retention is comfortable. It can be repeated up to ten times.

Concentration: On the vishuddhi chakra.

Time: Ideally, it should be practiced in conjunction with prāṇāyāma and mudrās, but if practiced alone, it should follow āsana and prānāyāma practice, and precede meditation.

Precautions: Do not inhale or exhale until the chin lock has been released and the head is upright.

Limitations: Persons with high blood pressure, abnormal intracranial pressure, or heart ailments should not practice without expert advice.

Benefits: Body and mind relax. The heart beat is slowed as the chin lock compresses the carotid sinus (the autonomic nerves around the sinus connected with the medulla oblongata and other centers in the brain which control the heart beat). The thyroid and parathyroid glands, which influence the growth of the body's reproductive systems, are also stimulated by the chin lock and breath retention, improving their functioning. This bandha is useful for removing or reducing stress, anxiety, and anger, and is an excellent pre-meditational practice.

(2) *Mūla bandha* (perineum contraction lock)

Sit in a meditational pose with the knees firmly on the ground. Siddhasāna or siddha yoni āsana are best, since these press the heel into the perineum and thereby directly aid the performance of the bandha.

Relax the whole body with the palms on the knees and eyes closed. Inhale deeply, retain the breath, and perform jālandhara bandha. Then contract the muscles of the perineum (the area between the external genitalia and the anus) and draw them upwards. This is the final pose. It should be held as long as the breath can be retained comfortably. Release the perineum contraction, slowly raise the head, and slowly exhale. Repeat the process.

This bandha can also be performed by initially exhaling and holding the breath out while executing the locks, or by maintaining the contraction for long periods with normal breathing but without jālandhara bandha.

Duration: As long as the breath can be retained without strain. Repeat up to ten times.

Concentration: On the mūlādhāra chakra.

Sequence: Practice after āsana and pranāyāma, but before meditation; ideally, in conjunction with the mudrās and pranāyāma.

Precautions: This bandha must be practiced carefully under expert guidance.

Limitations: Refer to jālandhara bandha.

Prepatory technique: Beginners may find it difficult to contract the muscles of the perineum strongly and maintain the contraction during breath retention. Such people should regularly practice ashvinī mudrā (see Chap. IV), to strengthen the perineal muscles and develop control over them.

Benefits: The perineum (the region of the mūlādhāra chakra) is contracted and pulled upwards. This forces the apāna vāyu (the vital energy acting in the part of the body below the navel) to ascend and thereby unite with the prāna vāyu (the vital energy acting in the region of the body between the larynx and the base of the heart). This generates energy of a higher dimension. This bandha facilitates the awakening of kundalinī, and it helps to maintain celibacy by acting to sublimate sexual energy and raise it to higher chakras.

The pelvic nerves are stimulated and the associated urogenital organs are toned. Constipation and hemorrhoids show improvement because the sphincter muscles of the anus are strengthened and intestinal peristalsis is stimulated. The benefits of jālandhara bandha are duplicated.

(3) *Uddiyāna bandha*

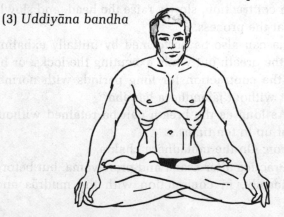

Sit in any meditational pose, resting the knees on the floor. Relax the whole body with the palms on the knees and the eyes closed. Exhale deeply and hold the breath outside. Perform jālandhara bandha and contract the abdominal muscles, pulling them upward. This is the final pose and should be held as long as is comfortable. Slowly release the stomach muscles and then jālandhara bandha, and inhale. When the breathing has returned to normal, the process may be repeated.

Duration: For as long as the breath can be retained without strain. Repeat ten times.

Concentration: On the manipūra chakra.

Time: Practice after āsana and prānāyāma, but before meditation; ideally, in conjunction with the mudrās and prānāyāma.

Precautions: Practice this bandha only when the stomach and intestines are empty. Release the chin lock before inhalation.

Limitations: Persons suffering from heart problems, peptic or duodenal ulcers, and pregnant women should not practice this āsana.

Preparation, Alternative: Agnisara kriyā (see Chap. IV) may be practiced as a preparatory technique or as an alternative.

Benefits: The diaphragm is pulled up into the thoracic cavity and the abdominal organs are drawn toward the spine. This bandha therefore benefits all abdominal ailments, providing relief from constipation, indigestion, worms, and diabetes. The "digestive fire" of the manipūra chakra is stimulated, improving the function of the abdominal organs. The liver, pancreas, kidneys, and spleen are all massaged, enhancing their functioning, and regular practice of the bandha can eliminate associated diseases. The adrenal glands are normalized, so that a lethargic person gains vitality and an anxious or overwrought person is calmed. The sympathetic nerves of the solar plexus are stimulated and the abdominal organs they control, are stimulated.

As mentioned above, the manipūra chakra, located in the region of the navel is stimulated. As the manipūra is the center of prāna in the body, the distribution and flow of prāna throughout the body—especially prāna which rises through the sushumnā nādī—is improved.

Now that we have discussed the three basic bandhas, let us turn our attention to our next topic, the mudrās.

IV
The Mudrās and the Awakening of the Chakras

Now that we have discussed the three basic bandhas, let us turn our attention to the mudrās. Not merely physical postures, these are practices which generate a strong psychic effect upon the inner being of the student, facilitating spiritual advancement. Their specific aims are to aid in the awakening of kundalinī, to bring about the awareness and control of prāna in the astral dimension, and to generate siddhis (paranormal abilities). When these goals have been attained, the student is able to transmit prāna at will through the subtle chakras and nādīs to cure a diseased area of his own or another's body. This type of paranormal ability inevitably appears when a degree of advancement has been attained.

In its broadest sense, the term "mudrā" encompasses all methods for awakening the chakras, including pratyāhāra (sense withdrawal). Of course, in addition to their spiritual benefits, the mudrās effectively promote physical health. It is important that they be studied under the guidance of an experienced teacher. Here we shall briefly describe some of the basic mudrās.

95

(1) *Jnāna and Chin Mudrās*

Sit in a meditation āsana and bend the index finger of each hand so that the tip touches the inside of the root of the thumb. Keeping the other three fingers of each hand straight, place the hands on the knees with the palms turned down and the three unbent fingers and thumb of each hand pointing at the floor in front of the feet.

This is jnāna mudrā.

Chin mudrā is performed in the same way as jnāna mudrā except that the palms of both hands face upward.

Duration: Either of these mudrās may be performed in any of the meditation poses for the duration of that pose.

Benefits: Jnāna and chin mudrās are simple but important psycho-neural finger locks which complete the meditational āsanas such as padmāsana and siddhāsana and make them more powerful.

My long experience of yoga and acupuncture theory suggests this explanation: Prāna or ki energy absorbed through the manipūra chakra reaches and sustains the lungs, and then flows along both lung meridians to the thumbs. Some of this prāna is emitted from the sei ("well") point of the lung meridian at the tip of the thumb. When the index finger and thumb are touching in jnāna and chin mudrās, the energy that would otherwise be discharged is transferred to the large intestine meridian that begins at the tip of the index finger. As the body's vital energy is conserved by these mudrās, the student can meditate for long periods.

In the traditional Indian explanation, symbolic significance is attributed to each of the fingers. The little finger represents tamas (inertia, lethargy); the ring finger represents rajas (activity, action, passion); the middle finger, sattva (purity, wisdom, peace).*

The index finger represents the jivātma (the individual soul in each person) and the thumb signifies the paramātma (the all-pervading Supreme Consciousness). The position of the index finger and the thumb symbolizes the ultimate goal of yoga—the union of the individual soul and the Supreme Consciousness.

(2) *Shāmbhavī mudrā* (Eyebrow-center gazing)

Sit in a meditation āsana with the spine erect and the hands on the knees in chin or jnāna mudrā. Gaze forward at a fixed point and then upward as high as possible, without moving the head. Then focus the eyes at a point directly between the eyebrows and concentrate on that point. Let the thought process cease and meditate on the self (Ātman) or the Supreme Consciousness (Paramātma).

---

* *According to yoga theory, in its unmanifest state prakriti (the primordial energy of the universe, the most basic substance) is composed of three gunas, or qualities, which are: tamas, rajas, and sattva. When observed by purusha (Pure Spirit), these gunas begin to act, influencing and combining with each other, so as to create the material aspect of the universe.*

Duration: As long as possible. At first, for a few minutes; but with practice, the time can be slowly extended.

Benefits: This is one of the most highly regarded practices in yoga. One who is proficient in the technique of shāmbhavī mudrā can transcend the mind, the intellect, and the ego, entering the psychic and spiritual realms of consciousness. It is a powerful technique for awakening the ājnā chakra, the seat of union between the lower and higher consciousness. This mudrā brings calmness of mind and removes tension and anger. It also strengthens the eye muscles.

(3) *Ākāshī mudrā* (Consciousness of inner space)

Sit in a meditation pose and fold the tongue back against the palate, as in khechari mudrā (See Chapter IV p. 101). Practice ujjāyi prānāyāma and shāmbhavī mudrā. With the head tilted backward somewhat, but not to the fullest extent, breathe slowly and deeply. At first, ujjāyi prānāyāma in this position may irritate the throat, but with practice it will become more comfortable.

Duration: Maintain the final position for as long as possible. If it is difficult for more than a short time, stop practicing ujjāyi prānāyāma, khechari mudrā, and shāmbhavī mudrā; rest for a short time, then repeat.

Concentration: On the ājnā chakra.

Precautions: As with all mudrās, it must be learned gradually under expert guidance,

Benefits: When this mudrā is perfected, the student goes into a kind of trance. This is not a trance in the Western sense but in the yogic sense, one in which the student achieves a state of heightened consciousness. Calmness and tranquility of mind result, and the benefits of ujjāyi prānāyāma, shāmbhavī mudrā, and khechari mudrā are duplicated.

(4) *Bhujangani mudrā* (Snake breathing)

Sit in a meditation pose, relaxing the whole body. In this mudrā, the student must try to 'drink' air through the mouth into the stomach (*not* the lungs), as if he were gulping water. Expand the stomach as much as possible, hold the air inside for a short period of time, then expel the air by belching. Repeat the process.

Duration: Do as many times as desired, though three to five times is usually sufficient. It may be repeated more often to ease specific ailments. This mudrā can be performed at any time, though it is more effective when performed after the hatha yoga practice of shankha prakhalana.*

Benefits: The esophageal walls and the digestive secretory glands are rejuvenated. The whole stomach is toned, stagnant gases are eliminated, and gastric disorders improve. When air is retained in the stomach, the student can float in the water for any length of time without sinking.

(5) *Ashvinī mudrā* (Horse mudrā)

Stage 1: Sit in a meditation āsana, relax the whole body, close the eyes, and breathe normally. Contract the sphincter muscles of the anus for a few seconds, then relax them for a few seconds. Repeat this process as many times as possible.

---

* *A gentle, systematic method for complete washing of the entire alimentary canal from the mouth to the anus.*

Stage 2: Sit as in Stage 1, contracting the anus during inhalation. Retain the breath and hold the contraction, then exhale, releasing the contraction. Repeat this process as many times as possible.

Duration: For as long as is comfortable without strain. May be practiced at any time of the day and at any stage during yoga practice.

Concentration: On the mūlādhāra chakra.

Benefits: Control is gained over the sphincter muscles of the anus (as a horse has). When this mudrā is properly performed, the escape of prāna from the body is prevented, and this energy can therefore be conserved and directed upwards for higher purposes. It is very useful for those who suffer from piles or prolapse of the rectum or uterus, though in these cases this mudrā is most effective if done in conjunction with an inverted pose. Intestinal peristalsis is also stimulated and constipation is eased. This is an excellent preparatory exercise for mūla bandha.

(6) *Kakī mudrā* (Crow beak)

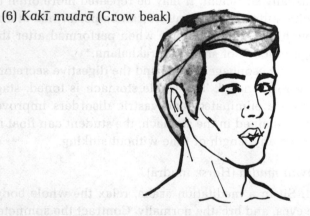

Sit in a meditational pose and make a narrow tube by pursing the lips. Concentrate the eyes on the tip of the nose. Inhale slowly and deeply through the mouth and then slowly exhale through the nose. Again inhale through the mouth and repeat the process.

Duration: For as long as possible.

Benefits: The influx of air touches the walls of the mouth and stimulates the digestive secretions. This mudra is effective in awakening the mūlādhāra chakra and for cooling the whole body.

(7) *Khechari mudrā* (Tongue lock)

Close the mouth and roll the tongue backwards so that the underside of the tongue touches the back of the palate. Take the tongue-tip as far back as possible without strain (in this position ujjāyi prānāyāma may be performed) and hold it there for as long as possible. If beginners feel discomfort after a short time, they should relax the tongue for a few seconds, and then resume the position. (With practice, the tongue can be stretched enough to be rolled backwards to stimulate the larynx and pharynx. This stimulation is then conveyed to the various nerve centers in the brain.)

Breathing: Beginners may breathe normally during the practice, but over a period of months they should gradually try to reduce the rate of respiration until after two months or more it is only five to eight breaths per minute (normal breathing being about sixteen per minute). With careful practice, preferably under expert guidance, the respiration rate can be reduced even further.

Duration: For as long as possible or desired, preferably at peaceful, relaxed times. Khechari mudrā can be performed in conjunction with other yoga practices.

Precautions: If this mudrā is performed during physical exercise and a bitter taste is felt in the throat, stop the practice to avoid any harmful effects.

Benefits: This mudrā has a subtle influence on the human body. There are various pressure points and glands in the cavity behind the palate which have extensive control over the activities of the body, and the secretions from these are stimulated by the folded tongue. Saliva is also produced, which removes feelings of thirst and hunger. Yogis who are buried underground for long periods of time perform khechari mudrā for the duration. This allows them to retain the breath for as long as they wish without any harm. The mudrā helps to awaken the kundalinī shakti, and also to preserve the vital energy of the body.

The form of kechari mudrā described here is, properly speaking, a practice of rāja yoga. In the full hatha yoga form, the tendon beneath the tongue is gradually stretched over a period of several months until the rear passages can be completely blocked with the folded tongue. When perfected, this practice can cause detachment of the astral body from the physical. The consciousness thereby dwells in ākāshā, the "space" between the astral and physical dimensions. This mudra is regarded as very important in the ancient yoga texts.

(8) *Prāna mudrā*

Starting
Position

Stage 2

Sit in a meditation pose with the spine erect. Close the eyes and place the hands on the lap.

Stage 1: Exhale as deeply as possible, contracting the abdominal muscles to expel the maximum amount of air from the lungs. Perform mūla bandha while retaining the breath and concentrating on the mūlādhāra chakra. Retain the breath for as long as is comfortable.

Stage 2: Release mūla bandha and slowly begin a deep inhalation, expanding the abdomen to its fullest extent and drawing as much air as possible into the lungs. Simultaneously raise the hands in front of the navel. The hands should be open with the fingers pointing at each other but not touching, and with the palms facing the trunk.

During this stage, try to feel the prāna being drawn from the mūlādhāra to the manipūra chakra as you inhale.

The movement of the hands should be coordinated with the abdominal inhalation.

Stage 3: Continue the inhalation by expanding the chest and simultaneously continue the upward movement of the hands. At the end of this expansion the hands should be directly in front of the heart. During this stage, try to feel prāna being drawn from the manipūra to the anāhata chakra.

Stage 4.

Try to draw even more air into the lungs by raising the shoulders. During this action, try to feel the prāna being drawn up to the vishuddhi chakra and then spreading like a wave to the ājnā chakra and eventually to the sahāsrāra. Coordinate the hand movements with the breath by raising the hands in front of the throat.

Stage 5.

Stage 5: Retain the breath inside while moving the hands out to the sides. In the final position, the hands should be at the same height as the ears, the arms outstretched but not straight. Concentrate on the sahasrāra chakra. Try to visualize an aura of pure light emanating from the head. Feel your whole being radiating vibrations of peace to all beings. Maintain this position for as long as possible without straining the lungs. Then return to the starting position while exhaling, *repeating Stages 1 to 5, but in reverse order.* During the exhalation, feel the prana coming down from the sahasrāra to the mūlādhāra via each chakra. Relax the body for a short time, breathing deeply and slowly.

Concentration: The awareness should move with the breath and hand movement from the mūlādhāra to the sahasrāra and vice versa. When this mudrā is perfected, the student can see the breath extrasensorily as a stream of white light ascending and descending in the sushumṇā nādī. Prāṇa mudra should be performed before meditation.

Precautions: Do not strain the lungs. Slowly increase the duration of inhalation, retention, and exhalation with regular practice.

Benefits: This is a compact mudrā, combining prāṇāyāma with the symbolic gesture of a mudrā. It is an excellent practice for awakening the dormant vital energy (prāna shakti). It distributes this energy throughout the whole body, thereby increasing strength, personal magnetism, and health.

(9) *Navamukhī Mudrā* (The mudrā of nine gates—yoni Mudrā)

Sit in a meditational āsana, relax the whole body, and inhale slowly and deeply. Simultaneously concentrate on each chakra in turn for a few seconds, feeling the slow ascent of the breath (prāna) and consciousness from the mūlādhāra to the sahasrāra. Retain the breath inside and raise both hands to the face. Close the ears with the thumbs, the eyes with the index fingers, the nostrils with the middle fingers, and the mouth by placing the ring and the little fingers above and below the lips. Perform mūla bandha and vajroli mudrā (see p. 91 and 114). Concentrate on the sahasrāra while retaining the breath inside. Hold the breath for as long as possible without strain, then release the finger pressure on the nostrils and slowly exhale. During this exhalation release mūla bandha and vajroli mudrā, but keep the fingers in position. Maintain awareness of the sahasrāra. At the end of the exhalation, relax for a few seconds and then repeat the whole process.

Duration: For as long as possible without strain.

Notes: In the body there are nine openings through which sensory experiences of the external world enter and waste matter is excreted: the two ears, the two eyes, the two nostrils, the mouth, the anus, and the urinary passage. These openings are called the nine "gates" in the "temple" of the body. By closing these gates and withdrawing the mind inward, one is able to pass through the tenth gate—that of spiritual awakening—thereby transcending mundane consciousness. The mystical tenth gate is in the crown of the sahasrāra chakra and is known as the gate of Brahma (higher conscousness).

Benefits: As the mind is drawn within from the external world, awareness develops of the nāda, psychic sounds which originate in the sahasrāra chakra and emanate from an important center in the brain called bindu-visargha.

(10) *Agnisar Kriyā* (Vahnisar Dhauti: "purification by fire breathing").

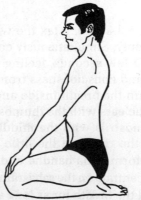

Vajrāsana

Sit in vajrāsana (note diagram, p. 106), keeping the toes together and separating the knees as far as possible. Place both hands on the knees and lean the upper half of the body forward slightly, keeping the arms straight. Open the mouth and extend the tongue from the mouth. Breathe rapidly in and out by contracting and expanding the abdomen. The breathing should resemble the panting of a dog. Repeat this rapid breathing 25 times.

Advanced form: Take the same pose as in the sample form. Exhale as deeply as possible and perform jālandhara bandha. With external retention, rapidly contract and expand the abdominal muscles.

Precautions: Wait at least four hours after eating to practice this mudrā.

Limitations: Those with high blood pressure, heart disease, or peptic or duodenal ulcers should not do this practice.

Benefits: Abdominal conditions such as excessive wind (flatulence), constipation, depressed liver function, etc., are relieved, the abdominal organs are toned, and the appetite is stimulated. This serves as a good preparation for uddiyāna bandha (see Chapter III p. 92) and nauli kriya (abdominal massage, see Chapter IV, p. 120).

Although described here with the basic mudrās, aginsāra kriya, which can be used as a substitute or preparation for uddiyāna bandha, is not a mudrā proper, but a part of hatha yoga practice. With it, this section is concluded, and we proceed to the methods for awakening the chakras.

Methods for Awakening the Chakras

One traditional approach to the awakening of the chakras is exemplified by the *Gorakshashatakam*, a brief treatise written in the tenth century by the guru Goraknath. This text will be presented in detail in Chapter VI-B. The principle technique described is the concentration on each chakra while gazing at the tip of the nose. For example, Goraknath

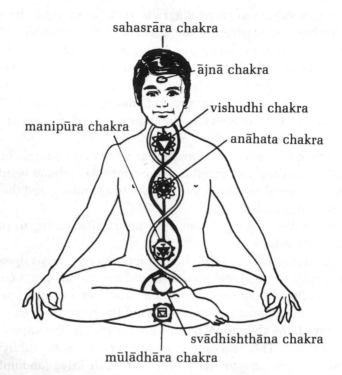

sahasrāra chakra

ājnā chakra

vishudhi chakra

manipūra chakra

anāhata chakra

svādhishthāna chakra

mūlādhāra chakra

writes, "The first chakra, called ādhāra (the mūlādhāra), is like burnished gold. Meditating on it with the gaze fixed on the tip of the nose, one is freed from sin. The second chakra is the svādhisthāna, as beautiful as a genuine ruby. Meditating on it with the gaze fixed on the tip of the nose, one is freed from sin."

The effectiveness of this practice can be explained by the location of the idā and pingalā nādīs, which originate in the mūlādhāra chakra — the seat of kundalinī — and terminate in the left and right nostrils, respectively. Gazing at the tip of the nose therefore stimulates these nādīs and the mūlādhāra chakra, as well as the kundalinī it houses. When using this method while concentrating on another chakra, the practitioner can cause kundalinī to rise and further energize that chakra, already activated by mental concentration. This technique of nose-gazing, then, is a powerful method which can potentially double the effects of concentration.

However, since this practice is so simple and monotonous, a beginner finds himself easily distracted by thoughts and desires which emerge from the subconscious. His mind becomes restless, and his concentration is easily broken. For these reasons, the practices recommended here are of a more comprehensive and varied nature. Indian yoga has devised and handed down other effective methods for awakening the chakras which combine chakra concentration with āsanas, prānāyāma, and mudrās. The mechanism of these practices follows a distinct pattern: first, prāna is absorbed through prānāyāma; next, the chakra is stimulated physically and phychically through specific āsanas and mudrās; and finally, the chakra is activated by the infusion of channeled prāna and direct mental concentration.

The following descriptions of practices for awakening the chakras are largely based on *Tantra of Kundalini Yoga* by Swami Satyananda Saraswati. Please realize that the practices enumerated here traditionally have been taught only to outstanding students under the careful guidance of a guru.

Practicing alone from a book can easily lead to a misunderstanding and thus considerable danger. It is essential that the instructions recorded here be followed only under the most expert guidance.

(1) Awakening the Ājnā Chakra

Sit in siddhāsana (women in siddha yoni āsana) with the eyes *gently* closed. If siddhāsana is impossible, sit in half siddhāsana, with one heel—whichever feels more comfortable—pressing against the perineum. Place the hands on the knees in chin mudrā and make sure the spine is erect. It is important to keep the eyelids closed *gently*; the unconscious strain generated when the eyes are closed tightly prevents entry into deep meditation. Concentrate between the eyebrows or on the tip of the nose, fixing the eyes themselves on either spot behind the closed lids. At the same time, alternately contract and relax the perineum gently, where the heel is pressing. Continue for 5 to 10 minutes.

Next, become aware of the breath and adjust to the rhythm so that the perineum is contracted during inhalation and relaxed during exhalation. Breathe at a natural speed in this way for 50 breaths, maintaining awareness of both the perineal contractions and the breath. This is the first half of the method.

Next, remaining in the same position, concentrate on the ājnā chakra between the eyebrows. Inhale slowly and deeply, imagining the absorption or prāna between the eyebrows as you chant OM* in your mind. Then exhale slowly, imagining that you are radiating prāna from the eyebrow center, returning it to the universe, as you continue to chant OM. Continue for as long as possible (30 minutes to two hours).

There are two reasons why stimulation of the perineum, the location of the mūlādhāra chakra in the physical body, is helpful in awakening the ājnā. First, this practice helps to awaken the kundalinī which resides within the mūlādhāra. No chakra can be awakened unless it is energized by an activated kundalinī. Secondly, the ājnā is directly connected to the mūlādhāra by the idā, pingalā and sushumnā nādīs, which converge at these two points. Direct stimulation of one of these chakras generates a contingent effect upon the other. Thus, the activation of the mūlādhāra in the first part of the practice described here is an excellent preparation for the direct concentration on the ājnā which follows.

Concentration on the ājnā chakra is strongly recommended before attempting to awaken other chakras, for the following reasons. Each chakra is said to possess its own latent karma, which is brought to the surface and activated to some extent when it is stimulated through ascetic practice. The

---

* Pronounced like "home" without the "h".

awakening of the ājnā chakra avowedly enables the practitioner to purify the karma of the lower chakras, in addition to that of the ājnā itself. Thus, if the ājnā is awakened first, the overpowering and potentially dangerous karmic forces hidden in the lower chakras may be safely controlled.

Furthermore, by first activating the ājnā the practitioner strongly stimulates the kundalinī residing in the mūlādhāra, owing to the direct connection between the two chakras.

The only way to discover the precise location of the ājnā is through direct experience, but the sensation is often reported as follows. When the perineum is repeatedly contracted and relaxed in coordination with the breathing, the area becomes hot and a subtle vitration is felt there. At the same time, a similar sensation is felt at a point between the eyebrows, the location of the ājnā chakra. As the student maintains concentration on this point, visualizing the absorption and diffusion of prāna while chanting OM, the ājnā is gradually activated. After months or years of continued practice, awakening should take place.

(2) Awakening the Mūlādhāra Chakra (Mānduki Kriya)

Sit in vajrāsana (Japanese seiza posture—sit on the heels, knees pointing forward) with the knees slightly separated. Interlock the hands and hold them below the navel, wrists on the thighs. With the eyes closed, direct your gaze to the tip of the nose, concentrating there. Then open the eyes slightly and continue to concentrate. Even though the nose-tip may not be visible, a sensation should be felt there. When the eyes become tired, close them for awhile, continuing mental concentration. When they are rested, resume visual concentration. Repeat this process for 10-20 minutes. Next, shift your attention to the perineum. Alternately contract and relax it for a period of 30-60 minutes. These two techniques, practiced together, comprise the method for awakening the mūlādhāra chakra.

112

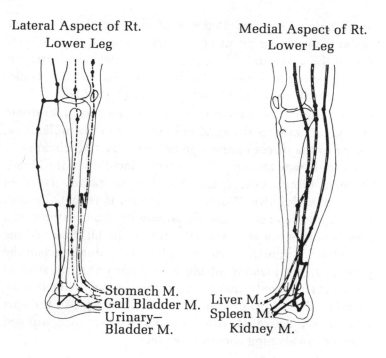

Lateral Aspect of Rt.
Lower Leg

Medial Aspect of Rt.
Lower Leg

Stomach M.
Gall Bladder M.
Urinary–
Bladder M.

Liver M.
Spleen M.
Kidney M.

The value of sitting in vajrāsana to stimulate the mūlādhāra chakra can be explained in terms of acupuncture theory. The mūlādhāra controls the functions of the urogenital organs, which, in terms of Chinese medicine, are governed by the urinary bladder and kidney meridians.

The urinary bladder meridian runs down the back of the leg, with the kidney meridian somewhat to the inside. These meridians are stimulated by the weight of the upper half of the body in vajrāsana, and this stimulation is transmitted to the mūlādhāra chakra, helping to activate it.

We have already seen how concentration on the tip of the nose stimulates the mūlādhāra, due to the idā and pingalā nadis which connect the two areas (see Chapt. IV, p. 108). In fact, when an acupuncture needle is inserted into the perineum (the location of the mūlādhāra in the physical body),to a depth of 1 cm., a tingling sensation is often felt at the tip of the nose, and nasal blockages are cleared. After 5 to 10 minutes, ki energy which has stagnated in the head flows downward, and the balance of ki-flow throughout the body is restored.

The above information suggests that before attempting to awaken a given chakra, it is useful to concentrate first on a complementary chakra at the opposite end of the interconnecting nādīs. This resembles a common pattern in acupuncture treatment: to treat a given problem area, a point located at the opposite end of the body but closely related through the meridian network is strongly stimulated. For example, a needle may be inserted in the hyakue point (Paihui, GV20) at the top of the head to treat hemorrhoids. Techniques based upon this principle—either in acupuncture treatment or yoga practice—promote the improved functioning of the internal organs and increased prāna flow. In the case of yoga, chakra awakening is facilitated by strengthening the mutual interaction of the individual chakras.

(3) Awakening the Svādhishthāna Chakra

Sit in siddhāsana, placing the upper heel at the lowest point of the abdomen, in the center. This point is the location of the svādhishthāna chakra. With both hands on the knees, assume chin mudrā. Close the eyes and keep the body perfectly still. Then concentrate directly on the svādhishthāna. Practice khechari mudrā (see Chapter IV, p. 101), releasing it whenever tired. While concentrating, slowly contract and relax the surrounding muscular area. The contraction starts from the point of svādishthāna itself, but eventually should cover a larger area which includes the genitals. However, make certain that the mūlādhāra area stays relaxed, unaffected by the contraction process. At first it may be difficult to isolate the various muscle groups, but continued practice will bring results. Both contraction and relaxation should be slow and deliberate, performed with full awareness. Uddiyāna bandha (Chapter III, p. 92), shlabhāsana (Chapter IV, p. 118), and dhanurāsana (Chapter II, p. 61), are recommended to help develop conscious control of the contraction-relaxation process.

Another technique often suggested to facilitate concentration on the svādhishthāna is as follows. Press the palms against the knees, raising the shoulders a little but keeping the elbows straight. Bend the neck forward as in jālandhara bandha (Chapter III, p. 89), and perform the same contraction and relaxation described above. (The breath retention of jālandhara bandha is unnecessary.) After practicing in this pose for a few minutes, return to the standard erect posture and continue.

This contraction and relaxation, performed with a deeply meditative attitude and in complete stillness, is called vajroli. After practicing vajroli for 30-60 minutes, release khechari mudrā and chant OM three times.

The beneficial effects of khechari mudrā and the posture of jālandhara bandha—both of which stimulate the throat area—upon the svādhishthāna chakra can be explained as follows. Like the mūlādhāra, the svādhishthāna is related to the urogenital organs, and thus to the kidney and urinary bladder meridians of acupuncture. The kidney meridian flows through the larynx and pharynx, which are stimulated by the forward bending of the neck in jālandhara bandha, and by pressure from the tip of the tongue in the complete form of khechari mudrā. This stimulus is transmitted along the kidney meridian to the urogenital organs, improving their function and helping to activate the svādhishthāna chakra. In addition, the heart meridian passes through the tongue, and therefore is stimulated by khechari mudrā. The heart meridian is directly related to the kidney meridian, together they form the "lesser yin" meridian (heart in the upper body, kidney in the lower). Therefore the stimulus to the heart meridian indirectly affects the kidney meridian and thus the svādhishthāna chakra.

Shalabhāsana (the "locust" pose), mentioned above, is helpful in awakening the svādhishthāna.

Method: Lie on the stomach with the hands beside the thighs, palms facing down. Stretch and raise the legs, together with the abdomen, as high as possible, by pressing the arms against the floor. Make sure the knees do not bend. Hold for a few seconds, then lower the legs carefully.

Breathing: Inhale deeply in the prone position. Retain the breath inside while raising the legs and abdomen. Exhale while returning to the starting position. Perform in conjunction with bhujangāsana (Chapter II, p. 60) and dhanurāsana (Chapter II, p. 61).

Duration: Perform up to five times.

Concentration: On the vishuddhi chakra.

Limitations: Those who suffer from peptic ulcers, hernia, intestinal tuberculosis, or poor heart function should not practice this āsana.

Benefits: This āsana tones and regulates the liver, intestines, pancreas, and kidneys, and stimulates the appetite. It is especially useful in treating diseases of the stomach and intestines. In addition, it strengthens the lower back and tones the sciatic nerves.

(4) Awakening the Manipūra Chakra

The following practice, consisting of four stages, is recommended by Swami Satyananda as a powerful method for awakening the manipūra chakra. The main technique is a variation of mūla bandha, but three other techniques are included to increase its effectiveness. The four parts are:

1) the same as the first half of the ājnā chakra awakening method;
2) vajroli mudrā (for svādhishthāna awakening);
3) the main technique, in which prāna and apāna* are unified in the navel area, generating shakti power which activates the manipūra chakra in the spine;
4) māndūki kriya, also used to awaken the mūlādhāra.

Part 1: Sit in siddhāsana and assume chin mudrā with the eyes closed and spine erect. Concentrating on the perineum, alternately contract and relax it in a comfortable rhythm for five minutes.

Part 2: Contract and relax the lower abdomen, including the genital area, with full awareness for five minutes, concentrating on the svādhishthāna chakra.

Part 3: Inhale deeply. Imagine prāna being absorbed through the throat and flowing down to the navel, and apāna

---

*Two varieties of prāna within the body which control respiration and excretion, respectively. See Chapter V.

flowing up from the mūlādhāra chakra to the navel. Slowly assume mūla bandha (Chapter III, p. 90). Hold the breath, concentrate on the navel, and visualize there the unification of apāna and prāna. Continue to hold the breath as long as possible and then exhale. This cycle should be repeated for 10 minutes.

Part 4: Change from siddhāsana to vajrāsana and separate the knees a little. Clasp the hands with fingers interlocked, close the eyes and be still. Concentrate attention on the tip of the nose for a while, directing the closed eyes at the same point. Slightly open the eyes and gaze attentively towards the tip of the nose. Again close the eyes, maintaining concentration. Repeat the process for ten minutes.

After this, return to siddhāsana and again repeat part (3) for 20 to 30 minutes. This is the final stage of this practice.

The techniques for Parts 1 and 2 are useful because they stimulate the two lowest chakras, facilitating the rise of kundalinī to the manipūra. As stated, Part 3 is the main practice, as the unification of prāna and apāna—which may be imagined as the vital energy in the upper and lower sections of the trunk—is the key to awakening the manipūra chakra.

The effectiveness of the mānduki kriya and vajrāsana in Part 4 in stimulating the manipūra is an interesting phenomenon. Swami Satyananda explains it by stating that the manipūra is directly connected with the eyes and the feet, but he gives no details. However, the connection is easily explained in terms of the acupuncture meridians, as follows.

The manipūra chakra is said to control the digestive organs; the relevant meridians are the stomach, large intestine, liver, gallbladder, and spleen. The large intestine meridian passes beside the ala of the nose, where it interconnects with the stomach meridian. The latter starts in the orbital cavity directly below the pupil, descends the face, the front of the trunk, and the lateral side of the front of the leg, terminating at the second toe. The gallbladder meridian flows from beside the lateral corner of the eye, around the back of the ear, back into the temporal region, then down the side of the neck, trunk, and leg (lateral to the stomach meridian) to the end in the fourth toe. A yin-yang relationship exists between the spleen and stomach as well as between the liver and gallbladder meridians; consequently, these complementary meridians exert a strong influence on each other. Further, the spleen and liver meridians flow up the medial side of the leg. All this indicates that the meridians controlling the digestive organs are closely connected with the eyes, nose, and legs; and these meridians, as stated above, have a close relationship with the manipūra chakra.

Therefore, when the eyes and nose are stimulated through mental and visual concentration on the tip of the nose in mānḍūki kriya, this stimulation activates the manipūra chakra through the digestive organ meridian framework. Similarly, through direct pressure on the legs, vajrāsana stimulates the meridians located in the legs which are related to the manipūra.

The following practices of trāṭaka, uddiyāna bandha, and nauli kriya are also recommended as techniques which help to awaken the manipūra chakra.

(4a) Trāṭaka

The following is the easiest and most common of a wide variety of forms of trāṭaka—the practice of gazing at an object.

In a dark or darkened room sit in siddhāsana or some other comfortable position. Place a lit candle at eye level 45-60 cm. (18-24 inches) away. Relax the whole body with the eyes closed and spine erect. Once a comfortable position is found, keep still. Do not move in any way or for any reason throughout the entire practice. Open the eyes and gaze intently at the brightest spot of the flame just above the top of the wick.

With practice, it becomes possible to gaze at the flame for a few minutes without moving the eyeballs or blinking. Gaze at the flame so intently that awareness of the body is lost. The gaze should be absolutely fixed on one point. After a few minutes, the eyes will probably become tired or begin to water, and then they should be closed and relaxed. Again, do not move the body, but concentrate on the after-image of the flame in front of the closed eyes. Hold it just in front of, or a little above, the center of the eyebrows. When it begins to fade, open the eyes and again concentrate on the actual flame.

Trātaka may be performed by gazing at a variety of objects: a small dot, the full moon, a shadow, a crystal ball, the nose tip, water, darkness, an empty space, a shining object that is not excessively bright, and many other things. If appropriate, you may concentrate upon an image of your personal deity or a photograph of your guru's face, while trying to feel his spiritual presence and grace. The rising sun, one's own image in a mirror, or the eyes of another person may also be used as an object of concentration. These practices should be done under expert guidance, however, as there are certain risks involved.

Trātaka practice can be divided into two categories: bahiranga (outer) and antaranga (inner). The methods mentioned above are all "outer" practices. Inner trātaka is the practice of inner visualization (for example, of a chakra or a personal deity), generally performed with the eyes closed. Even if the eyes are left open, the concentration is directed inward to such an extent that no external objects are perceived.

Duration: Generally 15-20 minutes is sufficient. This period may be lengthened considerably for spiritual purposes, or to correct eye defects. Sufferers of insomnia or mental tension are advised to practice trātaka for 15 minutes before going to bed at night. Specifically, the best time for trātaka is 4-6 A.M., after āsana and prāṇāyāma practice, but it is beneficial at any time. Preferably, the stomach should be empty as this facilitates concentration.

Precautions: There is no danger in the simple form of trāṭaka (on the candle flame), but undue strain must be avoided in the beginning stages. The ability to keep the eyes open without blinking will gradually develop with practice.

Benefits: The benefits of trāṭaka are many—physical, mental, psychic, and spiritual. Physically, it aids weakness and certain defects of the eyes, including nearsightedness. It calms and stabilizes the mind, and provides relief for insomnia. Furthermore, it develops the power of concentration necessary for true meditation practice. The eyes are the gates to the mind; when they are steady the mind itself becomes steady, and the thinking process automatially ceases as concentration deepens. Trāṭaka is one of the most powerful methods for controlling a restless mind filled with waves of constantly changing thoughts. This control is a prerequisite for effective spiritual practice.

Satyananda does not explain why trāṭaka is effective in awakening the manipūra chakra. However, as explained previously, the stomach and gall bladder meridians flow around the eyes, and we can therefore postulate that the stimulation the eyes receive in trāṭaka is transmitted along these meridians to the manipūra chakra.

(4b) Uddiyāna Bandha

Satyananda recommends uddiyāna bandha (Chapt. III, p. 92), in conjunction with agnisar kriya (Chapt. IV, p. 106) and jālandhara bandha (Chapt. III, p. 89), as a method to awaken the manipūra. The stimulus provided to the manipūra should be evident from the descriptions of these practices in the relevant sections.

(4c) Nauli Kriya

Stand with the feet a little less than a meter (1 yard) apart.

Stage 1: Contract the recti abdomini muscles (the two columns of muscles on either side of the navel), in isolation from the other abdominal muscles (madhyāma nauli). When this is mastered, proceed to Stage (2).

Stage 2: Perform isolated contraction of the left rectus abdomini muscle only. This is vāma nauli.

Stage 3: As before, contracting only the right rectus abdomini muscle (dakshina nauli).

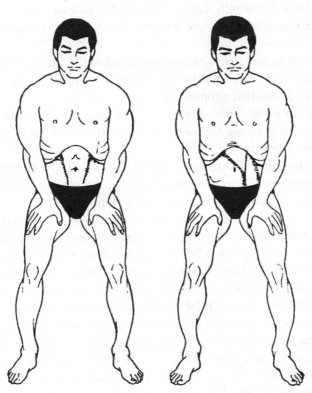

Stage 4: The practitioner must, before attempting this, be able to perform Stages 1, 2 and 3 without difficulty. In a standing position, do uddiyāna bandha. Then begin to churn or roll the recti abdomini muscles so that they move from the left across center to the right in one smooth motion. Repeat the movement in succession as many times as possible while holding the exhalation. Then relax the abdominal muscles and breathe in. When breathing has returned to normal, repeat the process, from right to left.

Preliminary practices: Before attempting Stage 1 of nauli, the student should perfect agnisar kriya and uddiyāna bandha.

Duration: Practice the stage 4 technique for as long as you can hold the breath, and, counting this as one round, do up to six rounds, three from left to right and three from right to left.

Period of practice: This technique takes time to perfect, and regular daily practice is important. If Stage 4 is mastered within 3 months, progress is good.

Precautions: This kriya is best practiced under the guidance of a yoga teacher. Do not perform until at least four hours after a meal.

Limitations: Those who are suffering from high blood pressure, peptic or duodenal ulcers, hernia, or any other serious digestive ailments should not practice nauli.

Benefits: This is the most powerful method of relieving abdominal ailments since it massages all the organs in the abdomen, keeping them healthy and free of malfunction. It is very useful in cases of constipation because it encourages intestinal peristalsis. It is also effective in treating sexual ailments and keeping the sexual organs in good condition.

The powerful massage given by nauli kriya to the digestive organs controlled by the manipūra chakra stimulates the associated meridians, and this stimulation seems to be transmitted to the manipūra chakra, triggering the activation of the chakra in a higher dimension.

(5) Awakening the Anāhata Chakra

In this practice, it is more important to breathe with full awareness than to maintain one āsana for a long time. Therefore, if a posture is uncomfortable it may be changed; if an itch is felt, there is no reason why it should not be scratched.

Sit in a meditational āsana with the eyes closed, concentrate on the throat, and become fully aware of the in-breath.

Feel the breath going down deep into the chest cavity. The outgoing breath does not require any particular attention.

Next, direct the awareness to the ākāsha, the space just above the diaphragm; then, become aware of the space being filled by the inhalation, and the filling process itself. Gradually, you will come to feel the space around the heart itself. Once awareness of this "heart space" has developed, you will feel it expanding and contracting in time with the breath. Breathing should be normal, without any forced retention or unusually long breaths.

If the awareness of the heart space and of its contraction and expansion is constant, after some time something will be seen there. One must not try to produce the vision with the imagination; it comes of its own accord. The practitioner has only to wait and prepare for it with constant awareness. It is a vision of a lake and a blue lotus. It is good if you can feel the space of the heart contracting and expanding, but if this is impossible, just try to feel the breath filling up the space—the first stage. Then proceed to the second and third stages, remembering that the vision in the latter appears by itself in its own time.

(5a) The Practice of Ajapa-Japa

This is another method helpful for awakening the anāhata chakra. It consists of awareness of the mantra SO during inhalation and HAM during exhalation.* Be at ease during this practice. Satyananda says that the mantras SO and HAM, inherent in the natural breath, may be felt in the nostrils, rising and falling between the navel and throat, in the throat itself, or in the heart space, or in all at once, or in each in turn.

During this practice of ajapa-japa, a psychic sound (nāda), which is inaudible in the ordinary sense, is sometimes heard.

---

* Pronounced like English "so" and "hum."

This is a sign of the awakening of the anāhata chakra. This experience demonstrates the literal meaning of "anāhata": "unbeaten (sound)."

(6) Awakening the Vishuddhi Chakra

To awaken the vishuddhi, Satyananda recommends the repetition, in turn, of the methods described above for awakening the other chakras, and finally, concentration on each chakra in turn from the mūlādhāra up to the ājnā, and then back down to the mūlādhāra. A summary of these methods follows.

For the ājnā chakra: Sit in siddhāsana or siddha yoni āsana, hands in chin mudrā, eyes closed and spine erect. Contract and relax the perineum in a natural rhythm, neither too slow nor too fast. In a few days, you may sense the ājnā between the eyebrows; if so, concentrate on that spot. Practice this stage for four minutes.

For the mūlādhāra chakra: Sit in vajrāsana and place the hands, with fingers interlocked, below the navel. Concentrate the eyes and mind on the tip of the nose with the eyes closed. Continue mānḍūki kriya for three minutes.

For the svādhishthāna chakra: Practice vajroli mudrā for three minutes.

For the manipūra chakra: Practice Part 3 of the first method for awakening this chakra. During inhalation bring prāna from the throat down to the navel and at the same time, āpana from the mūlādhāra up to the navel. Hold the breath and unify prāna and āpana in this area. Then exhale. Practice for four minutes.

For the anāhata chakra: first concentrate on the throat and feel the ingoing breath filling up the cavity of the chest. Be aware of the heart space and its contractions and expansions, which follow the natural breath. Wait for the vision to come spontaneously. Practice for four minutes.

Next concentrate in turn on the mūlādhāra, svādhishthāna,

manipūra, anāhata, vishuddhi, and ājnā; then return to the mūlādhāra in the reverse order. Practice this for three minutes.

This whole process is Satyananda's teaching for awakening the vishuddhi chakra. The practitioner should stimulate the lower chakras in ascending order before concentrating on the vishuddhi itself, because the upper chakras cannot truly awaken until the awakening of the lower chakras has taken place.

However, the ājnā is a special case. As mentioned in the section devoted to it, it should be activated first, in order to lessen the serious dangers that may be encountered when the karma of a lower chakra is activated. Also, the ājnā is directly connected with the mūlādhāra (and kundalinī), and the awakening of these is interrelated, as detailed previously.

After following the sequence given above, assume khechari mudrā and concentrate on the thyroid gland in the throat for thirty minutes (the tongue may be relaxed at times). This will greatly intensify the effect on the vishuddhi.

(6a) Viparīta Karani Mudrā

This is a very effective mudrā for activating the vishuddhi chakra.

Lie flat on the back with the feet together and the arms by the sides, palms flat on the floor. Raise the legs and trunk using the arms as levers. Then bend the elbows and prop up the trunk with the hands. In the final pose, the legs should be vertical and the trunk at a 45° angle to the floor. Relax the whole body and close the eyes. Perform ujjāyi prānāyāma with khechari mudrā.

Inhale slowly, feeling the breath and the consciousness move from the manipūra chakra to the vishuddhi; keep the attention on the vishuddhi during exhalation. Repeat as many times as is comfortable.

Duration: On the first day, practice for a few seconds only. Increase the time daily, until the mudrā can be easily performed for 15 minutes or more.

Sequence: Practice after āsanas but before meditation.

Precautions: Should not be practiced after heavy physical exercise or less than three hours after eating.

Limitations: This technique should not be attempted by those with an enlarged thyroid gland, high blood pressure, or heart ailments.

Benefits: This mudrā causes subtle changes in the prāna flow in the body. In particular, it facilitates the flow from the manipūra chakra (the center of subtle prāna), to the vishuddhi (the center of purification). This helps to purify the astral body and prevents physical disease caused by defective prāna flow. It is also an important practice for subliminating sexual energy from the lower to the higher dimensions.

(7) Awakening the Bindū-Visargha

A description of how to awaken the sahasrāra would seem to be in order here, but first we will present Satyananda's technique related to the bindū-visargha (see p. 234), a psychic center between the ājnā and the sahasrāra.

Sit in a meditational pose with the eyes closed. Be aware of the natural breath for two minutes (a kind of ajapa-japa). As awareness of the breath grows, the SO-HAM sound becomes audible. The breath and the SO-HAM mantra may be felt anywhere—either in the throat, in the nose, or between the navel and the throat. If after awhile the mantra changes to another sound such as OM, it does not matter, but unbroken awareness of the breath and the mantra must be maintained for four minutes. Remain fully aware of the breath, whichever mantra is present. Feel the close relationship between breath and mantra for four minutes.

Next, feel the breathing and the mantra in one straight line up and down between the vishuddhi chakra and the bindū-visargha (located at the back of the head, near the top) for three minutes.

As the practices for awakening the vishuddhi chakra and bindū-visarga are continued, these centers awaken and ordinarily inaudible psychic sound (nāda), is heard around the bindū-visarga, indicating more precisely its location.

(8) Awakening the Sahasrāra Chakra

The following is the method used by the author for several years to awaken the sahasrāra chakra and open the Brahman Gate.

As preparation, (i) pawanmuktāsana (the "wind-releasing" āsanas), the sushumnā regulating exercises, and bhastrikā prānāyāma (this directly stimulates the kundalinī—see Chapter III), should be practiced.

The main practice is performed as follows:

Sit in siddhāsana and chin mudrā, with the eyes closed. Gently contracting the perineum during inhalation, raise kundalinī up the sushumnā and let it stream out into the universe through the Brahman Gate at the top of the head, chanting SO. Hold the breath for about two or three seconds, visualizing the unification of kundalinī with the

Creator in Heaven. During exhalation, absorb prana from the Creator through the Brahman Gate, making it descend the sushumnā to the mūlādhāra, while chanting HAM. Visualize the unification of prāna and kundalinī as you retain the exhalation for two or three seconds. Continue this practice for 10 to 20 minutes.

After that, concentrate on the top of the head (the sahasrāra chakra) for 30 minutes or more, chanting OM.

Satyananda does not describe any method to awaken the sahasrāra, apparently because he believes it transcends the limits of the human psyche, and thus is not a chakra in the true sense. Gorakhnath, however, teaches the following method in Gorakshashatakam:

> While gazing at the tip of the nose, concentrate the mind and meditate on Lord Shiva in Heaven, or on the small cavity in the sahasrāra at the top of the head (the dwelling place of Lord Shiva).

Diligent daily practice of the methods described above will bring about various changes in the body, mind, and spirit of the practitioner. The characteristic effects of awakening each chakra will be detailed in later chapters. However, the following general effects can be observed:

• In the early stages of chakra activation and awakening, unusually sensitive physical and mental states may be experienced. These are only temporary, however, and should not cause anxiety. Without fail, such phases pass.

• The physical body becomes healthy, and the constitution improves.

• The practitioner gains control over his feelings, at the same time experiencing richer emotions and deeper sympathy for others.

• Due to increased powers of concentration—thinking, judgment, and discernment become deeper, more constant, quicker, and more reliable.

• The mind is freed from its attachments.

• Impartiality and insight beyond surface appearances are acquired.

• The ability to take effective action toward the fulfillment of one's goals is strengthened.

• Psychic abilities appear.

• A direct relationship with the divine world can be established, at a level corresponding to the practitioner's spiritual state.

• The freedom of mind attained makes it possible to exist in the realm of enlightenment while living in this world.

---

* *Āsana, Prānāyāma, Mudrā Bandha* and *Tantra of Kundalinī Yoga* by Swami Satyananda Saraswati have been used as source material for chapters II, III and IV.

V

The Chakras and Nādīs
as Described
in the Upanishads

The classic presentation of the eight-fold path of yoga practice described in Chapter I is found in the well-known *Yoga
Sutras* of Patanjali, probably composed in the 2nd century.
However, this text barely mentions the subtle body and its
component chakras and nādīs. We do find these two brief
verses in the third chapter which deals with the attainment
of siddhis (spiritual powers):

> Through samyama (concentration and medita-
> tion) on the navel wheel, one obtains a knowledge
> of the constitution of the body. (v. 30)

> Through samyama on the kurma nādī, one obtains
> unshakable patience. (v. 32)

The "navel wheel" refers to the manipūra chakra (*chakra* can
be translated "wheel" or "circle"); the kurma nādī is located
in the throat, and is associated with the vishuddhi chakra.

However, more detailed accounts of the chakras, nādīs,
and the subtle body can be found in a group of the Upani-

shads, known as the *Yoga Upanishads*. The Upanishads are properly considered a part of the Vedas, the oldest canonical literature of Hinduism which dates to the early part of the first millennium B.C. However, the Upanishads under consideration here were clearly composed at a much later date, probably in the 6th century A.D. or later. In this chapter we will focus upon descriptions found in four texts: *Shri Jābāla Darshana Upanishad, Cūdamini Upanishad, Yoga-shikkā Upanishad,* and *Shāndilya Upanishad.* For the sake of comparison, we will also have occasion to refer to passages in the texts presented in Chapter V: *Shat-chakra-nirūpana* and *Gorakshashatakam.* In later sections, comparisons will be drawn also with the meridian system of Chinese medicine, in order to clarify the nature of the nādīs and other aspects of the subtle body described in these Upanishads.

The *Yoga Cūdamani Upanishad* explains the significance of man's three bodies. It records that at primordial creation, an empty space (or ether) was created from Brahman, the One, the highest principle of the universe. From this, air, fire, water, and earth were sequentially created. These five "elements" pervade all things and underlie their manifest form. The presiding deities of these five realms are Shiva, Ishvara, Rudra, Vishnu, and Brahma respectively. Brahma, the lord of the earth, is believed to be the creator of gods, angels, humans, plants, and the like.

Lord Brahma endows man with a body composed of the five elements and divided into three parts. The portion composed of physical elements is called the "gross body" (sthūla-sharīra); that portion made up of subtle elements is called the astral (or subtle) body (sūkshmasharīra); that part which contains the causes of all that each human being is as an individual, is known as the casual body (karānasharīra). It is said that all things in existence possess these three bodies. Within the causal body, the three gunas (qualities)—*sattva* (purity, wisdom, peace), *rajas* (activity, passion), and *tamas*

132

(inertia, lethargy)—exist in a harmonious state of perfect equilibrium. However, in the astral and physical bodies, this balance among the gunas is lost, resulting in dynamic interaction among the three. The seven chakras are the centers of the energy system in the astral body, and the nādīs are the channels that distribute this energy.

This Upanishad implies that those who wish to attain liberation must learn the location of the chakras through personal experience, asking "How can he who does not recognize the chakras in his own body attain liberation?" In general, the four Upanishads under consideration seem to share this attitude, as the descriptions of the location, structure, and functions of the chakras are extremely brief.

The *Yoga-shikkā Upanishad* contains the most detailed passages concerning the chakras. For example, it says:

> The human body is the abode of Lord Shiva. It is said to give fulfillment to all beings endowed with it. The mūlādhāra chakra, which lies between the anus and the genitals, is of a triangular shape.

> —Chapter I, verse 168

The area referred to is the perineum. Kundalinī shakti, the primordial material force of the universe, often represented by the symbol of an inverted triangle, resides here. In the meditational posture known as siddhāsana (see Chapt. II, p. 72), the heel is pressed firmly against the perineum to help awaken this power.

Other chakras are described in this text as follows:

> The svādhishthāna chakra, which is hexagonal, lies at the root of the genitals. The wheel set up at the navel is ten-sided and is called manipūraka (the manipūra chakra).
> —Ch. I, v. 172

The great twelve-sided wheel located at the heart
is called Anāhata (unbeaten, the anāhata chakra).
—Ch. I, v. 173

Inside the throat cavity there lies a wheel of sixteen sides called the vishuddhi (purity). The seat
named Jālandhāra is held steadfast in there.
—Ch. I, v. 174

Ājnā (command), which lies between the eyebrows and has two petals, is the highest of the
wheels. It is here that is set up, upside down, the
great seat called Uddāyāna.
—Ch. I, v. 175

The *Yoga Cūdamani Upanishad* also locates the ājnā chakra
between the eyebrows, in accordance with most later teachings.
The *Yoga Kundalinī Upanishad*, however, states that the ājnā is
located at the top of the head, the area normally associated
with the sahasrāra.

This most detailed text, *Yoga-shikkā Upanishad*, omits men-
tion of the sahasrāra, but it is referred to in the *Yoga Chūdamani
Upanishad:*

At the top of the head (the Brahman Gate), or at
Mahabatin, there are one thousand petals.
—v. 6

No detailed, systematic description of the actual sensations associated with chakra awakening is to be found in the
Upanishads. The *Yoga Chūdamani Upanishad*, however, does
record:

He who perceives a disc of light like a jewel at the
navel is a knower of yoga. It flashes with a golden
light like lightning.
—v. 9

This description of a bright disc perceived at the navel corresponds to the actual appearance of the aura of an activated manipūra chakra. It has been observed through extrasensory perception by innumerable yogis, both Eastern and Western, throughout the ages.

Yoga-shikkā Upanishad describes the psychic sounds associated with the mūlādhāra, anāhata, and vishuddhi chakras this way:

> A sound arises in her (kundalinī shakti in the mūlādhāra chakra), as if a sprout were shooting out from a tiny seed. The yogi knows that she is witnessing all. In such a manner does a true yogi emerge.
>
> —v. 3

> The low sounds (ghosā) and high sounds (garjā) like a thunder storm manifest in the heart, where shakti resides.
>
> —v. 4

> Then through the breath and through that which is known as the musical scale, vaikharī (the universal pure sound) arises, through the rhythm of the lips and tongue in their dance about the palate and teeth.
>
> —v. 5

> Sounds of varying qualities manifest themselves from the initial A throughout the range of Ksha. From these sounds, each syllable, from these syllables, each word is born.
>
> —v. 6

To interpret a bit, kundalinī shakti has the power to manifest an ordinarily inaudible sound, as if germinating a seed. This sound first arises in the mūlādhāra chakra. When the shakti reaches the anāhata, it is perceived by those persons gifted with clairaudience as a voice heard through a silken veil, or as an ocho in a deep valley. This is a common psychic experience which has been recorded in many traditions from ancient times. When kundalinī shakti reaches the vishuddhi chakra in the throat, the sound can be manifested through the vocal cords in the conventional manner.

We will not dwell further on the chakras as described in the Upanishads due to the lack of detailed passages. Fuller accounts of the chakras recorded in traditional and modern sources will be presented and compared in later chapters. The chakras have been directly experienced by those who have perfected the siddhis (supernormal powers) throughout the ages. There is universal agreement about the major aspects of these experiences, as we shall see.

Now let us turn to the passages in the Upanishads about the nādīs. There is no general concensus concerning the number of nādīs which exist in the body: figures from 1,000 to 350,000 are mentioned. The number which appears most often, however, is 72,000. Of these, ten, fourteen or fifteen—depending on the text—are deemed most important.

Table I shows the nādīs described in seven different yoga texts: the four Upanishads discussed in this chapter, the Shatchakra-nirūpana and Gorakshashatakam presented in Chapter VI, and one other text.

As you can see, the descriptions vary considerably, both in particulars and degree of detail. Furthermore, only the terminal points and general directions of flow are enumerated. Determining the actual pathways of the nādīs from these descriptions alone is a difficult task, and consequently many differing interpretations have arisen.

Some yoga teachers and researchers maintain that the nādīs are an intrinsic element of the astral body, because the nādīs are composed of subtle matter. Other researchers claim that the nādīs are identical with the cardio-vascular

Table 1: The Explanation of the Nadi's Flow

		Jabala Darshana Upanishad	Yoga Cudamani Upanishad	Yoga-shikka Upanishad	Gorakshashatakam
1.	Sushumna	Up the spine, to the top of the head	In the middle	In the middle, Brahmanadi	In the middle
2.	Ida	On the left of Sushumna, its mouth over Brahmarandhra; terminates in the left nostril	On the left	On the left of Sushumna from the "navel wheel", flowing toward the root of the navel to join Vilamba	On the left
3.	Pingala	On the right of Sushumna, its mouth over Brahmandhra	On the right	On·the right of Sushumna from the "navel wheel" flowing toward the root of the navel to join the Vilamba	On the right
4.	Gandhari	Behind Ida, to one side, ending at the edge of the left eye	The left eye	From the "navel wheel" to the eye	Ending in the left eye
5.	Hastijihva	Behind Ida, to one side, ending at the tip of left big toe	The right eye	From the "navel wheel" to the eye	Ending in the right eye
6.	Pusha	From behind Pingala, up one side of it to the right eye	The right ear	From the "navel wheel" to the ear	In the right ear
7.	Yashasvini	On one side of Pingala between Pusha and Sarasvati, ending at the tip of the left big toe	The left ear	—	In the left ear
8.	Alambusa	In Kandasthana and surrounding the anus	The mouth	From the "navel wheel" to the ear	Ending at the mouth
9.	Kuhu	On one side of Sushumna located in the bow shaped curve before Sushumna and Raka, the nadi flows downwards, then up to terminate at the right edge of the nose.	The genitals	Flowing downwards from the navel to discharge impurities	Ending in the penis
10.	Shankhini	Between Gandhari and Saraswati, ending in the left ear	Muladhara	In the throat, conveying nourishment to the head	In the anus, i.e., in Muladhara
11.	Sarasvati	On one side of Sushumna, flowing upwards	—	Ending at the tip of the tongue	—
12.	Varuni	Between Yashasvini and Kuhu	—	Flowing downward from the navel to convey excrement	—
13.	Payasvini	Ending at the edge of the right ear	—	—	—
14.	Shura	—	—	From the "navel wheel" to between the eyebrows	—
15.	Visvodari	Between Kuhu and Hastijihva, located inside Kandasthana	—	From the navel. Gets the four kinds of nourishment	—
16.	Saumya	—	—	—	—
17.	Vajra	—	—	—	—
18.	Citrini	—	—	—	—
19.	Others	Jihva also courses upwards		Raka drinks water instantaneously, causes sneezing and collects phlegm to the throat; Citra flows downwards from the navel to discharge semen.	
	Notes	The root of all nadis, Kandasthana is nine fingerbreadths above the muladhara chakra and the center of it is the navel. The nadis leave Kandasthana horizontally and vertically.		The beautiful nadi called Vilamba is around the navel. The nadis originate there and flow horizontally and vertically. It is called the "navel wheel" and looks like an egg.	

Siddhasiddhantapaddhati	Shandilya Upanishad	Shatcakra-Nirupana	Meridians (tentative)
Through the palate up to Brahmarandhra	At the back of the anus up to the head and ending in Brahmarandhra	From the middle of Kanda up to the head	The governor vessel meridian (from the upper lip to the perineum)
Ending in the nostrils	On the left of Sushumna	On the left of Sushumna	The second line of the urinary bladder meridian (See explanation in the text)
Ending in the nostrils	On the right of Sushumna, up to the end of the right nostril	On the right of Sushumna	The second line of the urinary bladder meridian
Ending in the two ears	From behind Ida, ending in the left eye	—	The third line of the urinary bladder meridian
Ending in the two ears	—	—	The first line of the urinary bladder meridian (left)
Ending in the two eyes	From behind Pingala	—	The third line of the urinary bladder meridian (right)
—	In between Gandhari and Sarasvati, ending in the right ear and at the tips of the toes	—	The first line of the urinary bladder meridian (right)
—	Running upwards and downwards from the root of the anus, through the tonsils	—	The conception vessel meridian (from the perineum to the mouth)
The anus	At the side of Sushumna, running to the end of the penis	—	The liver meridian (from the tip of the big toe to the eye passing through the penis and the nose) (?)
At the end of the penis	Running upwards to the tip of the right ear	Below Sahasrara, supports sushumna on its stalk above the neck	The kidney meridian
At the corner of the mouth	Behind Sushumna, to the tip of the tongue	—	The spleen meridian (?)
—	Lying in between Yashasvini and Kuhu, reaching all parts above and below Kundalini	—	—
—	Between Pusha and Sarasvati	—	The gall bladder meridian (see explanation in text)
—	—	—	—
—	—	—	The stomach meridian
—	To the very tips of the toes	—	—
—	—	Inside Sushumna	—
—	—	Inside Vajra	—

and nervous systems. As stated in the Introduction, the latter theory may sound plausible at first, because the sushumnā nādī superficially seems to correspond to the central canal of the spinal cord, and the idā and pingalā nadīs to the sympathetic nerve trunks. However, this theory does not evidence a realistic correspondence with the traditional descriptions of the nādīs. For example, the *Jābāla Darshana Upanishad* states that idā starts at the mūlādhāra, goes up the left side of the sushumnā, and ends in the left nostril. Actually, though, the upper ends of the sympathetic nerve stems lying on either side of the spine do not terminate anywhere near the nostrils.

Likewise, the sushumnā, although it could possibly lie in the central canal of the spinal column, cannot be the same as the nerve itself. It is said that all nādīs originate at the kandasthāna, a spherical region centered around the navel. From there, the other nādīs follow paths on all sides of the sushumnā—right and left, front and back. Some terminate in the eyes or ears, others in the genital or perineal area, still others in the mouth or tongue. These ideas are at odds with Western medical knowledge, which considers the brain and the spinal column to be the nervous system.

From the point of view of embryology, as well, it is clear that the navel and the formation of the nervous system are not related. The navel and its surrounding organs develop from the endoderm and mesoderm. For example, the connective tissues of the following anatomical structures develop from the mesoderm: kidneys, adrenal glands, sexual glands, uterine tubes, womb, vagina, notocord, supporting structures (bone, cartilage, and connective tissue in the broad sense), dentine, heart, blood vessels, lymphatic vessels, lymph nodes, hemolymph nodes, spleen, striated muscles, smooth muscles, etc. On the other hand, the central nevous system develops from the ectoderm. Thus, even at the embryonic stage, the navel and the nervous system are not closely related. This evidence leads me to believe that the nādīs are not identical with the nervous system.

Statistical Diagram of Susceptibility to Disease

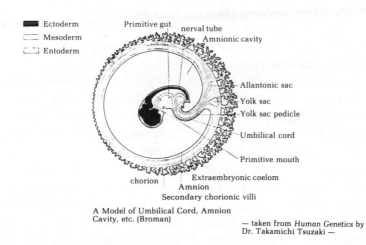

A Model of Umbilical Cord, Amnion
Cavity, etc. (Broman)

— taken from *Human Genetics* by
Dr. Takamichi Tsuzaki —

Some researchers attempt to resolve these contradictions by positing two types of nādīs, gross and subtle. The former are said to correspond to the nervous and vascular systems of the physical body, while the latter are composed of subtle matter and belong to the astral body. I find this a plausible view.

However, another possibility is to posit a close correspondence between the nādīs and the meridians of Chinese medicine. In the next section we will investigate this hypothesis, comparing the traditional description of the nādīs with those of the acupuncture meridians.

As noted above, the Upanishads agree that the nādīs originate in the navel. For example, in the *Shri Jābāla Darshana Upanishad* it is said that the kandasthāna lies nine fingers (18-20 cm.) above the mūlādhāra chakra, with the navel at its center. From here, the nādīs spread out in all directions (see Table 1). The *Yoga-shikka Upanishad* confirms this, stating "there (at the navel) start the nadis, some flowing vertically and others horizonally. It is called the 'navel wheel' (manipūra chakra) and is shaped like an egg."

In fact, Chinese meridian theory is in perfect agreement with this conception. The meridian network is said to originate at the chūkan (chung-wan, CV12) point, which lies midway between the navel and the bottom of the sternum. The word "kan" means "stomach," and there are actually three "kan" points in acupuncture: upper, middle, and lower. These are the jōkan (shang-wan, CV13, 3-4 cm. below the bottom of the sternum on the midsternal line); chūkan, mentioned above, and gekan (hsia-wan CV10, 3-4 cm. above the navel). Of these three, chūkan and gekan are within the circumference of the manipūra chakra and the kandasthāna.

Like the nādīs, acupuncture meridians are also deemed to be channels for the circulation of vital energy. Electrophysiological experiments have been conducted to verify the existence of the meridians, and to establish the directionality of the energy flow. The results of these experiments suggest that the meridians are energy channels quite dissimilar to the nervous system; that they form a network which spreads throughout the connective tissue of the body; and that they are filled with body fluid. In this last respect, also, the meridians seem to correspond to the nādīs described in the *Upanishads*. For instance, the *Chandogya* Upanishad states that the gross nādīs (those of the physical body) are filled with a body fluid which is responsible to the suns rays.

The number of nādīs and meridians may be similar. Although there are twelve ordinary and eight extraordinary meridians, vast numbers of minor meridians also are said to exist. It is quite possible that if all these were counted, the total number of meridians might reach 72,000, the figure usually associated with the nādīs.

The nādīs and meridians are also similar in that they function both physiologically and psychologically. In common Japanese usage, the word ki, used to indicate the energy which flows through the meridians, can also refer to other types of both physical and emotional or mental energy. Furthermore, ki energy may be directed mentally within one's own body, as well as physically by needle stimulation. Expert acupuncturists are said to perceive intuitively the movement of ki when they are in a state of mental concentration. Similarly, the prāna which flows through the nādīs may be directed mentally by various meditation techniques, as well as exercises such as āsanas and prānāyāma which directly stimulate the physiological system. The distinction often made between gross and subtle nādīs also bears witness to the dual physiological and psychological nature of this energy flow.

We shall now attempt to correlate, by comparative study, the main nādīs with the principal meridians. We shall first examine the relationship between the three "great nādīs"—the sushumna, idā, and pingālā—and certain major meridians.

The Sushumnā Nādī

As shown in Table I, the sushumnā, or Brahman nādī, is a canal which follows the spine. Descriptions of its starting point are not entirely consistent. Shāndilya Upanishad states that it starts at the mūlādhāra chakra, whereas Shat-chakra-nirūpana says it originates in the kandasthāna. According to the Chhandogya Upanishad, the sushumnā nādī begins at the heart. However, most yoga scriptures and other Upanishads seem to agree that the mūlādhāra is its starting point. The terminal point is always described as the Brahman Gate at the top of the head, through which prāna and kundalinī shakti are said to enter and exit.

In Chinese medical theory, there is a major "extraordinary" meridian, known as the governor vessel meridian, which seems to correspond closely to the sushumna. Its function is said to be the overall governance of the six yang meridians. It starts at the tip of the coccyx (the approximate location of the mūlādhāra chakra), courses up the center of the back to the top of the head, and terminates in

Governor Vessel Meridian (GV)

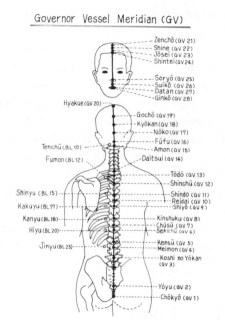

the upper lip. It is said that ki energy is stored in this meridian like water in a lake: the flows of ki through the twelve ordinary meridians are likened to rivers, which distribute vital energy to the various organs and tissues. In the event of an energy imbalance or insufficient ki in a particular organ or part of the body (due to disease or other malfunction), the energy stored in the governor vessel meridian is mobilized to supplement the flow in the related ordinary meridians. In such cases, the stored energy usually flows downward. Likewise, the normal energy flow in the sushumnā is said to be in a downward direction. These are some of the aspects of these two main energy channels which lead me to believe they correspond.

There are also similar spiritual practices within the two traditions of tantra yoga and Taoist meditation which suggest a close correspondence. In many of the tantric yoga practices, kundalinī shakti is directed upward from the mūlādhāra chakra to the ājnā chakra or Brahman Gate, utilizing various breathing and visualization techniques. In the Taoist practice known as shōshūten (sometimes called the "Circulation of Light"), ki energy is raised from the tip of the coccyx to the top of the head along the governor vessel meridian. In both cases, this physiological energy is sublimated into higher psychological or spiritual energy (known as ojas in the yoga tradition). Thus, the functions of the sushumnā and the governor vessel meridian in spiritual practices of their respective traditions exhibit a high degree of correspondence.

The Idā and Pingalā Nādīs

Many yogis, gurus, and Western researchers teach that the idā and pingalā start at the mūlādhāra and spiral about the sushumnā up to the ājnā, intersecting at each chakra along the way. The idā is said to start from the left side of the mūlādhāra, passing through the left nostril on its way to ājnā; the pingalā starts on the right side and passes through the right nostril (sometimes these two nādīs are said to terminate in the nostrils). It has been suggested that these two nādīs may correspond to the pair of sympathetic nerve trunks which wrap around the spinal cord, due to a structural resemblance to the intersecting nādīs. However, none of the seven traditional sources listed in Table I describes the idā and pingalā as intersecting at all. *Shri Jābāla Darshana Upanishad* records that these two nādīs cover the mūlādhāra chakra, and the Brahma knot within it, with their mouths. The idā is said to be located on the left of the sushumnā, the pingalā on the right. *Yoga-shikka Upanishad* states that they originate in the navel wheel (kandasthāna), rather than the mūlādhāra, but it agrees that they lie on the two sides of the sushumnā. In general, most sources, ancient and modern, agree that the idā and pingalā nādīs originate in the

144

mūlādhāra chakra, and lie on the left and right sides, respectively, of the sushumnā. Only *Shandilya Upanishad* and *Shri Jābāla Darshana Upanishad* state that they terminate in the nostrils; it is not specified whether they run in straight or intersecting lines.

Urinary Bladder Meridian (BL)

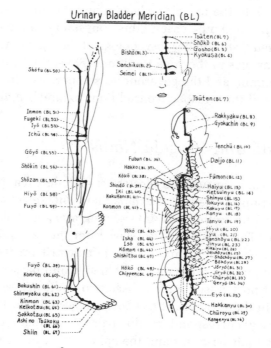

I have come to the conclusion that the idā and pingalā nādīs flow beside the sushumnā in straight lines, and that they correspond to the second lines of the urinary bladder meridian for the following reasons. On each side of the body this meridian originates near the bridge of the nose, flows up over the head, enters inside, and emerges at the back of the head. It then divides into two branches: one line, usually called the third, courses down the back approximately 9 cm. from the spine, passes along the back of the leg, and terminates in the fifth toe; the second line passes down the back about 4.5 cm. from the spine, going through the lumbar region to the urinary bladder itself. Situated along this second line are the *yu* ("associated") points, each of which is said to reflect the condition of a specific organ. The yu point for a givon organ is the meeting point between the meridians and the autonomic nerves which control that organ in the related section of the spine. Therefore, yu points simultaneously reflect the condition of the associated autonomic nerves and the relevant meridians. For example, acupuncture treatment at the stomach yu point (iyu or wei-shu, BL21, the associated point for the stomach on the urinary bladder meridian), influences concurrently the condition of the stomach, the stomach meridian, and the spinal nerves which control stomach functions. Like the idā and pingalā nādīs—second in importance only to the sushumnā—these secondary lines of the urinary bladder meridian are extremely important and are used with great frequency in acupuncture treatment. Therefore I have concluded that they correspond to these two nādīs.

It is interesting to note that in our sources, nādīs located in the limbs are barely mentioned. Surely, if these are the channels for the vital energy of the body, they must extend to the extremities. The acupuncture meridians in these areas are clearly defined. However, we will have to content ourselves with analyzing the following nādīs within the trunk and head, as they are described in the yoga texts.

Gāndhārī Nādī

The gāndhārī nādī flows beside and behind the idā nādī and terminates in the left eye, according to six of our seven sources. (Only *Siddhasiddhāntapaddhati* claims that it ends in the ears.) Therefore, it might correspond to the third line of the urinary bladder meridian on the left side of the body. The rationale for this will be discussed in the following two sections. The first line of this meridian (see diagram) lies approximately 1.5 cm. on either side of the spinal column; the second and third lines lie about 4.5 cm. and 9 cm. away, respectively. These three lines run parallel to the spine all the way down to the buttocks.

Hastijihva Nādī

According to Shri Jābāla Darshana Upanishad, the hastijihva nādī also lies beside and behind the idā nādī, terminating at the tip of the left big toe. Other sources state that it terminates either in the right eye or in the ears. In acupuncture theory, only the liver and spleen meridians are known to terminate in the big toe, but they flow along the front of the body, and consequently cannot correspond to this nādī. In fact, only the urinary bladder meridian has branches running parallel to the spine. If the hastijihva nādī actually ends in the eyes (where the bladder meridian starts), as some sources claim, then it might correspond to one of these lines. But which line is it? In my opinion it is the first line, for reasons given in the next section.

It is important to note that Shri Jābāla Darshana Upanishad places the gāndhārī and hastijihva lateral to the idā, presumably on the left side, with the pūshā and yashasvinī nādīs (described below) simultaneously situated in relation to the pingalā on the right. Furthermore, the hastijihva and yashasvinī are both described as terminating in the left big toe; the terminal points of the pushā and gāndhārī are not mentioned. Therefore it may be inferred that these two latter groups form complementary left-right pairs.

The Yashasvinī Nādī

The yashasvinī nādī lies on one side of the pingalā between the pūshā (which runs behind the pingalā, up to the right eye) and sarasvatī nādīs. The sarasvatī is said to lie to one side of the sushumnā, but which side is not specified. However, since we are told that the shankhinī nādī lies between sarasvatī and gāndhārī (on the left of the sushumnā), the sarasvatī probably also lies on the left. It follows, then, that the yashavinī, which is situated between the pūshā (on the right side of sushumnā) and sarasvatī (on the left) must lie closer to the posterior median line, the path of the sushumnā.

One may therefore conclude that yashasvinī corresponds to the first line of the urinary bladder meridian and the pūshā to the third, both on the right. On the left, the hastijihva, which forms a pair with the yashasvinī, is the first line, and the ghāndhārī, paired with the pūshā, is the third.

As mentioned earlier, only the spleen and liver meridians connect with the big toe—the terminal point of the hastijihva and yashasvinī nādīs according to *Shri Jābāla Darshana Upanishad*—but they do not run along the back. However, the urinary bladder meridian, which corresponds with these nādīs in other respects, terminates in the small toe. When the general lack of detail concerning the nādīs' paths in the limbs is taken into account, I feel it is not unreasonable to match these nādīs with the various branches of the urinary bladder meridian. In this case, perhaps they actually terminate in the small, not big, toe.

Alambusā Nādī

According to *Shri Jābāla Darshana Upanishad* the alambusā nādī runs from the anus to Kandasthāna (which encompasses the manipūra chakra); *Shāndilya Upanishad* adds that it courses upward through the tonsils. *Yoga Cūdamani Upanishad* and *Gorakshashatakam* state that it terminates in the mouth, while *Yoga-shikka Upanishad* maintains that it continues to the ear.

In acupuncture theory, of the fourteen major meridians only the conception vessel meridian starts in the anal area and runs along the anterior median line to the mouth. The yin

148

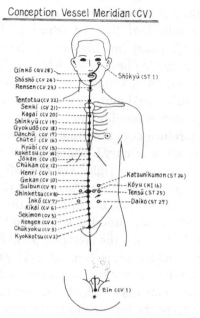

Conception Vessel Meridian (CV)

cognate of the yang governor vessel meridian (shown earlier to correspond to the sushumnā), this conception vessel meridian plays a vital role as the central connecting channel for all the yin meridians. Although the alambusā nādī is not considered among the three most important nādīs (sushumnā, idā, and pingalā) in yoga theory, its position definitely shows a strong correspondence to the conception vessel meridian.

Kuhū Nādī

Again, according to Shri Jābāla Upanishad and Shāndilya Upanishad, the kuhū nādī is supposed to lie to the side of the sushumnā. The former also states that it starts at the bow-shaped area between the sushumnā and the rākā (probably near the pharynx; see below), runs downward and then up to terminate at the nose tip. This account seems to imply that the nādī lies to the front of the sushumnā, rather than parallel to it along the back.

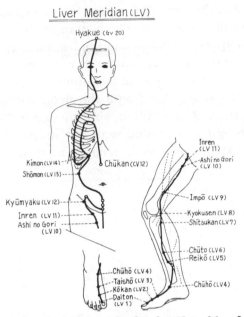

Liver Meridian (LV)

On the other hand, other Upanishads, the *Shāndilya* for instance, state that the kūhū nādī ends in the genitals. The acupuncture meridian on the front of the body which passes through the genitals is the liver meridian: it starts at the tip of the big toe, runs up the medial side of the leg into the genital area, follows a curved path to the side of the anterior median line and then reaches the top of the head, passing through the throat and eyes. If these Upanishad descriptions are followed, the kuhū ñadī may reasonably be assumed to correspond to the liver meridian. Of course no path along the leg is described in these sources, but as we have previously noted, the routes of the nādīs in the limbs are not usually described.

Shankhinī Nādī

The descriptions of the shankhinī nādī recorded in Table I suggest that its pivotal point is in the throat, that it is connected with the mūlādhāra chakra, anus, and penis, and that

150

it ends at the ears. This seems to correspond to the course of the kidney meridian, which starts at the tip of the little toe, passes up the medial side of the leg, through the pubic area, and then runs slightly to one side of the median line up to the throat to end at the root of the tongue. (A second branch connects the kidney itself with the main meridian line in the pubic region.) In addition, abnormality in the kidney meridian is often associated with ear disorders, a fact which might explain the shankhinī nādī's reputed connection to the ears.

Kidney Meridian (KI)

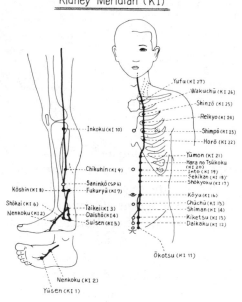

However, we must note that *Shri Jābāla Darshana Upanishad* states the shankhinī lies between the gāndhārī (behind the idā to one side), and the sarasvatī (probably on the left of the sushumnā). If the shankhinī is in fact situated on the left side of the back, it cannot correspond to the kidney meridian, as only the urinary bladder meridian is located there.

As Table I shows, our two most detailed sources—*Shri Jābāla Darshana Upanishad* and *Shāndilya Upanishad*—describe an unexpectedly large number of nādīs as lying along the back, parallel to sushumnā, idā, or pingalā. If these descriptions are taken literally, one must conclude that these nādīs all correspond to the various branches of the urinary bladder meridian (which has three on each side of the back). Here we run into major difficulties in our efforts to match the nādīs and meridians, difficulties largely due to the scarcity and ambiguity of the nādī descriptions. Perhaps many of the nādīs are described in relation to the sushumnā, idā, and pingalā simply because these were the most widely known and identifiable reference points. However, another important reason comes to mind. The nādīs were originally identified through extrasensory perception which, in humans, is rarely developed to the extent of ordinary vision. When observed in this way, the nādīs usually appear in the form of lines or bands of light. Therefore, beyond recognizing which side of the sushumnā, idā, or pingalā a given nādī lies on, it may have been difficult for the ancients to identify precisely its location.

Spleen Pancreas Meridian (SP)

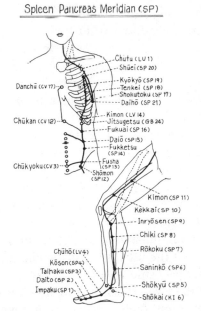

Sarasvatī Nādī

The sarasvatī nādī is said to flow up one side of the sushumnā to terminate in the tongue or mouth. Only *Shāndilya Upanishad* states that it lies behind the sushumnā. If this nādī actually lies to the front of the sushumnā, it probably corresponds to the spleen meridian. The spleen meridian starts at the tip of the big toe, goes up the medial side of the leg, and enters the abdomen, where it circulates through the spleen by way of the stomach. It then penetrates the diaphragm, rises through the chest and throat, and finally disperses at the root of the tongue.

Vārunī Nādī

Varying descriptions of this nādī are given. One source says that it flows down between the yashasvinī and kuhū nādīs, pervading all areas above and below kundalinī. Another says it flows down from the navel to promote the process of excretion. In either case, this nādī seems to be related to the functions of the lower abdomen.

According to *Yoga-shikkā Upanishad*, the vārunī nādī itself conveys excrement, a statement which implies it comprises the large intestine, colon, rectum, and anus. If this is true, the nādī would be a gross physical structure, yet not a gross nādī in the conventional sense of nerves and blood vessels which convey physical energy. This is a possibility. In fact, the *Ayur Veda*, an important Hindu scripture on medicine, uses the term nādī in reference to the deferent duct in the male and the uterine tubes in the female. Furthermore, *Yoga-shikkā Upanishad* implies that the deferent duct and urethra are nādīs, and that the citra nādī is the channel which conveys and discharges semen. In light of these descriptions, it is possible that the large intestine might be termed a nādī. If this is the case, I don't believe there is any meaningful correspondence between the vārunī or citra nādīs and the acupuncture meridians.

Payasvinī Nādī

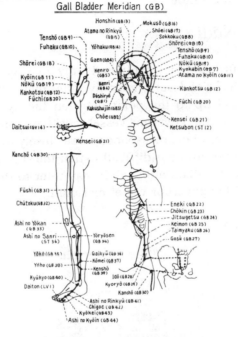

Gall Bladder Meridian (GB)

The *Shāndilya Upanishad* states that the payasvinī nādī runs between the pūshā and sarasvatī nādīs. If the pūshā corresponds to the third line of the urinary bladder meridian on the right side, as discussed earlier, and if the sarasvatī corresponds to the spleen meridian in the front of the body, the nādī between these two should correspond to the right branch of the gall bladder meridian. According to *Shri Jābāla Darshana Upanishad*, the payasvinī nādī terminates at the edge of the right ear. In this respect it closely resembles the gall bladder meridian, which also travels up to the ear. I therefore believe that these two channels correspond. The gall bladder meridian starts at the outer corner of the eye, travels across the side of the skull — first above the ear, then around it—and next, passing through the neck, runs downward in a zig-zag fashion along the side of the trunk, the lumbar area, and finally the outside of the leg to terminate at the tip of the fourth toe.

Shūra Nādī

The shūra nādī is mentioned only in *Yoga-shikkā Upanishad*. The brief description only states that it runs from the navel wheel up to the point between the eyebrows. This point lies on the governor vessel meridian, but as we have seen, this meridian corresponds more closely to the sushumnā nādī. Therefore it is difficult to pair the shūra nādī with a particular meridian, although it may refer to this particular section of the governor vessel meridian.

Visvodāri Nadī

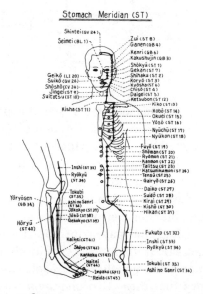

The visvodāri nādī is said to run between the kuhū (which tentatively corresponds to the liver meridian) and the hastijihva (the first line of the urinary bladder meridian on the left side). Among the acupuncture meridians which run through a horizontal cross-section of the body at the hip level, the second and third lines of the urinary bladder meridian, as well as the gall bladder, spleen, stomach, and kidney meridians, are found between the two mentioned above.

According to *Shri Jābāla Darshana Upanishad*, the visvodāri nādī resides inside the kandasthāna, and *Yoga-shikkā Upanishad* notes that it receives "four kinds of nourishment." Since the kandasthāna is the area which encloses the manipūra, the chakra which controls the digestive system, these statements suggest that this nādī is related to the stomach and other digestive organs. Of the eligible meridians, the stomach meridian seems most likely to correspond to the visvodāri nādī.

The Remaining Nādīs

According to *Shat-chakra-nirūpana*, the vajrā and cītrini nādīs are finer channels contained within the sushumnā nādī.

As mentioned earlier, *Yoga-shikka Upanishad's* description of the citra nādī seems to identify it with the deferent duct or the ureter.

The rākā nādī, as described in *Yoga-shikkā Upanishad*, "drinks water instantaneously, causes sneezing, and collects phlegm." Thus, it probably corresponds to the esophagus or pharynx.

Another nādī, called jihvā, is mentioned in *Shri Jābāla Darshana Upanishad*. It is impossible to accurately describe its location, however, since it is merely said to "flow upwards."

This completes our study of the nādīs and meridians. As we have seen, the lack of detailed descriptions in the yoga sources makes it difficult to make accurate correspondences. It is my intention to gather other source materials to render more precise these attempts to correlate the two systems of energy circulation. I also intend to conduct scientific experiments to substantiate the ideas presented here.

Although the traditional descriptions of the nādīs in the yogic texts are extremely brief, I believe that much more detailed knowledge has been transmitted orally throughout the ages, and that modern yogis have experiential knowledge of the nādīs and their functions. In fact, as we have seen in previous chapters, many of the yoga āsanas and mudrās effectively redirect the circulation of vital energy, thereby strengthening the functions of the related meridians. I believe that accomplished yogis are fully aware of these effects.

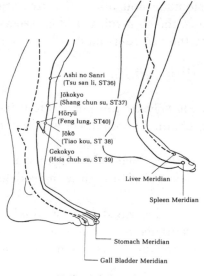

Meridians in the Legs and Feet

For instance, it is widely taught that vajrāsana (Japanese "seiza" posture, see Chapt. IV p. 107) promotes good digestion. As I noted in Chapter IV, although yoga authorities offer no rationale for this effect, it can be easily explained in terms of meridian theory. When one sits in vajrāsana, the medial and lateral areas of the leg below the knee touch the floor and are thus stimulated. The meridians which traverse these areas are the very ones which control the digestive functions: the stomach and gall bladder meridians in the lateral area, and the spleen and liver meridians in tho medial reglon. The area which presses hardest against the floor contains points on the stomach meridian known to be particularly effective in improving stomach function: ashi no sanri (tsu san-li, ST36), jōkokyo (shang-chu-su, ST37), jōko (tiao-kou, ST38), gekokyo (hsia-chu-su, ST39), and hōryū (teng-lung, ST40). It has been demonstrated experimentally, through radiography and other means, that the stimulation of the ashi no sanri point with an acupuncture needle promotes peristaltic movement and gastric secretion in the stomach. In my opinion, yoga gurus are aware, at least experientially, of this connection between the nāḍīs along the leg and their connection with the digestive organs.

Let us now turn our attention to the different varieties of prāna which function in the body, as described in our sources.

The Five Major Prānas

According to yoga theory, prāna or vital energy is absorbed into the body through respiration or directly through the function of the chakras. It is then distributed through the nāḍīs to all parts of the body, converting into different forms of pranic energy appropriate for the various organs and tissues. Usually, five varieties of prāna (or vāyu, "wind") are posited: prāna (that is, the sub-type of prāna associated with respiration), apāna, vyāna, samāna, and udāna. They function as follows:

prāna: serves the area between the throat and diaphragm. It controls the functions of respiration and speech, and in my opinion, the function of the heart.

apāna: governs the area below the navel. It controls the functions of the large intestine, kidneys, bladder, genitals, and anus; in particular, it generates evacuation.

vyāna: pervades the entire body. It spreads vitality through the system, maintaining a balanced energy flow.

samāna: governs the navel area, controlling the digestive and assimilative processes.

udāna: pervades the area above the throat, and the four limbs. It is said to govern the five senses and the functions of the brain. Also, it controls the upward flow of vital energy in the body. Overactivity of udāna causes such disturbances as dizziness and overheating in the head.

Tables II and III list the locations and functions of these five forms of prāna as described in our sources. Also included is information provided by Swami Satyananda, whose theories on the chakras are presented in detail in Chapter IX. Brief explanations of these pranic sub-divisions are also found in *Brhadāranyaka Upanishad*, *Taittiriya Upanishad*, and *Chāndogya Upanishad*, but they merely duplicate the material in the sources already cited.

Five Minor Prānas

As you can see in the above tables, five other sub-categories of prāna are often grouped with the five types described above, to form the "ten prānas." These latter five, called "upa prānas," supplement the functions of the major prānas. Their locations in the body are not described; *Shri Jābāla Darshana Upanishad* merely states that they are distributed throughout the skin and bones. They function as follows:

nāga: controls salivation and hiccupping.

kūrma: opens the eyes and controls blinking

krkara: causes sneezing and creates the sensation of hunger

devadatta: controls yawning and sleeping.

dhanamjaya: pervades the entire body, remaining even after death. Hair growth, which is occasionally observed some months after death, might be due to the function of lingering dhanamjaya.

As we have seen, these prānas are absorbed into the body through respiration and directly by the chakras, and distributed by the nādīs to the five regions of the body. However, the specific nādīs related to each region are not identified in the yoga texts. This clearly contrasts with Chinese medical theory, where the relationships between the meridians and internal organs, as well as the functional interrelationships among the various meridians, are clearly defined. Further research may enable us to more clearly understand the connections between the nādīs and the body's organs.

Is there anything in acupuncture theory which corresponds to the five prānas of yoga? I feel that the "triple heater," a conception which posits upper, middle, and lower systems of vital energy in the body, is the corresponding principle.

The upper heater works in the region above the diaphragm—the chest and up. It is said to govern the lungs and the respiratory function, and the heart and blood circulation. It thus resembles the prāna of respiration, both in location and function.

The middle heater lies in the area between the diaphragm and the navel. It controls the secretory, digestive, and assimilative functions of the stomach, spleen, pancreas, liver, and gall bladder. Thus it seems to correspond to samāna.

The lower heater operates in the region below the navel, and controls the functions of the large and small intestines,

Table II Locations of the Ten Prānas as Given in Upanishads and Other Sources

Source/Name of Prāna	Yoga Cūdamani Upanishad	Shri Jābāla Darshana Upanishad	Shat-chakra-Nirūpana Pāndukāpunchaka	Satyananda
Prāna	Heart	In constant movement in area between mouth and nose, at center of navel, and in heart	In the heart	Located in region between larynx and top of diaphragm
Apāna	Mūlādhāra	Works in large intestine, genitals, thighs and stomach; also at navel and in buttocks.	In the anus	In region below navel
Vyāna	Pervades entire body	Works from area between ears and eyes to heels; emerges at pharynx in place of prāna	Pervades whole body	Pervades whole body
Samāna	Navel	Pervades all parts of body	In navel	In the region between heart and navel
Udāna	Pharynx	Upper and lower limbs	In throat	In parts of body above larynx
Nāga	0	Pervades skin and bones	0	0
Kūrma	0	In skin and bones	0	0
Krkara	0	In skin and bones	0	0
Devadatta	0	In skin and bones	0	0
Dhanamjaya	Pervades entire body	In skin and bones	0	0

Table III Functions of the Ten Prāṇas as Given in Upanishads and Other Sources

Source/ Name of Prāṇa	Yoga Cūdamani Upanishad	Shri Jābāla Darshana Upanishad	Shat-chakra-Nirūpana Pandukapunchaka	Satyananda
Prāṇa	0	Exhalation and inhalation of air; coughing	Respiration	Associated with the respiratory organs, the organs of speech, together with the muscles and nerves that activate those organs; the force by which the breath is drawn inside.
Apāna	0	Excretion of feces and urine	Excretory functions	Provides energy to the large intestine, kidneys, anus and genitals; primarily concerned with the expulsion of prāna through the rectum.
Vyāna	0	Decomposition activities	is present throughout the body, effecting division and diffusion; resists disintegration; and holds the body together in all parts.	Regulates and controls the overall movement of the body and coordinates the other vital energies; harmonizes and activates all the limbs, and all associated muscles, ligaments, nerves and joints; is also responsible for erect posture of body.
Samāna	0	Draws all parts together	Governs process of digestion and assimilation	Activates and controls the digestive system: liver, intestines, pancreas and stomach, and secretions that they supply; also activates heart and circulatory system in general.
Udāna	0	Upward moving activity	Ascending vāyu	Controls eyes, nose, ears and all other sense organs, as well as brain. Without it, thinking and perception of external world would be impossible.
Nāga	Spitting	Hiccuping	0	• sneezing • yawning
Kūrma	Open eyes	Blinking	0	• scratching • belching
Krkara	Sneezing	Hunger	0	• hiccuping • hunger
Devadatta	Yawning	Sleeping	0	
Dhanamjaya	Pervades whole body; does not leave corpse	Glaring	0	

kidneys, urinary bladder, and genitals. It governs the excretion of feces and urine, and seems to correspond to apāna.

There is no counterpart in acupuncture theory for udāna, which, as we have seen, is related to sensory perception and the thought process. It also is said to affect directly the advancement of spiritual evolution through its capacity to direct energy upward. This helps the force generated when prāna and kundalinī are fused through yoga practice to rise along the sushumnā nādī and pass through the Brahman Gate at the crown. The lack of a Chinese counterpart to udāna is understandable, considering the fact that the primary focus of oriental medicine is the maintenance of health in the physiological system, rather than the manipulation of mental or spiritual states. (It is true that such emotional afflictions as depression or excessive fear can be treated through acupuncture, but these are viewed as symptoms caused by an imbalance in ki energy flow in the body.) Unlike the Indian system of chakras, nādīs, and prānas, which is described primarily in terms of the individual's spiritual advancement, meridian theory offers few clues concerning a possible functional connection between ki energy and the spiritual evolution of man.

Vyāna, which spreads and distributes vital energy to every minute part of the body, maintains the whole in a state of organic unity. This function is performed by the triple heater as a whole, which of course is represented by a single meridian in acupuncture theory. There is no correlation to yoga's claim that vyāna governs all voluntary movement, however, as this again is a mental function outside the sphere of Oriental medicine.

It is hoped that this discussion of the chakras, nādīs, and prānas as they are presented in the Upanishads, and their possible connection with the basic tenets of Chinese medicine, has shed light on both systems. In the next chapter we will present in detail the descriptions of the chakras in two of the major tantric texts.

VI-A
The Chakras and Nādīs as Described in the Shat-Chakra-Nirūpana

Many scholars and authorities on yoga regard the *Shat-chakra-nirūpana* (Descriptions of the Six Centers) as one of the best-written descriptions of the chakras and nādīs. It was compiled in 1577 by the pundit Pūrānanda, a guru from Bengal. His given name was Jagadānanda; he assumed the name of Pūrānanda upon initiation by his guru Brahmānanda. Later he went to Kamarupa in Assam. It is believed that he obtained his siddhi (state of spiritual perfection), in an ashram, the Vashishthashrama, which still exists today. Pūrnañananda never returned home. He lived the life of a holy man and compiled several treatises on tantra. *Shat-chakra-nirūpana* is, in fact, one section (from Part Six) of a much longer work entitled *Shri-tattva-cintāminī*.

The *Shat-chakra-nirūpana* was first translated into English by Arthur Avalon (Sir John Woodroffe) in 1918 and was published in his pioneering work, *The Serpent Power*. This same volume also includes Avalon's translation of another important tantric text, *Pādukā-panchaka (The Fivefold Footstool)*, as well as his commentaries on both.

The following excerpts represent the major portion of the text, adapted by the present author from Avalon's translation. I have grouped the verses by topic, and added the parenthetical explanatory notes.

Concerning the Idā, Pīngalā, and Sushumnā nādīs, Pūr-nānanda writes:

Verse 1

• In the space outside the spinal column, on the left and the right, are the two nādīs, Idā (moon, feminine) and Pīngalā (sun, masculine). The Nādī Sushumnā, whose substance is the threefold Gunas (qualities), is in the middle (its outermost part is the Sushumnā nādī; its middle is the Vajrā Nādī; its innermost part is the Chitrinī Nādī). The Sushumnā extends from the middle of the Kanda (the root of all the Nādīs) to the head, the Vajrā inside her extends from the penis to the head.*

Verse 2

• Inside the Vajrā is the Chitrinī, shining with the lustre of Om. She is as subtle as a spider's thread, and pierces all the Lotuses (chakras) which are placed within the backbone. She is pure intelligence. Inside the Chitrinī is the Brahma-nādī†, which extends from the orifice at the top of the Linga (the symbol of the phallus, also representing the astral body) in the Mūlādhāra chakra to the Bindū (spot or knot) in the pericarp of the Sahasrāra.

---

* American readers may be jarred by the use of the feminine pronoun throughout this translation, particularly when it is used in the same phrase with reference to the penis. Rather than changing Avalon's phrasing (from *The Serpent Power*) we will leave it and simply point out that the Sushumnā nādī is personified as a female deity, thus calling for "her", but the "penis" referred to belongs to the physical body of the practitioner. The Vajrā is a nādī inside the sushumnā.

† The Brahma nādī seems to be the hollow channel inside the Chitrinī, not a separate nādī.

Verse 3

- The Chitrinī is beautiful like a chain of lightning and fine like a lotus fiber, and shines in the minds of the sages. She is extremely subtle; the awakener of pure knowledge and the embodiment of all bliss, her true nature is pure consciousness. The Brahman gate shines in her mouth. This place is the entrance to the region sprinkled by ambrosia, and is called the Knot; it is the mouth of the Sushumnā.

Describing the chakras, the text continues:

Verse 4

The Ādhāra (Mūlādhāra) Chakra

- This Lotus is attached to the mouth of the Sushumnā, and is placed below the genitals and above the anus. It has four petals of crimson hue. Its head hangs downward. On its petals are the four letters from Va to Sa, of the shining color of gold.

Verse 5

- In this Lotus the square region of Prithivī (the earth element) surrounded by eight shining spears. It is of a shining yellow color and beautiful like lightning, as is also the Bīja (the mystical "seed" syllable of the chakra, here, "Lam") of Prithivī which is within.

Verse 6

- This Bīja is ornamented with four arms and mounted on the king of elephants. He carries on his lap the child Creator, resplendent like the young Sun, who has four lustrous arms and heads.

Verse 7

•Here dwells a Devī (goddess), Dākinī by name; her four arms shine with beauty and her eyes are brilliant red. She is resplendent like the lustre of many Suns rising at one and the same time. She is the carrier of the revelation of ever-pure Intelligence.

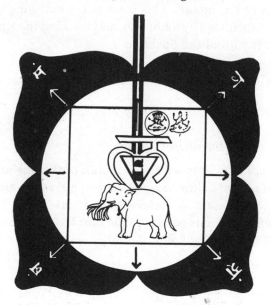

Mulādhāra

Verse 8

•Near the mouth of the Nādī called Vajrā, and in the pericarp, there constantly shines the beautifully luminous and soft, lightning-like triangle which is Kāmarūpa, also known as Traipura. There is always and everywhere the Vāyu (vital force) called Kandarpa (the god of love) who is very deep red, and is the Lord of Beings, resplendent like ten million suns.

Verse 9

- Inside the triangle is Svayambhu ("The self-originated") in his Linga-form (Shiva Linga), beautiful like molten gold, with his head downwards. He is revealed by knowledge (jnāna) and meditation (dhyāna) and is of the shape and color of a new leaf. As the cool rays of lightning and of the full moon charm, so does his beauty. The Deva (god) who resides happily here is in form like a whirlpool.

Verses 10, 11

- Over Shiva Linga shines the sleeping Kundalinī, fine as the fiber of the lotus-stalk. She is Māyā (the bewilderer) in this world, gently covering the hollow on the head of Shiva Linga. Like the spiral of a conch-shell, her shining snake-like form coils three and a half times around Shiva Linga, and her luster is that of a strong flash of young lightning. Her sweet murmur is like the indistinct hum of swarms of love-mad bees. She produces melodious poetry and all other compositions in prose or verse in Sanskrit and other languages. It is she who maintains all the beings of the world by means of inspiration and expiration, and shines in the cavity of the root Lotus like a chain of brilliant lights.

Verse 12

- Within Shiva Linga reigns dominant Parā, the awakener of eternal knowledge. She is the omnipotent Kalā [a form of Nādā (sound) Shakti] who is wonderfully skillful in creation and is subtler than the subtlest. She is the receptacle of the continuous stream of ambrosia which flows from the Eternal Bliss. By her radiance the whole universe is illumined.

Verse 13

• By meditating on Parā (or Kundalinī) who shines within the Mūla Chakra, with the lustre of ten million suns, a man becomes Lord of speech, King among men, and an Adept in all kinds of learning. He becomes ever free from all diseases, and his inmost spirit becomes full of great gladness. Pure of disposition by his deep and musical words, he serves the foremost of the Devas.

The Svādhishthāna Chakra

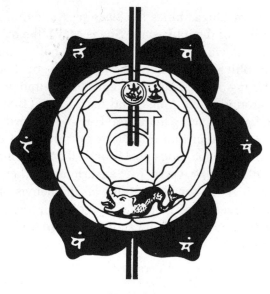

Svādhishthāna

Verse 14

• There is another Lotus placed inside the Sushumnā at the root of the genitals, of a beautiful vermilion color. On its six petals are the letters from Ba to La, with the

Bindū (spot) superimposed over each, of the shining color of lightning.

Verse 15

• Within this Lotus is the white, shining, watery region of Varuna, in the shape of a crescent, and therein, seated on a Makara (a legendary animal resembling an alligator), is the Bīja Vam (connected with the principle of water, just as the Bīja "Lam" of the Mūlādhāra is related to the earth element). It is stainless and white as the autumnal moon.

Verse 16

• Hari (Vishnu), who is within the Bindū of Vam, who is in the pride of early youth, whose body is of a luminous blue beautiful to behold, who is dressed in yellow raiment, is four-armed, and wears the Shrī-vasta (an auspicious curl on the breast of Vishnu) and Kaustubha (a great gem worn by him)—protect us!

Verse 17

• It is here that Rākinī always dwells. She is of the color of a blue lotus. The beauty of her body is enhanced by her uplifted arms holding various weapons. She is dressed in celestial raiment and ornaments, and her mind is exhalted with the drinking of ambrosia (which drips down from the Sahasrāra).

Verse 18

• He who meditates upon this stainless Lotus, which is named Svādhishthāna, is freed immediately from all his enemies such as lust, anger, greed, and so forth.

He becomes a Lord among Yogis, and is like the Sun illumining the darkness of ignorance. The wealth of his nectar-like words flows in prose and verse in well-reasoned discourse.

The Manipūra Chakra

Manipūraka

Verse 19

• Above the Svādhishthāna, at the root of the navel, is a shining Lotus of ten petals, of the color of heavy-laden rain clouds. Within it are the letters Da to Pha, of the color of the blue lotus with the Nāda and Bindū above them. Meditate there on the region of Fire, triangular in form and shining like the rising sun. Outside it are three Svastika marks (one at each side of the triangle) and within the Bīja of Vahni (i.e. the seed-mantra of Fire, "Ram") himself.

Verse 20

• Meditate upon him seated on a ram, four-armed, radiant like the rising Sun. In his lap ever dwells Rudra, who is of a pure vermilion hue. He (Rudra) is white with the ashes which he is smeared with; he is of an ancient aspect and three-eyed. His hands are placed in the attitude of granting boons and of dispelling fear. He is the destroyer of creation.

Verse 21

• Here abides Lākinī, the benefactress of all. She is four-armed, of radiant body, is dark of complexion, clothed in yellow raiment and decked with various ornaments, and exalted by drinking ambrosia. By meditating on this Navel Lotus the power to destroy and create (the world) is acquired. Vānī (the Devī of Speech, that is, Sarasvatī) with all the wealth of knowledge ever abides in the Lotus of his face (that of Fire, represented by the seed-mantra "Ram").

The Anāhata Chakra

Anāhata

Verse 22

• Above the Manipūra, in the heart, is the charming Lotus of the shining color (crimson) of the Bandhūka flower, with the twelve letters beginning with Ka, of the color vermilion, placed therein. It is known by its name of Anāhata, and is like the celestial wishing-tree, bestowing even more than is desired. The Region of Vāyu (wind), beautiful and with six corners, which is like smoke in color, is here.

Verse 23

• Meditate within the Region of Vāyu on the sweet and excellent Pavana Bīja (the principle of the Anāhata Chakra, the Bīja of Vāyu, "Yam"), grey as a mass of smoke, with four arms and seated on a black antelope. And within it also meditate upon the abode of Mercy, the stainless Lord who is lustrous like the Sun and whose two hands make the gestures which grant boons and dispel the fears of the three worlds.

Verse 24

• Here dwells Kākinī, who in color is yellow like new lightning, exhilarated and auspicious; three-eyed and the benefactress of all. She wears all kinds of ornaments, and in her four hands she carries the noose and skull and makes the sign of blessing and the sign which dispels fear. Her heart is softened with the drinking of nectar.

Verse 25

• The Shakti (power) whose tender body is like ten million flashes of lightning is in the pericarp of this Lotus in the form of a triangle. Inside the triangle is the Shiva Linga (see the verses on the Mūlādhāra chakra) known by the name of Bāna. This Linga is like shining gold, and on his head is an orifice minute as that in a pierced gem. He is the resplendent abode of Lakshmī (the Devī of prosperity).

Verse 26

• He who meditates on this Heart Lotus becomes like the Lord of Speech, and (like) Īshvara he is able to protect and destroy the worlds. This Lotus is like the celestial wishing tree, the abode and seat of Shiva. It is beautified by the Hamsa (here the Jivātmā, the individual soul) which is like the steady tapering flame of a lamp in a windless place. The filaments which surround and adorn its pericarp, illumined by the solar region, are exquisite.

Verse 27

• Foremost among yogis, he (who meditates on the Heart Lotus) is ever dearer than the dearest to women. He is pre-eminently wise and full of noble deeds. His senses are completely under control. His mind, in its intense concentration, is engrossed in thoughts of the Brahman. His inspired speech flows like a stream of clear water. He is like the Devatā who is the beloved of Lakshmī and he is able at will to enter another's body.

The Vishuddhi Chakra

• In the throat is the Lotus called the Vishuddhi which is pure and of a smoky purple hue. All the sixteen shining vowels on its sixteen petals, of a crimson hue, are distinctly visible to him whose mind is illumined. In the pericarp of this Lotus is the Ethereal Region, circular in shape and white like the full moon. On an

174

elephant white as snow is seated the Bīja of Ambara (the Ethereal Region; its bīja is "Ham") who is white of color.

Verses 28, 29

• Of his Bīja's four arms, two hold the noose and goad, and the other two make the gestures of granting boons and dispelling fear. These add to his beauty. In his lap there ever dwells the great snow-white Deva, three-eyed and five-faced, with ten beautiful arms, and clothed in a tiger's skin. His body is united with that of Girijā (a title of the Devī conceived as the daughter of the Mountain King), and he is known by what his name Sadā-shiva (Sadā — ever, Shiva — beneficence), signifies.

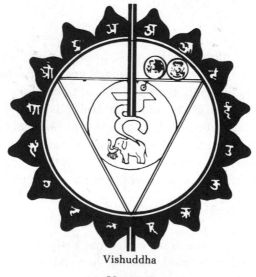

Vishuddha

Verse 30

• Purer than the Ocean of Nectar is the Shakti Sākini who dwells in this Lotus. Her raiment is yellow, and in her four lotus-hands she carries the bow, the arrow, the noose, and the goad. The whole region of the Moon without the mark of the hare (the hare is the Indian equivalent of the "man in the moon") is in the pericarp of this lotus. This region is the gateway of great liberation for him who desires the wealth of Yoga and whose senses are pure and controlled.

Verse 31

• He who has attained complete knowledge of the Ātmā (Brahman) becomes, by constantly concentrating his mind in this Lotus, a great Sage, eloquent and wise, and enjoys uninterrupted peace of mind. He sees the three periods, and becomes the benefactor of all, free from disease and sorrow, and long-lived, and, like Hamsa (here, Antarātmā, the true-self, that dwells by the pericarp of the Sahasrāra chakra), the destroyer of endless dangers.

Verse 31-A

• The Yogi, his mind constantly fixed on this Lotus, his breath controlled by Kumbhaka (breath retention), could move the three worlds, were he to get angry. Neither Brahma nor Vishnu, neither Hari-Hara (the combined form of Vishnu and Shiva) nor Sūrya (the god of the Sun) nor Ganapa (the God of Wisdom and protector from obstacles) is able to control his power.

The Ājnā Chakra

Verse 32

• The Lotus named Ājnā is like the moon, beautifully white. On its two petals are the letters Ha and Ksha, which are also white and enhance its beauty. It shines with the glory of Dhyāna (meditation). Inside it is the Shakti Hākinī, whose six faces are like so many moons. She has six arms, in one of which she holds a book (the gesture of enlightenment); two others are lifted up in gestures of dispelling fear and granting boons, and with the rest she holds a skull, a small drum, and a rosary (with which mantra recitation is done). Her mind is pure.

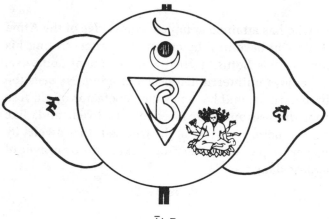

Ājnā

Verse 33

• Within this Lotus dwells the subtle mind (manas). It is well known. Inside the Yoni (which usually signifies the female genital organs, and here is symbolized by the triangle) in the pericarp is the Shiva called Itara in his phallic form. He here shines like a chain of lightning flashes. The first Bīja of the Veda (OM), which the abode of the most excellent Shakti and which by its lustre makes visible the Nādī Chitrinī, is also there. The Sādhaka (yoga practitioner on the path to realization) with steady mind should meditate upon these according to the order prescribed.

Verse 34

• The excellent Sādhaka, whose Ātmā (the True Self) is nothing but a meditation on this Lotus, is able quickly to enter another's body at will, and becomes the most excellent among Munis (those who are accomplished in dhyāna yoga), and is all-knowing and all-seeing. He becomes the benefactor of all, and is versed in all the Shāstras (sacred texts and commentaries). He realizes his unity with the Brahman and acquires excellent and unknown powers (Siddhi). Full of fame and long-lived, he ever becomes the Creator, Destroyer, and Preserver of the three worlds.

Verse 35

• Within the triangle in this Chakra ever dwells the combination of letters A and U which form the Pranava (the sacred syllable OM; see note below). It is the inner Ātmā as pure mind (Buddhi), and resembles a flame in its radiance. Above it is the crescent moon, and above this, again, is Ma-kāra (the letter M), shining in its form of Bindū (this M, together with A and U, form AUM — OM, the Bīja Mantra of the Ājnā Chakra). Above this is Nāda, whose whiteness equals that of the moon, diffusing its rays.

Verse 36

• When the Yogi closes the house which hangs without support (i.e., sever the mind's connections with the physical world by performing yoni mudrā, in which the mouth, ears, nostrils, eyes, and genital and anal orifices are closed—see Chapt. IV, p. 105) the knowledge whereof he has attained by the service of the excellent guru, and when the Cetas (outer-directed consciousness) by repeated practice becomes dissolved in this place which is the abode of uninterrupted bliss, he then sees within the middle of and in the space above (the triangle) sparks of fire distinctly shining.

Verse 37

•He then also sees the light which is in the form of a flaming lamp. It is lustrous like the clearly shining morning sun, and glows between the Sky (the Sahasrāra chakra) and the Earth (the Mūlādhāra chakra). It is here that Parama Shiva manifests himself in the fullness of his might. He knows no decay, and witnesses all, and is here as he is in the region of Fire, Moon and Sun (that is, as in the Sahasrāra chakra).

Verse 38

•This is in the incomparable and delightful abode of Vishnu. The excellent Yogi at the time of death joyfully places his vital breath (Prāna) here and enters (after death) the Supreme, Eternal Birthless, Primeval Deva, the Purusha, who was before the three worlds, and who is known by the Vedānta (the sacred texts dealing with the nature of Brahman).

Verse 39

•When the actions of the Yogi are good in all respects through the service of the Lotus feet of his Guru (i.e. when he is accomplished in service to his guru and in meditation upon the Ājnā) then he will see, above the Ājnā Chakra, the form of the Mahānāda (great Nada), and will ever hold in the Lotus of his hand the Siddhi of Speech (all powers of speech). The Mahānāda, which is the place of dissolution of Vāyu, is half comprised of Shiva and like a plough in shape; it is tranquil and grants boons and dispels fear, and makes manifest pure intelligence (Buddhi).

The Sahasrāra Chakra

Verse 40

• Above all these, in the vacant space wherein is the Shankhinī Nādī, and below the Brahman gate is the Lotus of a thousand petals. This Lotus, lustrous and whiter than the full moon, has its head turned downward. It charms. Its clustered filaments are tinged with the color of the young sun. Its body is luminous with letters beginning with A, and it is the absolute bliss.

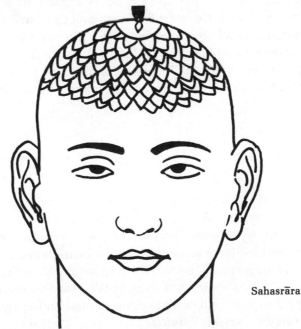

Sahasrāra

Verse 41

•Within the Sahasrāra is the full moon, without the mark of the hare, resplendent as in a clear sky. It sheds its rays in profusion, and is moist and cool like nectar. Inside it, constantly shining like lightning, is the Triangle and inside this, again, shines the Great Void (Bindū) which is served in secret by all the Devas.

Verse 42

•Well concealed, and attainable only by great effort, is the subtle Bindū (the "phase" of the moon representing Nirvana) with Amā Kalā (its "nectar-dripping" phase). Here is the Deva who is known to all as Parama Shiva. He is the Brahman and the Ātmā of all beings. In him are united both Rasa (the experience of supreme bliss) and Virasa (the bliss which is the product of the union of Shiva and Shakti). He is the Sun which destroys the darkness of nescience and delusion.

Verse 43

•By shedding a constant and profuse stream of nectar-like essence, the Lord instructs the Yati (self-controlled) of pure mind in the knowledge by which he realizes the oneness of Jīvātmā (the individual soul) and Paramātmā (the soul of the universe). He pervades all things as their Lord, who is the ever-flowing and spreading current of all manner of bliss known by the name of Hamsah Parama.

Verse 44

• The worshippers of Shiva call it the abode of Shiva;
the worshippers of Vishnu call it the place of Parama
Purusha (Vishnu); the worshippers of both Shiva and
Vishnu call it the place of Hari-Hara [the united selves
of Hari (Vishnu) and Hara (Shiva)]. Those who are
filled with a passion for the Lotus feet of the Devī
(Goddess Shakti) call it the excellent abode of the Devī;
and the worshippers of the Hamsah Mantra [Hamsah
is the union of Purusha (the true or pure Self, "Ham")
and Prakriti (the original substance, "Sah")] call it the
pure place of Prakriti-Purusha.

Verse 45

• That most excellent of men who has controlled his
mind and known this place is never again born in the
Wandering (this karmic world), as there is nothing in
the three worlds which binds him. His mind being
controlled and his aim achieved, he possesses complete power to do all which he wishes, and to prevent
that which is contrary to his will. He ever moves
towards the Brahman (or, "he is able to roam the
sky"). His speech, whether in prose or verse, is ever
pure and sweet.

Verse 46

• Here is the excellent sixteenth Kalā (phase) of the
moon (Amā-Kalā). She is pure, and resembles (in col-
or) the young sun. She is as thin as the hundredth part
of a fiber in the stalk of a lotus. She is lustrous and soft
like ten million lightning flashes, and is down-turned.

From her, whose source is the Brahman, the continuous stream of nectar flows copiously (or, "she is the
receptacle of the stream of excellent nectar which
comes from the blissful union of Shiva and Shakti").

Verse 47

• Inside it (Amā-kalā) is Nirvāna-kalā, more excellent
than the excellent (Amā-kalā). She is as subtle as the
thousandth part of the end of a hair, and in the shape
of the crescent moon. She is the ever-existent Bhagav-
atī who is the Devatā (divinity) who pervades all beings. She grants divine knowledge, and is as lustrous
as the light of all the suns shining at one and the same
time.

Verse 48

• Within its middle space (i.e. middle of the Nirvāna-
kalā) shines the Supreme and Primordial Nirvāna
Shakti. She is lustrous like ten million suns and is the
Mother of the three worlds. She is extremely subtle,
like the ten-millionth part of the end of a hair. She contains within her the constantly flowing stream of gladness, and is the life of all beings. She graciously carries the knowledge of the Truth to the mind of the
sages.

Verse 49

• Within Nirvāna Shakti is the everlasting place called
the abode of Shiva where there is neither kāla [time]
nor kalā [space]. It is free from Māyā (the world restricted by time and space), attainable only by Yogis,
and known by the name of Nityānanda. It is replete

with every form of bliss, and pure knowledge itself.
Some call it the Brahman; others call it the Hamsa.
Wise men describe it as the abode of Vishnu, and
rightoous men speak of it as the ineffable place of
knowledge of the Ātmā, or the place of Liberation.
(Here, liberation from the world of time and space
becomes possible.)

These, then, are the chakras as they are described in Pūr-
nānanda's *Shat-chakra-nirūpana*. As you can see, it is clearly
stated that each chakra has specific coloration, a fixed number of petals with a designated Sanskrit letter on each, a
geometric figure (yantra) within the pericarp of the lotus, a
designated animal and deity or deities whose iconography
represents aspects or powers associated with the chakra, and
a bīja mantra.

Superficially, these details may appear to be mere symbolic representations of certain functions of the chakras, or
perhaps figures which can be visualized to facilitate meditation. However, the reports of many persons who have undergone spiritual training verify many of the details described
here. For example, people who concentrate on the mūlādhāra or svādhishthāna chakras—even those with no prior
knowledge of chakra symbolism—often report seeing a
flame-like glow either around the perineum or below the
navel. This would seem to correspond to the red petals these
two chakras are said to possess. I find it plausible that the
designated colors of each chakra may represent the coloration of its aura in the astral dimension, and that the other
symbols may exist in some real way.

Of particular interest here is the experience of my mother,
a well-respected and highly-evolved religious personality. In
her 20s and 30s she practiced water asceticism frequently in
the depths of the mountains. During this practice she often
saw around her heart a character like an inverted sailboat,

surrounded by brilliant golden light. When she first asked me what it was I did not know, but a year or two later I began to study Sanskrit and read this *Shat-chakra- nirūpana.* I realized immediately that the "inverted sailboat" she described was none other than " य " (YAM), the bīja mantra of the anāhata chakra. Furthermore, the golden light she perceived is probably related to the golden triangle located within the bīja (see figure of Anāhata). In his book *The Chakras*, the Rev. C. W. Leadbeater (see Chapter VII), also describes the anāhata as glowing a golden color.

Therefore, in my opinion the descriptions of the chakras in *Shat-chakra-Nirūpana* are more than mere symbolic representations. I am in agreement with Swami Satyananda Saraswati, who states in his *Tantra of Kundalinī Yoga,* that there are numerous worlds beyond our everyday consciousness in the astral and causal dimensions where these geometrical figures, colors, and syllables may actually exist. Indeed, many of the iconographic details, as well as the paranormal abilities and mental states described here as associated with each chakra, correspond closely with the experiences of various ascetics of many religions throughout the world.

VI-B
The Chakras as Described
in the Gorakshashatakam

Gorakshashtakam is a yoga text written by the pundit Goraknath for the benefit of his disciples, probably during the tenth century. Widely respected and loved by the people of his time as the greatest living saint and guru in India, he was a man of great knowledge whose travels took him to areas outside of India such as Afghanistan and Baluchistan.

The descriptions of the chakras in the *Gorakshashatakam* resemble those in the Upanishads in most respects. Some additional information is provided, however, particularly concerning the paranormal abilities which accompany chakra awakening. Therefore, in this chapter I would like to present the following excerpts from the text, which I have adapted from the English translation edited by Swami Kuvalayananda and Dr. S.A. Shikla. The paranthetical remarks are mine, unless otherwise indicated.

Verse 78

•The first chakra, called ādhāra (mūlādhāra) is like burnished gold; meditating (on it) with the gaze fixed on the tip of the nose, one is freed from sin.

185

Verse 79

• The second chakra is svādhishthāna, beautiful like a genuine ruby; meditating (on it) with the gaze fixed on the tip of the nose one is freed from sin.

Verse 80

• The Manipūraka (manipūra) chakra is like the morning sun; meditating (on it) with the gaze fixed on the tip of the nose one can stir up the world.

Verse 82

• Fixing the gaze on the tip of the nose and meditating on (Anāhata), refulgent like lightning, in the Lotus of the heart, one becomes one with Brahman.

Verse 83

• In the center of the throat is the vishuddhi chakra, the source of nectar; meditating (on it) with the gaze fixed on the tip of the nose continuously, one becomes identified with Brahman.

Verse 84

• With the gaze fixed on the tip of the nose (and) meditating on the deity, resplendent as a pearl, that resides in the center of the brows (the ājnā chakra), one becomes full of Bliss.

Verse 85

• With the gaze fixed on the tip of the nose and meditating on the sky (the sahasrāra), on the absolute and peaceful Shiva, whose face is turned in all directions, one is freed from suffering.

Such are Goraknath's descriptions of the chakras and the effects he associates with their awakening. For a discussion of the nose-gazing techniques mentioned here, see Chapt. IV p. 100, 111. He further describes the meditations as follows:

Verses 86-87

•A student of Yoga obtains mastery over it after meditating upon the anus (corresponding to the mūlādhāra chakra), the penis (the svādhishthāna chakra), the navel (the manipūra chakra), the heart (the anāhata chakra), the throat and the uvula (the vishuddhi chakra), the Over-Lord in the middle of the eyebrows (the ājnā chakra), and the void (the sahasrāra chakra) as identical with the Ātmā that is all pervasive, pure, space-like and shining like a mirage.

Verse 88

•These centers of meditation which have been described, when associated with adjuncts (the letters, color, etc., of each chakra)* and the principle (i.e., Ātmā),* lead to the rise of the eight miraculous powers.

Verse 89

•The adjunct and the principle, these two only have been described — the former meaning color or letter while the latter means Ātmā.

---

* Notes appended by original translators.

188

Verse 90

• The adjunct implies (i.e., gives rise to)* perverse knowledge, while the principle is opposite in nature. The principle by its constant meditation leads to the destruction of all the adjuncts.

Verse 91

• A jewel when polished shines out in its true color. So the soul that is freed because of the awakening of Kundalinī is to be preferred (because then it sounds liberated)* and is freed from all adjuncts.

Verse 92

• The knowers of the principle know the principle to be free from pain, without any support, free from diversity, having no substratum, free from suffering and void of form.

In Verses 85-92, Goraknath seems to give us an important warning. To wit, if paranormal abilities are acquired by unifying the adjuncts (the various iconographical details of each chakra), with the principle (the Ātmā), through meditation, they must be approached with extreme caution. When activated, the adjuncts themselves have the propensity to give rise to "perverse" knowledge which deviates from the true goals of the spiritual aspirant. Only when the adjuncts have been finally merged with and dissolved into the absolute principle, Ātmā, can the yogi be freed from suffering and liberated from the concrete world of forms.

---

*Notes appended by original translators.

In the next chapter, we will turn out attention to Rev. C. W. Leadbeater's well-known study, *The Chakras*. This will prove quite interesting, as Leadbeater's descriptions of the chakras differ considerably from those contained in the material we have examined so far. The main point of contention is that Leadbeater, in his own experience of the chakras, did not perceive them to possess the various adjuncts described in the traditional Hindu literature. In fact, he contends that the Indian descriptions of the chakras are merely symbolic, and that the chakras he perceived in the form of wheels of multi-colored light, are the true ones. Let us examine his argument more closely.

VII

The Chakras as Explained
By Rev. Leadbeater

The Reverend Charles Webster Leadbeater, author of *The Chakras*, was born in England in 1847. He worked as a vice-rector of the Church of England, and became a member of the Theosophical Society in 1882. This society, founded by Madame Blavatsky in New York in 1875, promotes studies of comparative religion, philosophy and science and investigates the powers latent in man. In 1884 Leadbeater went to India to study under the guidance of his guru, and he practiced yoga while serving the society. After years of training he developed his clairvoyant faculties and investigated superphysical realms and man's inner constitution, which resulted in his book, *The Chakras*, published in 1927. He traveled and taught throughout the world, finally returning to India where he passed away in 1934, having written approximately thirty books.*

---

* For further information on Rev. Leadbeater, see *How Theosophy Came to Me* (Theosophical Publishing House, Adyar, Madras, India); also, *History of Theosophy and the Theosophical Society* (Theosophical Society, Wheaton, Illinois).

I would like to begin by presenting a summary of Lead-beater's views on the nature of human existence. Often, says Leadbeater, the physical body is considered tho oontor of the human being, with the soul a mere appendage. However, he contends that the physical body is actually the most superficial dimension of man's being: man is, in fact, a complex mechanism comprised of physical, etheric, astral, and causal bodies. These higher bodies, although invisible to the physical senses, play a vital role in man's existence, keeping his homeostasis intact and enabling him to reach higher spiritual realms.

Theosophy postulates an invisible physical matter known as the "etheric" which is differentiated from the normal physical body. The etheric is the vehicle which allows energy streams of thought, action, and feeling to flow from the invisible astral body to the denser physical matter, with the brain cells acting as receptors.* To the clairvoyant, the etheric body is clearly visible as a mass of faintly luminous violet-grey mist, interpenetrating the denser parts of the body and extending very slightly beyond it.

Now, the physical body becomes effete as time passes and requires three basic energy sources for its sustenance: food, air, and "innate vitality." This vitality is an invisible force which exists on all planes of the universe; however, in its physicalistic module it is most closely connected to the constitution and functioning of the etheric body. It, in turn, contacts the physiological body through the crucial medium of those invisible centers, the chakras.

Existing at the surface of the etheric double, which follows an outline of the physical body, these force centers serve as channels of energy between the physical and astral bodies. In their dormant state these chakras are small circles two in-

---

* In my opinion, the "etheric double" corresponds to the Ki energy flow of Chinese medicine.

ches in diameter which maintain a dull glow. However, when activated, as in a psychic person, they appear as blazing whirlpools of light.

Figuratively speaking, the chakras resemble flowers shooting forth at intervals from a stem, which is the spine. There are seven major chakras perpetually rotating towards the primary force. This force—the above-mentioned innate vitality—is sevenfold in nature, and all its forms correspondingly operate in each of the chakras. However, the operation of the centers is not uniform. For example, certain chakras in psychics or yogis might be awakened and functioning at a greater level of intensity than in an ordinary person.

Now, let us summarize Leadbeater's description of the chakras themselves. In his view, when the divine energy of the cosmos enters each chakra, it sets up secondary force emanations at right angles. These secondary forces undulate in a circular motion. At the same time, the primary force generates straight lines, which resemble stationary spokes on these wheels of undulating energy. These spokes help to bind together the astral and etheric bodies. Each force center has a different number of spokes, which determine the number of waves or "petals" within. Because of this pattern, the ancient scriptures describe each chakra as a lotus blossom.

The secondary forces move in undulations of various sizes, each with thousands of wave-lengths within it. These undulations weave under the radiating spokes of the primary force, creating flower-like oscillations of varying diameters which swirl about the vortex. Each of the resultant "petals" has a distinct predominant color, and resembles the shimmering gleam of moonlight on placid waters.

The chakras vary in size and brightness in different people. Furthermore, sometimes the distinct development of some chakras over the others within the same person is clearly visible. If an individual has certain superior traits which are related to a given center, that center is not only enlarged but also radiant, surrounded by brilliant golden rays.

Leadbeater divides the chakras into lower, middle, and higher groups, termed the physiological, the personal, and the spiritual, respectively. Those in the physiological group—the first and second chakras—have relatively few spokes and serve primarily as receptors to two principle forces which enter the physical body. These two forces are the "serpent fire," which comes from the earth, and vitality, which emanates from the sun. The middle group consists of the personal chakras, the third, fourth and fifth. The third chakra receives forces emanating from the lower astral level which enters man through his personality. In the case of the fourth chakra, the forces come from the higher astral; in the case of the fifth, they enter from the lower mental realms. All these centers seem to be connected with certain ganglia in the body. The sixth and seventh centers—the "spiritual" chakras—are activated only after a certain degree of spiritual growth has been realized.

Leadbeater is of the opinion that the various petals of these chakras are not necessarily related to the development of moral qualities, contrary to the view presented in the *Dhayānabindu Upanishad*. He had met persons in whom these centers were fully awakened even though their moral development was relatively low, while the centers of others who had attained considerable mental and spiritual development were scarcely vitalized.

To explain this seeming contradiction, Leadbeater puts forward a working hypothesis concerning the interrelationship between moral development and heightened activity of the chakras. According to him, the spokes around a given center differ in character due to subdivisions in the incoming primary force, which cause each spoke to radiate its own particular influence. In this process, the secondary forces passing through each spoke are modified by its influence and exhibit a variation of hue. Thus, each of the different petals manifests different radiations. A given moral quality may be indicated by a certain shade of color, which increases in luminousity and vibrational energy when that moral quality is strengthened. In other words, the conditions of individual petals, rather than the size or brilliance of the entire chakra, more accurately reflects moral development. Judging from this, the condition of each center and its constituent petals seems to be related to the interaction between the incoming primary force and the spokes it generates.

Leadbeater describes the individual chakras as follows:

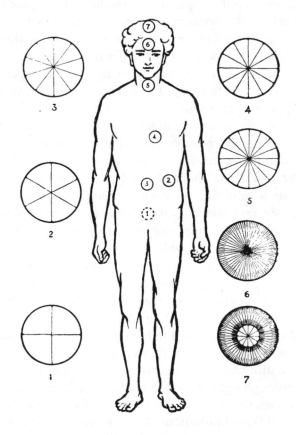

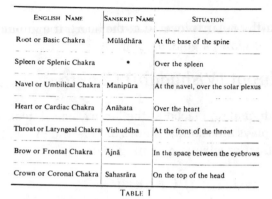

THE FORCE-CENTRES

English Name	Sanskrit Name	Situation
Root or Basic Chakra	Mūlādhāra	At the base of the spine
Spleen or Splenic Chakra	•	Over the spleen
Navel or Umbilical Chakra	Manipūra	At the navel, over the solar plexus
Heart or Cardiac Chakra	Anāhata	Over the heart
Throat or Laryngeal Chakra	Vishuddha	At the front of the throat
Brow or Frontal Chakra	Ājnā	In the space between the eyebrows
Crown or Coronal Chakra	Sahasrāra	On the top of the head

TABLE I

The Root (Mūlādhāra) Chakra

The first chakra is located at the base of the spine. It exhibits a primary force radiating in four spokes, producing the effect of quadrants of alternating red and orange hues. It becomes a fiery orange-red when strongly activated.

The Spleen Chakra

The second chakra originates in the spleen and is mainly concerned with the specialization, subdivision, and dispersion of the vitality obtained from the sun. Once absorbed, this vitality is again emitted in six undulations, each radiating a glowing color of the vital force, viz. red, orange, yellow, green, blue, and violet.

The Navel (Manipūra) Chakra

The third center is located at the navel or solar plexus. Receiving ten radiations from the primary force, it is thus comprised of ten undulations. Its predominant colors are varying shades of red and green. This chakra is closely connected with the emotions of the individual.

The Heart (Anāhata) Chakra

The fourth center is located at the heart. It exhibits twelve spokes, and glows a golden color.

The Throat (Vishuddhi) Chakra

The fifth chakra, placed at the larynx, has sixteen spokes, and it displays alternating shades of blue and green, producing the effect of silvery, gleaming water.

The Brow (Ājnā) Chakra

The sixth center, located between the eyebrows, is divided into two halves: pink mixed with yellow on one side, a purplish-blue on the other. Leadbeater notes that whereas the Indian scriptures describe the ājnā chakra as having only two petals, he himself perceived that each half of the chakra is subdivided into 48 undulations, making a total of 96.

In this connection, the sudden leap from the 16 spokes of the throat chakra to 96 here is noteworthy. Although the factors which determine the number of spokes are unknown, it is clear that they each represent a variation of the primal force. Thus, as we enter the higher spiritual realms which transcend the conventional bounds of human experience, we encounter complex, multiple manifestations of the primary force which cannot be easily labeled.

The Crown (Sahasrāra) Chakra

The seventh center, known as the crown or coronal chakra, is located at the top of the head. It is usually the last chakra to be awakened. Normally, it is nothing but a depression in the etheric body which allows the divine force to enter freely. However, as a person progresses in his spiritual development and begins to receive divine light, the chakra reverses itself, becoming a channel of radiation rather than reception. It emanates swift vibrations of various prismatic hues, among which violet predominates. The Indian scriptures describe the sahasrāra as thousand-petalled; Leadbeater is in virtual agreement, saying that it manifests 960 manifestations of the divine force. A unique feature of this chakra is a smaller whirlpool of energy at its center, consisting of twelve undulations of white and gold.

The sahasrāra chakra is often seen in Oriental representations of dieties and holy men, such as the statue of the Buddha at Borobudur in Java. The chakra is also sometimes depicted in Christian mythology: for example, the crowns worn by the twenty-four elders which they forever cast down before the throne of God.

In Leadbeater's opinion, it is not proper to identify the chakras with the nerve plexuses, because they are not physical entities in the usual sense. Rather, they act as intermediary conduits between the physical and astral bodies. However, each chakra is closely related to a specific nerve plexus. The figure p. 198 shows the location of the chakras in etheric double, and their corresponding positions in the spine ganglia. The "blossoms" exist on the surface of the etheric double; the stems act as channels to distribute vitality to the ganglia and spine. From these centers, vivifying energy circulates to the various internal organs.

The table below indicates the placement of each chakra in relation to the ganglia. For example, the heart chakra is located on the surface of the etheric double over the heart; its spinal counterpart is at the eighth cervical, and is closely connected to the cardiac, pulmonary, and coronary plexuses. The chakra is thus closely related to the functioning of the lungs, as well as the heart.

As we saw in Chapter V, the *Upanishads* state that prāna, the vital force, is absorbed through the digestive and breathing processes, and is distributed throughout the body along the nādīs. The chakras help to distribute and channel the prāna along the nadi system. Furthermore, prāna (or vāyu) is traditionally subdivided into five or ten categories, each individual variety being associated with a specific area of the body.

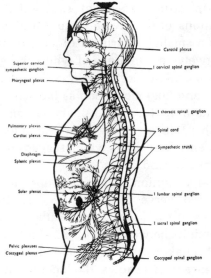

THE CHAKRAS AND THE NERVOUS SYSTEM

THE FORCES

Name of Chakra	Position on Surface	Approximate Position of Spinal Chakra	Sympathetic Plexus	Chief Subsidiary Plexuses
Root Mūladhāra	Base of spine	4th Sacral	Coccygeal	...
Spleen	Over the spleen	1st Lumbar	Splenic	...
Navel Manipūraka	Over the navel	8th Thoracic	Cœliac or Solar	Hepatic, pyloric, gastric, mesenteric, etc.
Heart Anāhata	Over the heart	8th Cervical	Cardiac	Pulmonary, coronory, etc.
Throat Vishuddha	At the throat	3rd Cervical	Pharyngeal	...
Brow Ājnā	On the brow	1st Cervical	Carotid	Cavernous, and cephalic ganglia generally

TABLE II

THE ROOT CHAKRA

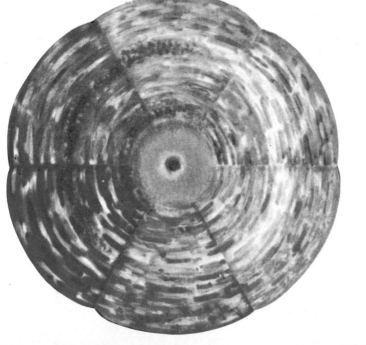

THE SPLEEN CHAKRA

THE NAVEL CHAKRA

THE HEART CHAKRA

THE THROAT CHAKRA

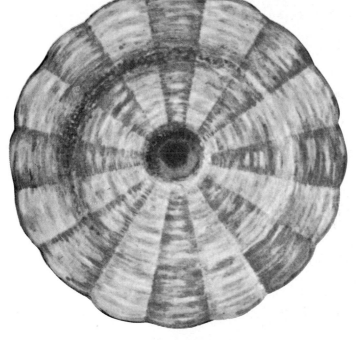

THE BROW CHAKRA

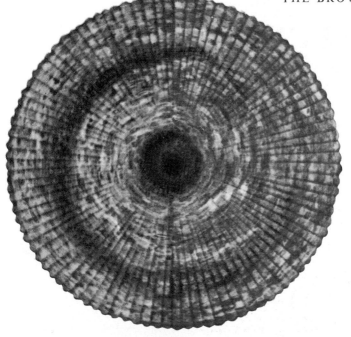

THE CROWN CHAKRA

Leadbeater's explanation of prāna, which he terms the "vitality globule," is as follows. The vitality globule originates in the sun, and radiates in all directions to permeate everything. In man, it is absorbed through the spleen chakra, where it is subdivided into streams of seven different colors: violet, blue, green, yellow, orange, dark red, and rose. These different colored streams flow to one or more chakras, whence they vivify the organs and other systems of the body. The following table, taken from Leadbeater's book, shows the correspondence between the five types of prāna within the traditional Indian system, and his own "rays of vitality."

PRĀNA AND REGION AFFECTED	RAY OF VITALITY	CHAKRA CHIEFLY AFFECTED
Prāna; heart	Yellow	Cardiac Anāhata
Apāna; anus	Orange-red	Basic Mūlādhāra
Samāna; navel	Green	Umbilical Maṇipūraka
Udāna; throat	Violet-blue	Laryngeal Vishuddha
Vyāna; the entire body	Rose	Splenic

TABLE IV

In my own research using the AMI device for measuring the acupuncture meridians (see Chapter IX), I have found that persons with ESP and other psychic abilities consistently show an abnormal yin state (the state of absorbing too much energy) in the spleen meridian. This would seem to correspond with Leadbeater, who states that the vitality globule is absorbed through the spleen chakra.

Leadbeater describes the seven individual rays of the primary force as follows:

The violet-blue ray: The violet-blue ray naturally flows to the throat, dividing into two shades: a light blue, which remains to vitalize the throat center, and a dark blue and violet which passes on to the brain. In the brain, the dark blue submerges into the lower and central parts of the brain, while the violet goes further up, invigorating the force centers at the top of the head.

The green ray: Enters especially into the solar plexus, filling the abdomen and vivifying the liver, kidneys, intestines, and the digestive system.

The yellow (golden) ray: Originally follows a pathway to the head, and after depositing substantial energy there, takes a route into the brain, directing itself mainly to the twelve-petalled flower which is situated in the midst of the highest force-center.

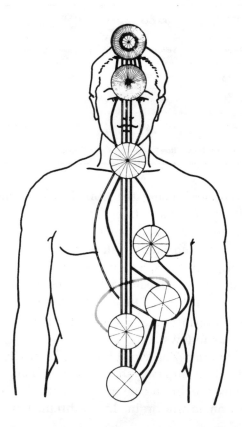

The rose-colored ray: Known as the nucleus or life-source of the nervous system. It is spread throughout the body in the entire nervous system. The unique characteristic of this ray is its ability to permeate and to radiate energy to other individuals. For example, a man of robust health constantly radiates these rose-colored atoms to the people around him, especially to those who are in need of this energy. Thus, certain people sometimes find themselves exhausted after spending time in close proximity to weak persons.

This phenomenon is found even among flora and fauna. For example, pine and eucalyptus trees radiate an intrinsic amount of energy, thus facilitating higher meditative powers.

The orange-red ray: Also containing shades of dark purple, this ray flows into the base of the spine and activates the urogenital organs; generally, it acts as a stimulant to the desires of the flesh and also helps to maintain body heat. However, when an individual develops an unyielding defense system, this ray can be directed towards the brain where all three shades of the ray (orange, red, and purple) undergo remarkable modification. The orange changes into a golden yellow which activates the intellect; the dark-red becomes crimson, engendering an altruistic state; while the third shade of dark purple is transformed into a pale violet, enhancing spirituality. Once these higher transformations have been realized, impeccable powers are developed which enable a person to transcend mundane sensual desires. Thus, when the serpent fire is stimulated, the severe dangers inherent in the awakening process can be avoided.

In Leadbeater's view, the centers exist in both the etheric and astral dimensions. The descriptions presented up to this point depict the centers as they exist and function in the etheric body. The vortices are located on the surface of the etheric body, and they are active in the average person to some extent, regulating physiological functions and helping him to lead a normal life.

Although the astral centers often resemble the etheric centers in appearance and location, they are fundamentally different entities. Existing within the astral body, they control sensory, mental, and spiritual functions in the astral dimension. The awakening of these astral centers can only begin with the activation of kundalinī—the serpent fire—located in the root chakra. In normal persons, this serpent fire is an unconscious, inert mass, devoid of any initiating or substantiating power of its own. However, when fully awakened it reaches unspeakable heights, enlightening the soul and enabling man to obtain the highest knowledge of the universe.

When the kundalinī reaches the second (spleen) chakra, a person is able to travel in the astral world with a vague sense of consciousness. When it reaches the third (manipūra) chakra, feeling in the astral body is gradually awakened. At the level of the anāhata chakra, the awakening of kundalinī enables a man to comprehend and reciprocate with other astral entities. As the power rises to the fifth center, the vishuddhi chakra, one acquires the power to hear on the astral plane. With the awakening of the sixth chakra, the ājnā, the power of full astral vision appears. As kundalinī rises to the sahasrāra, the seventh center, the adept acquires complete knowledge of astral life, endowing him with the perfection of all astral powers.

It is sometimes noted that the pituitary gland controls both the sixth and seventh chakras, acting as a converging point between the physical and higher dimensions. However, in certain exceptional cases, the centers are divided—the sixth in connected with the pituitary gland, while the seventh connects with the pineal gland—thus making possible direct communication from the higher planes to the lower mental states. In these instances, the intermediary astral planes are bypassed.

According to Leadbeater, the astral centers act almost like sense organs for the astral body. However, it should be remembered that these centers differ considerably from the physical sense orgains. First of all, the content of astral perception naturally differs considerably from that of physical perception; it is information from the astral dimension which is received. Furthermore, the astral organs of reception are not clearly differentiated in the way that the eyes, nose, ears, etc., are. Rather, the centers respond to vibrational information, which can be received from all directions. Therefore, a person functioning in the astral body has the power to see objects in any direction without turning his head. I would like to add that, judging from my own experience, visual astral information can also be received through chakras other than the ājnā. Thus, it seems that a given astral sense is not necessarily restricted to one astral center.

Leadbeater states that when the centers are awakened at only the astral level, the physical consciousness remains ignorant of this process. Information can be conveyed from the astral to the physical only through the etheric centers; thus, the etheric centers must be fully awakened for man to acquire consciousness of the astral dimension. Each of the major schools of Indian yoga has its own methods to awaken these centers. Rāja yoga emphasizes concentration and meditation on the chakras; in Karma yoga, the emphasis is on the dissolution of karma; in Jnāna yoga, one attempts to develop prajnā, or wisdom; in Laya yoga, one endeavors to acquire paranormal abilities and develop the interaction with divine beings; in Bhakti yoga, the practice is centered on self-redemption, love, and devotion to God; and in Mantra yoga, the chanting of mantras is practiced.

The following is a summary of Leadbeater's views on the awakening of kundalinī.

History records many spontaneous awakenings of kundalinī; however, it is generally believed that it is a gradual process, and most people who are attempting to awaken kundalinī for the first time will find it difficult in their present incarnation. The chances of successful higher awakening are greater for those individuals who have practiced yogic disciplines in their previous lifetimes.

During yoga practice, it is imperative to fully realize the value of one's Master's (or Guardian Angel's) guidance, and to follow it closely. Although age is no barrier to successful practice, good health is a prerequisite. The awakening process is strenuous, and only those in good physical condition can endure it.

During the spontaneous awakening of the serpent power, a dull glow is experienced at the coccyx, or in the abdomen or spine. This is followed by an excruciating pain in the spinal cord, the channel for the rise of kundalinī. Etheric dross is burned up during this painful process of purification. Despite strong resistance, kundalinī continues to rise, ultimately flashing through the head and encompassing the surrounding atmosphere. At this stage, except for a temporary loss of consciousness and slight fatigue, no adverse physical effects are experienced.

Once awakened, the serpent fire must be controlled carefully. The power must be made to move in an effective way, directed to the various chakras in a particular pattern. Normally, the adept concentrates upon a given chakra and activates it through the infusion of prāna, and then the kundalinī is aroused and directed to the chakra. As the optimum pattern differs considerably from individual to individual—due to differences in constitution, personality, and karmic factors—the close supervision by the Guru is indispensible.

During the second stage of its arousal, the serpent fire contacts the second etheric center. This acts as a prelude to conscious astral journeys which can be recalled later.*

---

* An accomplished yogi is able to consciously leave his physical body and travel to distant places through the astral dimension. This phenomenon is called astral projection. However, in individuals whose kundalinī is still dormant, dreams may act as a vehicle for astral travel. For example,

When the serpent fire reaches the third chakra, the practitioner experiences various kinds of astral influences in the physical dimension. He finds some experiences pleasant and others vaguely hostile—his feelings about certain places, for example—without any logical explanation.

With the awakening of the fourth center, the individual naturally begins to experience the joys and sorrows of others as if they were his own; at a later stage this experience may extend to bodily suffering as well.

As the serpent power reaches the fifth center, the practitioner becomes clairvoyant on the etheric and astral planes, acquiring the ability to hear various astral suggestions.

The vivification of the sixth sense enables a person to develop a unique faculty—a tiny etheric tube with an eye at its tip, stationed between the eyebrows. This tube can be expanded or contracted to examine objects of various proportions, in accordance with the needs of the individual. Leadbeater notes that this tube corresponds to a small snake depicted on the forehead of ceremonial headressess of Egyptian pharaohs.

Finally, the awakening of the seventh center revitalizes the kundalinī and enables it to pass easily through all the above-mentioned etheric centers. Once this has been achieved, a person acquires the ability to transcend the physical consciousness and experiences the beatitude of heaven.

An interesting related phenomenon Leadbeater discusses is what he calls "casual clairvoyance." In the casual clairvoyant state a person may experience glimpses of the astral world, despite the fact that the kundalinī has not awakened. This is due to irrevocably strong infusions of prāna which galvanize the chakras and activate them on higher levels. Intense inner concentration, resulting in the dharāna or dhyāna states of yoga, sometimes produces these spasmodic

---

a person who often dreams of flying through the air may actually be traveling through the astral dimension, but because his chakras are not fully awakened, he can have this experience only in dreams.

clairvoyant states, which are not related to the arousal of the serpent power. At other times, the partial awakening of kundalinī may be responsible for the onset of extraordinary psychic powers. When a person experiences these casual clairvoyant states, he should practice diligently to fully awaken the kundalinī force.

The prerequisite qualifications for the complete awakening of kundalinī are as follows:

1) A well-integrated, ethical, and virtuous life pattern.
2) A strong disposition to control and channel the kundalinī properly.
3) A well-developed sense of equanimity to endure the awakening of kundalinī without succumbing to injury.

If an individual attempts to awaken the serpent fire before fulfilling these criteria, the following dangers may be encountered:

1) Once awakened, the serpent power is uncontrollable. Its movement may generate excruciating pain which affects the whole somatic system and sometimes death results. In some cases, permanent damage is sustained in dimensions higher than physical.
2) Instead of moving upward along the spinal cord, the serpent power flows downward. In such cases, the reticent animal centers, located in the body's lower regions but unused by normal, virtuous people, are activated.* This results in an upsurge of the most undesirable passions.
3) The intensification of base, evil personality charac-

---

* Leadbeater omits the names of these chakras which are said to predominate in animals, but in the Indian tradition they are called the Atala, Vitala, Sutala, Talatala, Rasatala, Hahatala, and Patala. These lower chakras are located between the coccyx and the heels. The Mūlādhāra (the root chakra in humans) is said to be the highest of the chakras active in animals, while it is the lowest of the normally functioning human chakras.

teristics may occur. The traits of ambition, jealousy, selfishness, etc. are intensified to an incredible degree, deteriorating the very nucleus of the life process.

Thus, although awakening of the serpent power can lead the practitioner to spiritual liberation, serious dangers await him who is not adequately prepared. Leadbeater emphatically stresses the need to develop selfless love and to devote time and energy to the betterment of society before indulging in practice designed to awaken kundalinī. Furthermore, the expert guidance of a guru is necessary to avoid premature awakening and the accompanying dangers.

Leadbeater goes on to discuss the "etheric web," a single layer of minute physical atoms permeated by vital force which envelops the physical body like a sheath. This esoteric web acts as a strong barrier to all forces, with the exception of the divine force, which pass between the physical and astral bodies. Thus, a main function of the web is to protect the physical body from the influence of astral entities, while allowing the force of divine life to enter freely. It safeguards against the premature opening of the two bodies, which is potentially dangerous to a person whose chakras and nādīs are not adequately purified. Because this etheric web is the only barrier between the astral and etheric centers, any damage to its subtle fabric might result in emotional and physical disorder.

According to Leadbeater, the habitual consumption of alcohol, narcotics, drugs, tobacco, etc., may eventually weaken this protective web. These volatile stimuli harden the atoms so that the pulsation of the etheric web is greatly restricted and its growth is crippled. This leads to ossification of the web and a breakdown in the normal influx of vital energy. In turn, gross materialism, brutality, animalism, a loss of finer emotions, lack of empathy, selfishness, anger, and other such qualities are likely to manifest—in short, irresponsible and regressive behavior may result.

Leadbeater suggests that damage to the etheric web may affect the astral body directly, causing injury which remains even after death. In such cases, an individual's astral body might remain paralyzed and helpless for many weeks or months after physical death has occurred.

Thus, in order to progress spiritually within one's lifetime, it is important to give up all antisocial habits. The etheric and astral bodies must be purified, and the atomic matter of the etheric web kept scrupulously clean. This allows a natural, gradual opening of the etheric web, facilitating communication between the etheric and astral bodies; at the same time, the undesirable influences from the lower planes (i.e., the animalistic centers below the mūlādhāra chakra) are effectively screened out. So, the individual is able to experience spiritual awakening in the smoothest and safest possible manner.

Leadbeater's pioneering work, then, provides precise and comprehensible explanations of the chakras and their functions. In addition to describing the etheric centers as he perceived them, he elucidates their relationship with the nervous plexuses of the physical body, and their relationship to the astral chakras. Furthermore, his descriptions of the function of kundalinī and the etheric web are extremely succinct and valuable. To summarize, Leadbeater's views on the chakras form a pathway which leads to a basic understanding of esoteric knowledge.

In the next chapter we will present the chakras as described by Swami Satyananda Saraswati, an accomplished contemporary guru from India who has extensive knowledge of both conventional and tantric yoga.

VIII

The Chakras and Nādīs
as Described by Swami
Satyananda Saraswati

Swami Satyananda Saraswati is a widely respected Indian guru who has written extensively on tantra yoga and the chakras. Born in the Himalayas in 1923, he became a disciple of Swami Shivananda in 1947. After twelve years of spiritual practice with his master, he spent nine years wandering throughout India, perfecting his sadhana. In 1964 he settled in Monghyr and founded the Bihar School of Yoga. Under his guidance, many yoga centers and ashrams have been established throughout the world.

Swami Satyananda has distilled the essence of traditional yoga practice and teaches his own system of tantra geared to suit the needs of the modern age. Our Institute for Religious Psychology in Tokyo has established a mutual relationship with his organization, whereby we utilize his yoga teachings, and he has free access to our scientific research.

According to Satyananda, the word chakra refers to a center of psychic energy in the astral body, a center which controls certain higher or paranormal abilities. Each chakra is also closely related to particular systems and organs of the physical body, including the brain. Many of the brain centers are dormant or in a state of minimal activity in ordinary human beings. In the natural course of evolution these centers will gradually become more active and reach their full potential. The science of yoga, however, provides a safe means to shorten drastically this long process of human evolution—that is, the systematic development and awakening of the chakras. Satyananda emphatically states that the ultimate purpose of cultivating the chakras is none other than this acceleration of the evolutionary process.

The Ājnā Chakra

Satyananda recommends that the practitioner first attempt to activate the ājnā chakra before any other. His reason is that, once awakened, this chakra has the power to dissolve karma, thus helping to lessen any danger which might arise when the karma of the lower chakras is activated. The following is a summary of his understanding of the ājnā chakra.

Originally derived from Sanskrit roots meaning "to know" and "to follow", the word ājnā means "to command". Thus, the ājnā is often termed the "command center", where guidance is received from the guru (see below). It is located at the point where the three major nādīs (idā, pingalā, and sushumnā) merge to form a single passage, which then continues up to the sahasrāra chakra. Part of the combined life force which collects here from the throo nādīs fluws to the sahasrāra, while the rest is dispersed throughout the physical, astral, and causal bodies. At the ājnā the three nādīs form the Rudra-granthi or the "knot of Shiva", the third of the psychic "knots" which must be loosened for kundalinī to arise to the sahasrāra. In the physical body, the ājnā chakra is closely connected with the pineal gland, and the poin ' between the eyebrows. The latter is usually chosen for concentration upon the ājnā.

The ājnā is located at the opposite end of the sushumnā from t ə mūlādhāra chakra, and any change in one induces a a simi r change in the other. The symbols for the two chakras seem to support this: both contain an inverted triangle, he symbol of the creative, generative force.

Concentration on the ājnā brings one into contact with the great forces housed in the idā, pingalā, and sushumnā nadīs, and this leads to major psychic changes and purification of the mind. Once this purification has been achieved, concentration on the other chakras can be practiced safely. However, if this stage is bypassed, dangerous conditions may arise due to the activation of karma accumulated in other chakras, particularly the mūlādhāra, which is said to be the storehouse of karma. If the ājnā has been awakened, the practitioner is able to remain calm and unaffected when these forces are unleashed.

When the ājnā chakra is activated, the practitioner comes into contact with higher consciousness by releasing the great store of energy latent in the pineal gland. (Note that Satyananda associates the ājnā with the pineal gland, while Leadbeater assigns it to the pituitary gland.) "Contact with higher consciousness" may seem a nebulous concept to some, and indeed it is not an easy matter to explain. One of its meanings is direct contact with the "inner guru"—that is, an innate source of deep knowledge and wisdom which resides within the individual's ājnā chakra. Contact with the "outer guru"—one's guardian angel—also becomes possible. As the practitioner enters a state of deep concentration, self-awareness and ego-consciousness temporarily fade, and the voice of the inner and outer gurus may be heard. Thus the ājnā is called the "center of command." Telepathic communications with others and clairvoyant perception also develops as the ājnā is awakened.

Within the circle of the diagram which represents the ājnā chakra lies an inverted triangle. This symbolizes the creative, mother-force, material force, and manifestation. In contrast, the upright triangle (as found in the yantra of the anāhata chakra, ✡) represents conciousness—awareness without manifestation. Within the triangle, behind the letter " ই " lies a pillar-shaped form, known as linga. Although the linga is conventionally viewed as a phallic symbol, Satyananda says that in tantra yoga it is primarily a symbol for the astral body, termed linga shārira in Sanskrit. The circle symbolizes shūnya, the void. This is one of the three attributes of samadhi, the state of superconsciousness. The others are chaitanyā (fully awakened consciousness) and ānanda (bliss). The state of shūnya remains inaccessible to those whose consciousness is confined by the limits of space and time.

The astral body can be perceived extrasensorily in three forms, represented by Shiva-lingas at the mūlādhāra, ājnā, and sahasrāra chakras. At the mūlādhāra, it is seen as a smokey-grey column of gas, alternately forming and dispersing. As the depth of one's concentration increases, the astral body appears black, seen at the ājnā chakra. With continued concentration, this Shiva-linga becomes illumined, shining brightly at the sahasrāra. These three stages are known as dim, consolidated, and illumined astral consciousness, representing progressive purification and evolution of mind.

The syllable OM, the bīja mantra of the ājnā chakra, is located within the circle. It is the symbol of super-consciousness. Above the superimposed moon and bindū (dot) is a slight tail, representing the subtlest trace of consciousness. The two petals on either side of the circle contain the syllables Ham and Ksham, the bīja mantras of Shiva and Shakti, respectively.

Satyananda perceives the aura of the ājnā chakra as grey in color, although he notes that other commentators have described it as transparent. Leadbeater, on the other hand, states that the ājnā emanates an aura of dark violet. These descriptions are similar, in that dark colors are mentioned; the slight difference may be attributed to the fact that Satyananda is discussing the aura as it exists in the astral dimension, while Leadbeater describes the etheric.

The Mūlādhāra Chakra

The word mūlādhāra is derived from words meaning "root" (mūla) and "base" (adhāra); it is thus the root, the foundation of the seven chakras.

Satyananda says that mūla is best understood as mūla-prakriti, the transcendental basis of physical nature in the Sankhya tradition of Indian thought. (Prakriti is matter, characterized as feminine, in contrast to the masculine purusha—spirit). Mūla-prakriti is the primordial source of all the processes of natural evolution, the origin to which matter returns when it disintegrates. It is ultimately responsible for all aspects of man—whether physical, material, or psychological—including the conscious and unconscious minds. The mūlādhāra is the seat of mūla-prakriti, the great Shakti. Here this transcendent force lies, ready to be awakened.

In the physical body, the mūlādhāra chakra is located in the perineum (the area between the anus and the genitals). Directly connected to the testicles, it is associated with the sensory nerves which feed them. In the female body, it lies at the cervix. The ancient yoga scriptures associate the mūlādhāra with the earth element, whose principal attribute is smell; thus, on the physical level the mūlādhāra is associated with the sense of smell, and with the nose.

Traditionally, the mūlādhāra is represented by a lotus with four red petals, each containing a Sanskrit letter (Sam, Vam, Sham, and Śam); each letter represents the individual sound vibrations of associated nādīs. The bīja mantra of this chakra is Lam, the sound which represents the earth element. The presiding female diety is the red-eyed and fearsome Dākinī; her male counterpart is Ganesha, embodied in the form of an elephant.*

The inverted triangle in the diagram of the mūlādhāra symbolizes shakti, creative energy. As explained earlier, the Shiva-linga or phallic form within the triangle represents the astral body. The serpent coiled around it is the symbol of kundalinī. Kundalinī is upheld by an elephant with seven trunks, which signify the seven minerals indispensable for

---

* In Japan, Ganesha is known as Kangiten or Shōten-sama (holy deity of joy); he is often portrayed as a male and female couple embracing, each half human and half elephant.

the maintenance of the physical body. The yellow square inside the pericarp which contains these symbols is the yantra —symbol of specialized psychic energy—of the mūlādhāra chakra. This shape signifies the earth element and its particular type of energy.

Satyananda explains the significance of yantras in the following manner. Human existence is comprised of many bodies, each containing various nerve centers, hemoglobin, oxygen, carbon, etc., so the astral body—the psychic body, the great unconscious—is comprised of many aspects or dimensions. One of these is an aggregate of geometrical symbols; another is comprised of sound vibrations—the world of mantras. As one enters a state of deep meditation by concentrating on a chakra, thus transcending the ego-consciousness, one actually enters a realm where the sound vibrations of a single mantra, and nothing else, exists. Likewise, it is possible to experience a dimension where there is nothing but geometrical pattern—the world of yantras.

It is on the basis of such experience that Satyananda speaks of the reality of mantra and yantra. "Yan" and "tra" have the root meanings of "to conceive" and "to liberate," respectively. By concentrating upon a particular yantra, the individual conceives his consciousness in terms of that set pattern. As concentration increases, the yantra is activated and the consciousness gradually assumes its symbolic shape. Once total unification is experienced, the mind is liberated. Each of the seven chakras contains a yantra. By concentrating upon one of these, one can experience the mystical dimension of the personality where the yantras exist and, more particularly, the principle of the chakra itself.

An important function of the guru is to choose the appropriate chakra for the individual to concentrate upon which he does by chanting its mantra and visualizing the yantra. In my opinion, the guru bases his choice upon the karmic characteristics of the individual. The karma of past lives creates a set pattern of physical and psychological elements. In the dimension of yantra, these patterns can be perceived in geometric form. The individual's karma can be altered and purified most effectively by activating the appropriate chakra with its pervasive influence on all levels of being. One of the best methods for chakra activation is the direct stimulation of the yantric realm of consciousness through yantra visualization.

As we have seen, kundalinī lies dormant, like a coiled serpent, in the mūlādhāra chakra. Within the mūlādhāra is a knot-like formation, called the Brahmā granthi. When the knot is untied, shakti, the power of kundalinī, begins to rise up the sushumnā nādī within the spine. There are two other granthis along the sushumnā: the Vishnu granthi in the anāhata chakra, and the Rudra granthi in the ājnā. These psychic knots form an impediment to the rise of kundalinī, but once they are loosened, allowing the serpent power to continue its ascent, wisdom and power are bestowed upon the practitioner.

When the kundalinī awakens as the result of yoga practice or other spiritual disciplines, there is an explosive gushing forth from the realm of the unconscious. It is like an earthquake, in which things hidden underground are pushed to the surface. This emission may include the karma of many past incarnations, suddenly drawn out from the unconscious storehouse of the mūlādhāra. Again, please remember: the ājnā chakra should be awakened before the other chakras, so that these powerful unconscious forces can be safely controlled.

Kundalinī has two contrasting qualities. While lying dormant in mūlādhāra, it exits only in an unmanifest state, beyond the confines of time and space. Once activated, however, it is transformed into something resembling a material force, subject to the laws of the physical dimension. The same is true of the universal mūla-prakriti which, though it transcends time and space before the creation of nature, conforms increasingly to these laws as the evolutionary process progresses.

When the mūlādhāra awakens, a number of phenomena occur. The first thing many practitioners experience is levitation of the astral body. One has the sensation of floating upward in space, leaving the physical body behind. This is due to the energy of kundalinī, whose ascending momentum causes the astral body to disassociate from the physical and move upward. This phenomenon is limited to the astral and possibly mental dimensions, and this differs from what is normally called levitation—the actual displacement of the physical body.

Besides astral levitation, one sometimes experiences psychic phenomena such as clairvoyance or clairaudience. Other common manifestations include movements or increasing warmth in the area of the coccyx, and the sensation of something moving slowly up in the spinal column. These sensations result from the ascension of shakti, the energy of awakened kundalinī.

In most cases, when the shakti reaches the manipūra chakra, it begins to descend back to the mūlādhāra. Often the practitioner has the sensation that the energy ascends to the top of the head, but usually only a very small portion of the shakti is able to pass beyond the manipūra. Repeated earnest attempts are necessary for the kundalinī to ascend further. According to Satyananda, once the manipūra is passed, no further serious obstacles are encountered. However, during the stage when the kundalinī activates only the mūlādhāra and svādhishthāna chakras, many problems arise.

The awakening of the mūlādhāra chakra releases all kinds of repressed emotion in such an explosive manner that the practitioner is often rendered extremely irritable and psychologically unstable. One day he may sleep deeply for hours, another day he may wake up in the middle of the night to meditate or take a bath. He becomes passionate; at times very talkative or fond of singing, at other times so easily enraged that he may hurl objects at other people. During this stage of emotional and psychic instability, the guidance of a qualified, experienced teacher is essential. The awakening of the svādhishthāna chakra leads to a similar explosive release of repressed emotion: feelings of anger, sorrow, uncertainty, infatuation, etc. may increase to an almost unbearable degree. Rather than attempting to avoid these stormy periods, the practitioner should pass through them under the supervision of his guru. They are *not* signs of degeneracy or bad character, but rather an integral part of the evolutionary process. If these stages are avoided or suppressed, no further advancement is possible.

Subordinate to the mūlādhāra are the following lower chakras: Atara, Vitara, Sutara, Talatara, Rasatara, Mahatara and Patala. Located between the coccyx and the heels, they control the animal instincts. Although it is on a higher plane than these seven, passion and animal instincts predominate in the mūlādhāra as well. However, the divine shakti also resides there. The ordinary person may occasionally yield to the grip of the lower chakras, behaving instinctively like an animal, but it is said that he will always return to the mūlādhāra or another of the higher human chakras. The proper practice of kundalinī yoga, however, makes it impossible for the kundalinī to descend into these animal centers by transforming the shakti of the mūlādhāra into spiritual energy (ojas) and causing it to ascend the sushumnā.

The three major nādīs—idā, pingalā, and sushum-nā—originate in the mūlādhāra. These are the most important among the reputedly 72,000 nādīs in the body (one source gives the figure 300,000). Satyananda says that although the word "nādī" is often translated "nerve," it is derived from the root *nad*, "to flow." Therefore, it should be interpreted to mean the flow of psychic consciousness and not simply a physical conduit for this flow.

The idā nādī starts from the left side of the mūlādhāra chakra, the pingalā from the right, and the sushumnā from the center. Within the sushumnā is the more subtle chitra nādī and inside that is the Brahma nādī, subtler still. The sushumnā may therefore be considered a conduit for two other streams of conciousness. From the mūlādhāra, the sushumnā courses straight up to the ājnā chakra. The idā and pingalā wind their way up the spine in a spiral pattern, crossing each other at each chakra and reversing sides in the process. Finally, the idā enters the ājnā chakra from the left and the pingalā from the right. The idā is said to control mental and psychic activity, and the pingalā, prāna and various physical activities. The alternation of their relative positions at each chakra helps to maintain a balance between psychological and physical energy, ensuring harmony between the activities of the mind and body. Satyananda maintains that if an imbalance exists between the energy flow of the idā and pingalā nādīs, shakti cannot flow into and ascend the sushumnā.

The Svādhishthāna Chakra

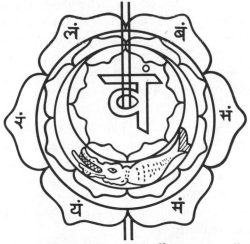

The word svādhishthāna literally means "one's own abode." This signifies that the original home of kundalinī was in this chakra. Only later did it descend to its present seat in mūlādhāra.

In fact, this theory corresponds with the physical migration of the male testes during the viviparous period. During the first months they are located in the interior of the lower abdomen, and then gradually descend to settle in the groin area. Of course, the sexual organs have a close relationship to shakti energy, and this movement is very similar to the alleged migration of kundalinī. Satyananda locates the svādhishthāna at the coccyx, adjacent to the mūlādhāra, and states that both are connected to the sacral and coccygeal nerve plexuses.

Of particular interest is Satyananda's discussion of the svādhishthāna and the unconscious. He states that the center in the brain connected to the svādhishthāna controls all phases of the unconscious mind, in particular the collective unconscious. This collective unconscious is more powerful than individual consciousness, and it controls much of human behavior, although most people are virtually unaware of it. Every experience in daily life, whether relevant to the individual's self-interest or not, whether conscious or unconscious, is recorded in the center of the unconscious, the svādhishthāna. Thus this center houses not only the karma of the individual's past lives, but all the experiences and associated karma which have contributed to the process of human evolution. Some of this karma is stored as dormant seeds, some is active. Whether active or inactive, the individual's conscious mind is seldom aware of his karma at all. However, when the awakened kundalinī begins to ascend, triggering the process of psychic evolution, both dormant and active karma are unleashed and flood into the consciousness. If the individual cannot analyze or control this karma stored in svādhishthāna, then the kundalinī retreats back to the mūlādhāra.

In this sense, the svādhishthāna chakra and the karma it houses are a serious impediment to human spiritual evolution. The best method to overcome this obstacle is first to awaken the ājnā chakra. The superconsciousness housed in the ājnā is fuly aware of the workings of the unconscious mind in the svādhishthāna, and can control the unleashed karma.

At this juncture, it may be useful to summarize Satyananda's views on human evolution.

Life is created when prakriti (original substance) is manifested, ordered by the observing consciousness of purusha (spirit, the True Self). As matter becomes increasingly ordered, successive stages of animal evolution are realized and the seven minor chakras which exist in humans below the mūlādhāra are gradually developed and activated. Once the mūlādhāra is reached, animal evolution ends and human evolution begins. The six higher chakras represent the full range of possible human development. According to the Tibetan tantric tradition, above the sahasrāra there exists another series of seven chakras which correspond to the evolution of divine beings. Thus, just as the mūlādhāra is considered the highest animal but the lowest human chakra, the sahasrāra may be viewed as the crossover point between human and divine evolution.

In tantra, then, the infinite process of evolution from the Absolute—the state before creation, before the interaction of purusha and prakriti—through the creation of the phenomenal world, the animal and human realms, the dimension of divine beings and beyond, is described in terms of the chakras. This conception is grounded in the belief in the ongoing spiritual evolution of all created things and acknowledges the importance of the chakras in this process. This system underlies the esoteric traditions of yoga and Buddhism in India, Tibet, and Nepal.

In this context, Satyananda contends that much of the common experience undergone during the process of animal evolution is stored within the mūlādhāra chakra, in the form of karmic propensities and latent abilities. For example, most of man's physical activities—sleeping, eating, defecating—are functions developed during the stage of animal evolution, and they are still at work due to the activity of this chakra. In this sense, the karma of man's animal nature is active and functioning in the mūlādhāra.

In contrast, the karma of the svādhishthāna is almost completely inactive without manifest form. It exists only as the collective unconscious, the residual karmic force of past evolution. In this sense it is even more basic than the mūlādhāra, the original source of the latter's animal karma. The forces hidden within the svādhishthāna are very powerful and irrational, and form a strong impediment to the further rise of kundalinī. Often the kundalinī will return to its dormant state in the mūlādhāra, beaten back by the impenetrable karma of the svādhishthāna. However, when the latter chakra is awakened and controlled, the animal karma of the mūlādhāra is subjugated, and further advancement becomes possible.

In a broader sense, as well, it is said that whenever a higher chakra is activated by kundalinī, its functions and scope of activity begin to predominate over those of the lower chakras. The relationship between these two lowest chakras is both unique and particularly close, however, and should be noted carefully.

The traditional diagram for the svādhishthāna chakra contains a crocodile residing within a crescent moon. The crocodile represents the forces of unconscious, formless karma. The crescent moon is formed by two circles, the larger with outward-turned petals, the smaller with petals facing inward. The inner circle represents the phantom-like existence of the unconscious, carried on the back of the crocodile.

The presiding deity is Brahmā, the creator. He is sometimes described as the Hiranya-garba, the "golden womb" from which all creation issues. Satyananda equates the Hiranya-garba with the collective unconscious of the svādhishthāna. The female deity of the chakra is Sarasvatī, the goddess of knowledge;* she also appears in the form of Rākinī, the goddess of the vegetable kingdom. The svādhishthāna chakra is closely related to the vegetable world, and the observance of a vegetarian diet is said to be an important practice to awaken it.

The syllables on the chakra's six vermilion petals are Lam, Ram, Yam, Mam, Bam, and Bham. The governing principle (tattva) is water (āpas); the yantra is the white crescent moon. Its bīja mantra is Vam.

The svādhishthāna is associated with the sense of taste, and thus its "organ of knowledge" is the tongue. Its "organs of activity" are the sex organs and kidneys. It is closely connected with the prostatic nervous plexus.

When the svādhishthāna is awakened, the following paranormal abilities appear: increased powers of intuition, knowledge of the astral body, and the ability to create taste sensations in oneself and others (without actually eating).

The Manipūra Chakra

---

* In Japan she is known as Benzaiten, the goddess of learning, poetry, music, etc. Usually enshrined near bodies of water, she is customarily depicted holding a lute.

Satyananda states that the manipūra is located in the spinal cord, behind the navel. The word "manipūra" carries the meaning "filled with jewels." In Tibet this chakra is known as "manipadma," meaning "jewelled lotus." (Cf. the well-known mantra of Avolokitesvāra, the Bodhisattva of Compassion: OM MANI PADME HŪM). In the Buddhist tradition manipūra is also called hara, meaning "to leave," because the kundalinī shakti is said to leave from the manipūra to ascend. As we have seen, there is a strong tendency for the kundalinī to descend after reaching the svādhishthāna chakra; however, once manipūra is reached, there is little chance this will happen. Accordingly, within the Tibetan Buddhist tradition, it is taught that the process of true spiritual evolution begins when kundalinī is awakened in the manipūra and begins its upward journey. In fact, the mūlādhāra and svādhishthāna chakras are not explicitly discussed, probably because they retain traces of animal life. In tantra yoga, as well, manipūra is considered the starting point for evolution toward higher human development.

The tattva of the manipūra chakra is fire, an element closely related to shakti and the awakening of kundalinī. In the physical body, the manipūra is said to be the center of the "digestive fire" which reduces food to ash (feces) and extracts vital energy. Also called the chakra of the sun, the manipūra is related to the solar plexus.

The awakening of this chakra entails both positive and negative aspects. As we have seen, once kundalinī rises to manipūra and establishes itself there, there is little possibility of a permanent recession back to the animal realms of consciousness. Satyananda calls this "confirmed awakening." Here the consciousness of Jīva, the personal soul, awakens. Underlying conventional human consciousness, the jīva is the personal spiritual consciousness which pervades all dimensions of evolution, from the creation of the lowest realms of nature through to the world of divine beings. Once this consciousness is awakened in manipūra, according to

Satyananda, it will not descend to the lower animal dimensions.

However, in my experience, it appears that shakti does sometimes return to the mūlādhāra after reaching the manipūra.

On the negative side, overstimulation of the manipūra can shorten the practitioner's life span. This is because the activated fire of this chakra burns up the life-supporting nectar which is said to be generated in the bindū—the psychic center at the back of the head, represented by a cool, crescent moon. Normally this nectar descends to a gland deep in the throat (closely associated with the vishuddhi chakra) and

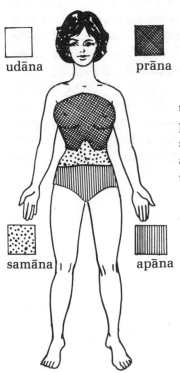

udāna

prāna

samāna

apāna

udāna vāyu: head region, limbs
prāna vāyu: chest area
samāna vāyu: upper abdomen
apāna vāyu: lower abdomen
uyāna vāyu: entire body

is stored there. However, the fire in the manipūra draws and consumes the nectar, causing accelerated decay of the body.

As described in Chapter V, prāna is said to divide into five sub-types or "winds" (vāyu) upon entering the body, each governing a different area, as follows:

According to Satyananda, the conscious joining of prāna and apāna in the navel region is an important practice to awaken the manipūra chakra. Normally, during inhalation prāna flows from the throat to the navel, and apāna moves downward from the navel to the anus. However, when apāna is consciously directed upward from the mūlādhāra during inhalation to meet prāna at the navel (see p. 116, 157), these two energies collide, generating a great force. As apāna is raised from the mūlādhāra, it is also accompanied by kundalinī shakti; this shakti is energized by the union of apāna and prāna, and the resulting supercharged energy flows directly from the navel to the manipūra in the spine.

It is said that the mūlādhāra is associated with the physical realm, the svādhishthāna with the realm between the physical and the spiritual dimensions, and the manipūra with the spiritual world—the realm of heaven. Satyananda assigns these three chakras to the first three of seven possible planes of evolution, which are:

the three
main planes
$\left\{\begin{array}{l}\end{array}\right.$
Bhu — earth
Bhuvana — intermediate space
Svaha — heaven
Mahaha
Janana
Tapaha
Satyam — the truth

Consequently, the paranormal abilities which result from the awakening of the svādhishthāna—telepathy, clairvoyance, clairaudience, etc.—may not be entirely free of self-interest, negativity, personal emotion, and other undesirable mental attributes. This is because the subject's personality remains within the second stage of evolution, and the earthbound egotistical self still occasionally manifests its influence. However, when the individual evolves beyond the limits of mortal existence and enters the realm of the manipūra, he reaches a state of higher consciousness full of infinite beauty, truth, and felicity. This chakra has been traditionally described as jewel-like in a variety of cultures to symbolize these incomparable qualities. Here, no trace of prejudice or personal bias remain. Thus, the siddhis (supernatural powers) realized when the manipūra awakens are of a benevolent and compassionate nature. They include the ability to locate hidden treasures, the mastery of fire, the ability to see the body from within, freedom from disease, and the ability to send prāna to the sahasrāra. In addition, concentration on the manipūra improves digestion.

The lotus of the manipūra chakra contains ten dark blue petals, each inscribed with a Sanskrit letter. These sound vibrations, each corresponding to a nādī, are: Dam, Dham, Nam, Tam, Tham, Dam, Dham, Nam, Pam. The presiding female deity is Lakshmi (or Lākinī) who drips fat and blood from her mouth. The male deity is Vishnu. The tattva of the manipūra is fire, whose bīja mantra is Ram; within the diagram, it rides on the back of a ram. Its yantra is an inverted triangle, often depicted with T-shaped protuberances on each side.

The Anāhata Chakra

The anāhata chakra is said to be located in the area of the astral body which corresponds to the heart. Thus, in the physical body it is closely connected with the heart and the cardiac nervous plexus, and is often referred to as the "heart chakra." However, in contrast to the small area occupied by the physical heart, the astral space of the anāhata chakra is vast and formless. It is normally dark, but when activated becomes radiantly bright. It is said that purity resides here.

The word anāhata means "unbeaten" or "unbroken." Anāhata nāda manifests here, a non-physical sound which continues without beginning or end.

To understand the import of the anāhata chakra, we must first summarize Satyananda's views on karma.

Derived from the root "kri" meaning "to work," the word karma denotes the law of cause and effect, by which every action generates its own result. However, it is commonly used to describe a kind of indebtedness for one's actions which must be worked out or paid for at some future time. Therefore, there are both individual karma and social or collective group karma, because actions may be performed either by individuals or a group or society as a whole. Satyananda further distinguishes individual karma, which

originates from one's own past incarnations, and that derived from one's parents or ancestors. Thus, there are three
major categories of karmic debt: a) that accruing from an individual's past incarnations; b) that inherited from his fami-
ly; and c) that resulting from actions of his society or social
group. All these factors contribute to an individual's karma;
they must be dealt with. It is impossible to avoid one's karma.

The three lowest chakras—mūlādhāra, svādhishthāna, and
manipūra—are closely related to the senses and consciousness which govern the physical body and its maintenance.
Functioning within the phenomenal world, the mind of these
chakras is bound by the law of karma. In other words, at this
level the jīva (individual soul) is not free from the causal
relation between actions and their consequences; its functions depend on karma, and are bound by it. Regardless of
whether its origin lies in the individual's past lives, that of
his forbearers, or in the actions of the society to which he
belongs, karma totally dictates the individual at the levels of
the mūlādhāra and svādhishthāna, until it is somehow either
worked out or purified. However, at the level of manipūra,
the jīva begins to assume partial control, and can exercise its
own will to a limited degree.

In contrast, the mode of being which functions in the
anāhata chakra completely transcends the realm of worldy
existence. Unlike the previous three, it is not subordinate to
the karma of this world. Therefore an individual with an
awakened anāhata chakra can directly perceive the workings of earthly karma, and at the same time free himself of it.
At this level the jīva can control worldy karma and exert its
own will in this realm to fulfill its wishes. Here lies the major
difference between the anāhata and the lower chakras. At
the lower levels, the individual soul merely accepts what is
presented by karmic circumstance, but at the anāhata it can
exercise its free will.

This power of wish fulfillment is symbolized by the
"wishing tree'—an evergreen called Kalpavriksha—

represented within the similar lotus beneath the anāhata in the symbolic diagram. Although present in all persons, this tree only functions when the anāhata chakra has awakened. When this power is acquired, it is said that the subject's wish will be granted, whether good or evil. Therefore Satyananda issues the following admonitions.

Before attempting to awaken the anāhata chakra, it is imperative to develop the capacities of correct thinking and judiciousness. Evil thoughts and misjudgments tend to create disharmony and conflict; this is especially true when a subject with an awakened anāhata wills his mistaken thoughts and desires into full actualization.

In addition, an attitude of constant optimism must be maintained. Inner peace and harmony in relations with others should be practiced, regardless of any confusion, conflict, or malicious intent one encounters. Negativity and pessimism are obstacles to the awakening of the anāhata. Thus, even a hedonist or a murderer should be regarded as an innately good person; such negative conditions as poverty, disease, emotional conflict, etc., should be considered ultimately beneficial occurrences. In fact, the cultivation of such a consistently positive attitude is considered a method for awakening the anāhata. According to Satyananda, it is also important to keep in mind the thought, "The whole world is within me. I am in everyone. Everyone is in me." His recommendation is probably based on the Hindu belief that Brahman, the absolute being of the cosmos, resides in the anāhata chakra as Ātman, the individual true self. Brahman and Ātman are, in essence, the same. Indeed, this realization is important both for awakening the anāhata, and for the realization of the universal Absolute.

Satyananda further admonishes his disciples in the following way. In general, after the awakening and ascension of kundalinī shakti to a given chakra, when any negative or pessimistic attitude arises in the mind, the kundalinī will return to the mūlādhāra. If it only reaches the manipūra and then descends, it can be raised again by yogic or other practices. However, if it should descend after having reached the anāhata, it is extremely difficult to raise it again. Clearly, those wishing to awaken the anāhata should not for one moment lose their optimism, regardless of the circumstances encountered. Anyone who endeavors to awaken the kundalinī should take this admonition seriously.

A number of paranormal abilities result from the awakening of the anāhata chakra. The ability to control air (vāyu) is acquired. Non-individualistic, cosmic love is awakened. The practitioner becomes eloquent, and poetic genius develops. As mentioned before, he acquires the power to have his wishes fulfilled.

The anāhata controls the sense of touch. When it is awakened, one's sense of touch becomes increasingly subtle, and even astral matter can be felt, using the astral sense of touch. This sensation can then be communicated to others. Thus the anāhata's sense organ is the skin, and its active organ is the hands.

In addition to these paranormal abilities mentioned by Satyananda, powers of psychic healing also develop when the anāhata awakens. Prāna can be transmitted through the palms and directed to the diseased area of another person's body. The well-known technique of "laying-on of hands" is probably related to the close connection between the anāhata and the hands. Psychokinetic powers also develop when the anāhata is awakened.

The lotus of the anāhata chakra has twelve vermilion petals, containing the letters Kam, Khan, Gam, Gham, Ngam, Cham, Chham, Jam, Jham, Nyam, Tam and Than. The associated tattva is vāyu (air or wind) and is symbolized by a hexagonal star, the yantra of the anāhata. As previously mentioned, the inverted triangle represents shakti, material force, while the erect triangle represents Shiva, or consciousness. The yantra is smoky in color, and the bīja mantra is Yam. It rides on the back of a black antelope, a symbol for alertness. Satyananda says that the mantra Om Shanti (shanti means inner peace) belongs to the anāhata. The female deity is Kali (or Kākinī), wearing a necklace of human bones. The male deity is Īsha or Rudra.

The anāhata contains the Vishnu granthi (knot). As described earlier, the chakras containing granthis (mūlādhāra, anāhata, and ājnā) are of special importance. Only when they are awakened and the knots are loosened can the kundalinī rise to further the process of spiritual evolution.

The Vishuddhi Chakra

In the physical body, the vishuddi chakra is located in the throat, corresponding closely to the thyroid gland. It is related to the pharyngeal and laryngeal nerve plexuses. "Vishuddhi" is derived from the word "shuddhi," to purify; it is considered the chakra of purification. In contrast to the ājnā and manipūra chakras, where the purification of thought and karma may take place, the vishuddhi is said to purify poison. The nature of this purification may be explained as follows.

In tantra yoga it is said that the moon excretes ambrosia, which is consumed by the sun of the manipūra. The moon here refers to the brain, the region of the sahasrāra, which is often symbolized by a moon or half-moon (perhaps corresponding to the ventricles of the brain) in both Hinduism and Taoism. The ambrosia or divine nectar formed there flows down to the manipūra, where it is consumed as fuel to sustain life.

The nectar secreted from the sahasrāra forms into drops at bindū visargha, the psychic "point" at the back of the head (see next section). It drips down to a minor chakra called lalana in the upper part of the epiglottis or the base of the nasal orifice, which serves as a reservoir for the nectar. It is secreted when such mudrās as khechari are practiced, and flows down to the vishuddhi chakra. If the vishuddhi has been awakened to some degree, the nectar undergoes purification and becomes the divine nectar which rejuvenates the body, bringing good health and longevity. However, it is said that if the vishuddhi is not active, the nectar becomes poison and flows downward. It slowly poisons the body, leading to decay and eventual death.

According to Satyananda, an awakened vishuddhi chakra also has the power to neutralize poisons which originate outside the body. In fact, the thyroid gland, which corresponds closely to the vishuddhi in the physical body, is medically recognized to perform an antitoxin function.

The awakening of the vishuddhi chakra results in telepathic powers. Although a person may feel that thoughts from others are received in the manipūra or elsewhere, the actual reception center is in the vishuddhi. From there, the thought waves are transmitted to other centers, in the brain and elsewhere, where conscious recognition may occur. Along with the mūlādhāra, the vishuddhi is the source of all the basic sounds: the vowels are said to originate here, as inscribed on the chakra's petals. Other associated paranormal abilities include indestructibility, full knowledge of the Vedas—the sacred texts which expound the Law of the Universe—the ability to know the past, present, and future, and the ability to endure without food or drink (see next section on the bindū).

The sixteen petals of the vishuddhi, violet-gray in color, contain the following letters: A, Ā, I, Ī, U, Ū, R̄, R, L̄, L, E, Ai, O, Au, Am and Ah. Its tattva is space (akāshā), represented by a circular or oval yantra. The bīja mantra is Ham, which sits atop a small white elephant within the circle. The female deity is Shakani, the male deity Sadashiva. The vishuddhi is associated with the sense of hearing. Thus, its organs of knowledge and action are the ears and the vocal cords, respectively.

Satyananda does not consider the sahasrāra a chakra in the true sense. He says that chakras operate within the human psyche, manifesting at different levels. The sahasrāra, however, is the totality beyond all individualization. Therefore, it is not discussed in *Tantra of Kundalini Yoga*. The bindū, however, is discussed, as follows.

Bindū Visargha

Bindū means "drop" or "spot", and bindū visargha literally means "the falling of the drop." Since "drop" refers to the nectar produced there, the entire phrase is perhaps best rendered "the seat of nectar."

According to tradition, the bindū is located near the top of the brain, towards the back of the head. A very slight depression or pit is found there, which contains a small amount of liquid secretion. Within this pit there is a slight elevation, the exact location of the bindū in the physiological structure. Cranial nerves emanate from this point including those connected to the optic system.

The process by which nectar is secreted from the bindū, stored in the lalana chakra in the nasal orifice, and purified by the vishuddhi chakra, has been described above. The bindu and lalana are best understood as minor psychic centers which are directly connected to the vishuddhi. Such minor centers cannot be awakened independently of the related major chakra. For this reason, only the six major chakras, from mūlādhāra to ājnā, are called "chakras of awakening."

As the divine nectar, purified by the harmonious functioning of the bindū, lalana and vishuddhi, begins to descend and pervade the entire body, extraordinary feats become possible. For example, a person is able to subsist for long periods without air, food, or water. There are documented cases of yogis who have been buried underground for forty days, voluntarily subsisting in state of hibernation, and have fully recovered. This is made possible by the practice of a special form of khechari mudrā, in which the tendon beneath the tongue is gradually severed over a two year period, until it can be curled back in the epiglottis to completely seal the respiratory passage. This directly stimulates the lalana center, and nectar falls to the vishuddhi, where it is purified and distributed throughout the body, supplying oxygen and other nutrients necessary for life. The bindū is induced to produce more nectar, and the body's need for air, food, and water is drastically reduced.* It is said that the nectar can slow down the body's metabolism, and in fact yogis buried underground exhibit no new hair growth.

At our institute in Tokyo we have conducted experiments which support the claim that an awakened vishuddhi chakra, in conjunction with the bindū and lalana centers, makes possible the conscious control of metabolism, respiration, food intake, digestion, etc. (For details, see my *Western and Eastern Medical Studies of Pranayama and Heart Control, Vol. 3, No. 1 of the Journal of the International Association for Religion and Parapsychology).*

According to Satyananda, the bindū controls visual perception. Cranial nerves connect it with the optical system. Therefore abnormality in the bindu can lead to eye disease.

The bindū is a center of nāda, or psychic sound. When the vishuddhi and bindū are awakened by such practices as Navamukhi mudra (Chapter IV), vajroli mudrā (Chapter IV), and murcha prānāyāma (Chapter III), a continuous non-physical sound comprised of innumerable subtle vibrations is heard. This experience pinpoints the exact location of the bindū.

Because it is not a chakra as such, the bindū is not represented by a lotus or resident deities. Its symbol is a full moon—representative of the point for which individualization begins—and also a crescent moon, expressing the fact that only a portion of the infinite totality which resides in the sahasrāra is manifest and perceptible to the practitioner at the bindū.

---

*The acquisition of these powers is sometimes attributed to the awakening of the Kurma ("tortoise") nādī, associated with the vishuddhi chakra.

Both the dot (full moon) and crescent moon may be seen in the upper right corner of some stylized versions of the written character OM:

This concludes our presentation of Satyananda's views on the chakras. This chapter is also the final installment in our review of the major extant literature on the chakras and nādīs. For the sake of clarification and as a summary, I would now like to present a discussion of my own experiences, experimentation, and theories in this field.

IX

Experience and Experiments
of the Chakras
by
Motoyama

After carefully studying the material described in the previous chapters, two questions troubled me.

The first question was, simply, *will ordinary readers believe that the chakras exist?* I believe that they do exist, and as part of the supporting evidence for this assertion, I would like to describe here the chakra-related experiences I, personally, have had over the last thirty years of practicing yoga. In addition, I wish to describe the scientific exploration into the possible existence of the chakras and their related systems which I have done. This discussion will make up the major portion of this chapter.

Before I begin that, however, I want to deal with the second question which emerged from the study. This is the problem I have with Leadbeater's assertion that the chakras he experienced were the true ones and that the traditional representations of the chakras are merely symbols.

I myself have not experienced the symbols as such in my own personal chakra awakening. However, my mother, a simple woman with no knowledge of Sanskrit, did. Specifically, she often commented on the fact that she saw a symbol which looked like an inverted sailboat inside a six pointed star at her anāhata chakra. We wondered what it meant. It was not until I studied Sanskrit years later that I was shaken by the realization that my mother had, in fact, seen the symbol traditionally associated with the anāhata chakra: —य—, the bija mantra "yam" surrounded by the star—✡—. It is, therefore, difficult for me to accept Leadbeater's view. Coupling this with Satyananda's statements that there are indeed dimensions in which the mantras and yantras do exist, I have come to feel that the chakras which Leadbeater experienced are probably those of his self-termed etheric double rather than the higher chakras of the astral or causal dimension. This also might somehow account for Leadbeater's outstanding omission of the svādhishthāna chakra, referring as he does only to the "spleen chakra", i.e., the manipūra. I do not know if he simply overlooked the svādhishthāna or if perhaps he purposely excluded it for some reason.

Returning to my own experiences, I was introduced to spiritual reality from an early age. My natural and foster mothers—both spiritual devotees—began taking me to temples and shrines in the mountains of Shōdo Island, my birthplace, when I was four. They taught me to chant Buddhist sutras and Shintō prayers, and the three of us chanted together for hours on end.

They also took me to places renowned as high energy centers for religious asceticism, such as the Kōbō waterfalls. This spot I remember particularly well. It was an eight kilometer walk through dense forest, dark even at midday, and the area was infested with water snakes. I found it quite frightening.

During this time with my mothers, I was taught about and experienced the existence of non-human entities, of entities who reside in higher dimensions. It must have been the combination of this environment and my karma that led me to aspire to the world of higher dimensional reality. This is why

I began to practice yoga thirty years ago. Let me now trace that history with you.

Awakening the Mūlādhāra Chakra

I was twenty-five years old. My early practice consisted of getting up at three a.m. every morning, practicing āsanas for about half an hour, and sitting for three or four hours. The first part of the meditation was devoted to prānāyāma, the latter to concentration on a specific chakra.

Here is this the initial method of prānāyāma I practiced.

Inhale breath (prāna) through the left nostril to the lower abdomen for four seconds. Hold the prāna in the inflated lower abdomen for eight seconds. Then raise the kundalinī from the coccyx to the lower abdomen (the svādhishthāna chakra) and contract the abdominal muscles. Visualize mixing and unifying the prāna and the kundalinī for eight seconds. Exhale through the right nostril for four seconds. One breath cycle, therefore, takes twenty-four seconds. Repeat the entire process, inhaling through the right nostril and exhaling through the left, and so on, alternately.

I performed this from fourteen to twenty-one times. After one or two months, I was able to prolong the period of kumbhaka (breath retention) to one or one and a half minutes. When I then concentrated on the svādhishthāna or ājnā chakra, worldly thoughts gradually ceased to enter my mind. I began to feel my body and mind fill with an extraordinary amount of energy.

As a result of the practice, my physical and psychological states began to show changes. I had often suffered from a stomach disorder and from an ear discharge. Also, I had been quite nervous and adversely affected both physically and mentally by bad weather. Within six months after I began yoga, these problems disappeared.

During continued practice, I began to notice some new sensations. I had an itchy feeling at the coccyx, a tingling feeling on the forehead and at the top of the head, and a feverish sensation in the lower abdomen. I could hear a sound something like the buzzing of bees around the coccyx. In ordinary daily life my sense of smell became so sensitive that I could not endure offensive odors.

These conditions continued for two or three months. One day, when I was meditating before the altar as usual, I felt particularly feverish in the lower abdomen and saw there a round blackish-red light like a ball of fire about to explode in the midst of a white vapor. Suddenly, an incredible power rushed through my spine to the top of the head and, though it lasted only a second or two, my body levitated off the floor a few centimeters. I was terrified. My whole body was burning, and a severe headache prevented me from doing anything all day. The feverish state continued for two or three days. I felt as if my head would explode with energy. Hitting myself around the "Brahman Gate" at the top of the head was the only thing that brought relief.

This, then, was the first time I had experienced the rising of the kundalinī shakti to the top of my head through the sushumnā. I did not experience as much physical or mental difficulty as is so often associated with this experience, probably because of the fortunate fact that my Brahman Gate was already open and the shakti was able to flow out into the astral dimension.

Awakening of the Svādhishthāna Chakra

The feverish feeling I had around the svādhishthāna, during the initial practice of prānāyāma some months before the awakening of kundalinī, was like a mixture of ice and fire. It was accompanied by a vision of white steam. A month or two later I began to see a round, crimson fire ball in my abdomen. Beginning at that time I began to often dream prophetic dreams, to have involuntary ESP experiences (such as telepathy), and to realize the spontaneous fulfillment of wishes.

I seem to have been able to activate the svādhishthāna, the manipūra, and the sahasrāra more easily than the other chakras. My ease at awakening the svādhishthāna may be due to the water asceticism I had practiced since my childhood. Traditionally, there is said to be a strong connection between the svādhishthāna and water, where the chakra is said to dominate the principle and power of water. Many modern psychics who practice water asceticism have thereby awakened the svādhishthāna chakra. Furthermore, it has been my experience that many psychics with inborn but uncontrolled PK or ESP also seem to have a more or less awakened svādhishthāna chakra.

After the awakening of this chakra, I became overly sensitive, both physically and mentally. During meditation, the smallest noise sounded like thunder and startled me. My emotions became unstable and I was excited easily. This period is sometimes called the "dangerous stage" of yogic discipline, during which it is generally important to have the guidance of an experienced guru. I managed to pass through it without too many problems under the guidance of both my mothers and with the aid of what may be termed divine protection.

The svādhishthāna chakra is thought to control the genitourinary system and the adrenal glands. The kidney, urinary bladder, and triple heater meridians are also thought to be connected with this system. It is interesting to note that when the condition of the meridians in my body is tested, there is a distinct abnormality in the kidney and urinary bladder meridians, though no malfunction is present. I have noticed such an abnormality in similar cases as well, and feel it is a possible indicator of increased svādhishthāna activity.

Awakening of the Manipūra Chakra

In my childhood, and until I started yoga, my digestion was poor. Fried foods gave me diarrhea. I suffered from frequent attacks of gastroenteritis at the transition period of spring or autumn which forced me to live on a simple diet of rice gruel and pickled plums. These conditions began to improve about six months after I began yoga practice.

After the same six months, a new series of sensations began. I often saw another reddish light centered on the navel that would become intensely white, seemingly much brighter than the sun. I grew dizzy and could see nothing for about ten minutes. I began to see a purple light shining between my eyebrows or in my abdomen.

Though I had often seen ghosts (lower astral beings) since my childhood, I began to see them with increased frequency during meditation at this time. I was occasionally able to ameliorate their suffering by chanting prayers of purification and Buddhist sutras for them, and by consciously emitting prāna. However, if the spirits were very strong and hostile, I was unable to help them and was adversely affected by them instead. When under the influence of such spirits, my body and mind became unstable. I became ill or got angry for no reason, and once had to stay in bed for a week with a fever. On the other hand, positive spirits (spirits who work to produce harmony with others), would affect me for the good, leaving me feeling very peaceful.

Another result of the awakening of the manipūra chakra was that I was endowed with such enhanced ESP abilities as clairvoyance, telepathy, and spiritual insight.

I had an impressive experience about that time which greatly affected my later life. One evening in November, 26 or 27 years ago, I was playing "kokkurisan" (a Japanese game which resembles the use of the Ouija board) with an old man, an assistant at the Shrine. After ten minutes I fell into a semi-trance. My body felt like it was on fire and I began to sweat profusely. My right hand started to move violently and I was unable to stop it. The trance became even deeper, but I did not lose consciousness.

Suddenly I had the extrasensory vision of a man wearing ancient white clothes. He was standing in a pine grove about 100 meters away through the shuttered doors. I saw him as clearly as if I had seen a real person. The ancient man was full of dignity and looked like a tribal leader. He beckoned to me, bowing. It felt as if he wanted to guide me somewhere.

The man introduced himself as Hakuō and told me that I had been the ruler of the tribes in this neighborhood, including his own, in a previous life. He said that he wished to invite me to the place where we had lived. I was able to understand this telepathically. As an academic researcher in philosophy and psychology, I found all of this extraordinarily strange. In another level of my being, however, in a higher part of my mind which makes no distinction between past, present, and future, I had the realization that what he was saying was true. I had been the lord of this area and Hakuō had been a follower of mine.

I think the spiritual dialogue with Hakuō continued for ten to twenty minutes. With my eyes open, I was able to see both the shutters and Hakuō. I saw this world and the spiritual world as if they were superimposed. When I shut my eyes, though, I could see only Hakuō, the pine grove, and the grass.

The next day I went by bicycle to Jindaiji temple, in front of which there is a mountain that has many old graves on it. Although I had never been there before, the place felt very familiar. To my surprise, there were ancient pot shards and stone implements on display in the temple, and a notice explained that a recent excavation had disclosed the existence of an ancient community around Jindaiji.

When I left Jindaiji, the autumn light was fading quickly into night. On my way home, I came across a dark place which somehow attracted me spiritually and I thought it might be the place where Hakuō had lived some thousands of years before. Going up about ten stone stairs, I indistinctly saw something which looked like a small shrine. I instinctively knew that, in fact, this had been the ancient dwelling of Hakuō and I simultaneously felt somehow that Hakuō was pleased at my discovery.

I went up to the shrine and began to pray, at which time I had a vision of the Buddhist deity, Fudōmyōō.* By this time it was completely dark. I felt very strange and hurried home. The next day, though, I went back to Jindaiji to visit the small shrine I had discovered the night before. As I was praying, the priest of this shrine came out after his morning prayer. I told him what had happened the previous evening. Surprised, he told me that, yes, Fudōmyōō was enshrined there and invited me in to worship. I entered the shrine and found that it was exactly as I had seen it.

Using the terms of parapsychology, this is an example of clairvoyance. But I also experienced something that I cannot describe with a word like "clairvoyance"—a strong affirmation of the existence of the spiritual world. This is the world which I believe enters the yogi's awareness through the awakening of the manipūra chakra.

I later had an experience with the manipūra chakra which taught me something else of importance: If one overuses the psychic ability attained by the awakening of the manipūra chakra—the ability to come into direct contact with the spiritual world—and neglects the development of the other chakras, or if one uses any one chakra to the exclusion of the others, one is apt to develop abnormalities and disease in both mind and body.

About 13 years ago (1967), seventeen years after I began yoga, my mother fell ill. In her place, I gave spiritual consultations to the members of Tamamitsu Shrine for about three years. At first, I was able to leave my body through the sahasrāra chakra during meditation to enter a state of higher

---

*The Japanese name for Achāla, one of the fire "brightness kings" of Esoteric Buddhism.

or divine union. However, about six months after I started giving these consultations, spirits would immediately appear before my manipūra or ājnā chakra when I went into concentration, and I had to negotiate with them constantly. I was unable to get past them in order to leave my body through the sahasrāra chakra and achieve this union—a predicament that continued for two or three years. Though I had not fallen ill since I began yoga, my stomach started to become easily upset and I began to tire easily.

At this juncture, I left Japan and went to lecture at Andhra University in India for three months. While I was there I developed a gastric ulcer, partly due to the spicy food, but also due to the deterioration brought on by the continual use of the manipūra. After I returned to Japan, my mother resumed the spiritual consultations and my gastric ulcer was cured in eighteen months by yogic discipline and acupuncture treatment.

From this experience, I realized that the contact with spirits at spiritual consultations had overworked my manipūra chakra, thus disturbing the balance with the other chakras and causing problems in the digestive organs. Many psychics who have overworked this chakra have died young or have had severe problems in the stomach and intestines. I feel sure that it is, in fact, dangerous to overuse any chakra.

Emotionally, the result of awakening the manipūra chakra was that my emotions became somehow richer and more under my control. I also acquired a much deeper level of sympathy with other people.

Awakening of the Anahāta Chakra

Although my digestion had been poor, I had never had any heart-related problems. However, about two years after I began yoga, I began to notice a pain where the line connecting both nipples crosses the midsternal line (the Danchū point of the conception vessel meridian, Shanchung, CV 17) and my heart seemed to be functioning abnormally. Rather than feeling ill, though, I was healthy, very active, and required only minimal sleep.

At this time, as is usual during the coldest period of winter, I was practicing the traditional water asceticism of rising at dawn, going outside, and pouring icy water over my semi-naked body for about an hour. As I was doing this, my mother stood by and prayed for me.

One morning the following occurred. I saw a kind of heat energy rising from my coccyx to my heart through the spine. My chest felt very hot and I saw my heart start to shine a brilliant gold. The icy water was warmed by this heat, steam rose from the surface of my body, but I did not feel cold. As the kundalinī rose from my heart to the top of my head, it became shining white. It left my body through the top of my head and I rose with it into a much higher dimension. My physical body was standing in the cold wind of this world, but I had forgotten it. I was half-unconscious, and yet I was aware of being in the heights and of worshiping the Divine. When I came to myself ten to twenty minutes later, my mother told me that she had seen a golden light shining at the top of my head and at my heart. I think this experience is the point at which my anāhata chakra was awakened.

Since then, I have been able to do psychic healing, and one or two years after this blessing, I had an experience which gave me the confidence to heal. A grandson of a member of our Shrine, then a child of three, had shown an allergic reaction to an injection. His condition became critical, and the doctor stated that it was hopeless. His grandmother telephoned me about 10 o'clock in the evening and implored me to pray and save him, so I immediately began to offer fervent prayers for him with my mother. Soon, the grandson appeared before the two of us. We continued our impassioned prayers, emitted energy to him and urged him to return to his body. About an hour later, he disappeared suddenly and we felt he had returned to his body and would recover. I telephoned the grandmother to tell her that he would be safe. Just then, in the hospital, his heart began to beat slowly but steadily and his respiration returned to normal. He steadily improved after that and recovered fully two or three days later.

After the awakening of the anāhata chakra, then, I recognized and learned to control the abilities both to emit psi energy and to perform psychic healing. In contrast to the situation after the manipūra chakra had awakened (when spirits entered me), after the awakening of the anāhata, my own spiritual energy or astral body was able to enter that of another person and to effect curative changes within that person. I was also able to expand my existence to include those whom I wanted to cure, or rather, other people could enter my expanded existence and live within me.

My mother, who I feel also had an awakened anāhata chakra, often performed psychic healing. For example, she once sent energy to a girl who was blind from birth by shouting at her. The girl's eyes suddenly discharged blood and pus. Later, on opening her eyes, she could perceive light, and about a week later, she began to see objects. At another time my mother prayed for an elderly paralyzed farmer who had been bedridden for more than ten years. After the prayer, she commanded him to stand, and he stood immediately.

I feel that many of the human beings who are able to perform miraculous healings do so through the agency of the anāhata chakra.

My psychological state also underwent some profound changes with this awakening. Notably, I developed an attitude of non-attachment to worldly things. Although I had become clairvoyant and telepathic after the awakening of the manipūra chakra, and though my emotions had become richer and more controllable, I had been unable to completely rid myself of attachment. With the anāhata, I began to feel a constant optimism about everything, deeply realizing the truths that all things come to him who waits, that bad times don't last, and that good always follows bad. I was enabled to see not only that good and bad co-exist inside and outside all things, but also that there is a world beyond this duality. After ridding myself of attachment, I became peaceful and my mind was free. For those who have once enjoyed this true freedom, the pleasures of this dualistic world seem meaningless.

After the awakening of this chakra, my wishes were often fulfilled spontaneously. For instance, we have a retreat in a place called Nebukawa in Odawara. The site covers about four acres, one of which was taken up by a deep valley with a river in it. I had often thought of making part of the valley into a parking lot for those who come to the retreat from various places in Japan. About a year later it so happened that a construction company did just this for us free of charge.

The former owner of our land was planning to build a big hotel at Yugawara hot spring. He had a problem with excess soil excavated during the construction and asked me if he could dump this soil in our valley, on the condition that he would build sturdy stone walls to contain it. I agreed at once, and, for one month, a steady stream of dump trucks showed up to fill our valley. Two big bulldozers leveled the site every day. Finally, about one third of the valley was made into a good, walled parking lot for at least fifty cars, an operation which would have otherwise cost us about $200,000.

Awakening of the Vishuddhi Chakra

I did not feel activity in the vishuddhi chakra as often as in the other chakras, but, during the fourth and fifth years of yoga practice, I began to concentrate on it after performing my daily prānāyāma. Very soon an irritation developed in my throat and breathing became difficult.

After several months, I saw a dark purple light spread

gradually around my head. Consciousness of my body vanished; I became quiet and calm. I experienced the state of nothingness.

The experience of the awakening of the vishuddhi chakra is like the feeling of a late autumn evening, when the sky is twilight purple and everything is silence itself. Pale purple light spreads and disperses. I enjoyed a feeling of absolute nothingness and my mind was totally still.

There is a Buddhist saying:

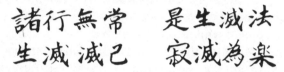

This means that everything, whatever it may be, is subject to change, because all things, once created, have to come to an end. Having transcended birth and death, having gone beyond them, we are in Shūnyatā, the absolute nothingness and the highest good.

After experiencing this state several times I found myself facing an abyss of absolute void. I experienced such a terrible fear that I wanted to stop yoga. I often felt that my attachment to this world was coming to an end; that I was leaving this world through this experience. My paralyzing fear gradually diminished as I learned to surrender myself completely to God—to totally entrust my life to Him.

During this process, I encountered a horrible devil-like being. It was an indescribably terrifying experience. However, I also had the realization that all things, even "gods and devils" are transient: ultimately there is nothing to fear. This realization is what enabled me to pass through this frightening and dangerous period.

When my fear was overcome and I could enjoy the feeling of total silence around me, I could clearly see that I was no longer attached to this world. I became able to work freely in this world without being attached to the results of my actions. I experienced a deeply wonderful feeling of non-attachment and freedom. With this attitude, I was able to see the past, the present, and the future in the same dimension by surpassing the distinction between them. When I now gave spiritual consultations to members of the Shrine, I could see their previous lives, their present situation, and their future as a continuous stream.

Another result of the Vishuddhi awakening had to do with my sense of hearing. It is said that when the vishuddhi awakens, the hearing becomes sharp. In fact, I have had a lot of difficulty in hearing due to tympanitis of both ears, which started when I was a child. In addition, the eardrum and the small bones in my left ear were surgically removed when I was young. However, since the vishuddhi awakened I have been able to hear much more clearly—not with my physical ear, but with that of the mind.

Awakening of the Ājnā Chakra

In connection with prānāyāma, I sometimes concentrated on the perineum, contracting it during inhalation and relaxing it during exhalation. In so doing, my perineal area would become hot. This sensation was usually accompanied by delicate vibration between the eyebrows in the spot which is the supposed location of the ājnā chakra and, of course, its connected organ, the pineal gland. To specifically accelerate the awakening of the ājnā chakra, I began the following practice.

Concentrating on the ājnā chakra, I visualized the absorbtion of divine energy through it while inhaling, and the diffusion of prāna out into the universe while exhaling, all the time chanting OM.

After performing this practice one hour a day for several months, kundalinī energy rose from my coccyx through my spine and my body became hot. My lower abdomen surrounding the svādhishthāna chakra became as hard as iron. My respiration became so easy and slow that I felt as if I could live without breathing. My body, especially the upper half of my torso, felt as though it disappeared. My ājnā chakra began to vibrate very subtly. I was completely immersed in a dark purple light while a bright white light shone from between my eyebrows. I heard a voice call me as if it were echoing in a valley. I was filled with ecstasy and a divine symbol of power was revealed to me. This state continued for one or two hours and, I think, indicated the initial awakening of the chakra.

This awakening was not frightening like that of the vishuddhi had been. I was simply filled with heavenly calm. I did not experience the dimming or loss of consciousness that had happened in the awakening of the other chakras. Rather, I found myself in a state of widened and deepened consciousness, a consciousness of a higher dimension sometimes referred to as superconsciousness. While in this state, the past, present and future are simultaneously knowable. The essence of objects, and the karma of other people, of previous lives, of nations and of the world become clear. Such knowledge is termed prajnā, or divine wisdom.

My various scientific studies originated from the wisdom obtained by concentration on the ājnā. I began to perceive that one of my tasks in this life is to help make this knowledge as clear as possible through scientific means, and to attempt to explain it in a way that others will understand. In this way my approach differs from that which employs the ordinary inductive methods of scientific research which were devised to examine physical phenomena in the effort to establish a synthetic scientific truth. I, rather, am attempting to manifest in the physical dimension, using deductive and scientific methods, the wisdom granted me while concentrating on the ājnā chakra.

Further concomitants of the ājnā's awakening were a number of psi abilities which seem to emanate from a different dimension than that of the abilities associated with the awakening of the anāhata and manipūra chakras. When my manipūra chakra awakened, for example, I was able to see and to be affected by spirits, and I could see the karma of individuals' previous lives. However, after the awakening of the ājnā chakra, I became aware of the suffering of the spirits and was able to help liberate them by praying to God on their behalf. Also, the understanding of karma received through awakening the ājnā chakra is not only that concerning individuals, but also that of larger entities such as families and nations. And the power to affect and alter others' karma was greatly enhanced by the awakening of the ājnā chakra.

In conclusion, I wish to add that the most important aspect of awakening the ājnā chakra is the ability to transcend and purify karma. For this reason, I feel it is absolutely necessary to awaken the ājnā and sahasrāra chakras for a human being to evolve to a higher level of being.

Awakening of the Sahasrāra Chakra

One of the practices I performed regularly in my initial program of discipline is a Taoist form called Shōshūten. This is a method of purifying the sushumnā by the circulation of energy in the upper part of the body, which is done by raising the kundalinī shakti along the sushumnā to the top of the head and letting it fall to the ājnā chakra during inhalation. Then keep the shakti there and hold the breath for two to three seconds. Let it fall to the svādhishthāna chakra along the midsternal line of the front of the body and keep it there, again holding the breath for two to three seconds. Maintain a circulation of the shakti from the mūlādhāra chakra up the sushumnā to the top of the head, back to the mūlādhāra, and so on.

While I was doing Shōshūten, I could see the inside of the sushumnā, the sahasrāra and two or three other chakras shining. After I had practiced yoga for six months or a year, a shining golden light began to enter and leave my body through the top of my head and I felt as if the top of my head protruded ten to twenty centimeters. In the astral, but not the physical dimension, I saw what looked like the head of Buddha, shimmering purple and blue, resting on the top of my own head. There was a golden-white light flowing in and out through the gate on top of the Buddha's crown. Gradually I lost the sensation of my body, but I held a clear awareness of consciousness, of super-consciousness. I could see my spiritual self gradually rise higher and leave my body through the top of my head to be restored in Heaven.

I was able to hear a powerful, but very tender, Voice resounding through the universe. While listening to the Voice, I realized spontaneously my mission, my previous lives, my own spiritual state, and many other things. Then I experienced a truly indescribable state, in which my entire spiritual existence became totally immersed within an extraordinary calmness. After some time, I felt it imperative that I return to the physical world. I descended, following the same path, and returned to my body through the gate at the top of my head. I consciously had to permeate my whole body with spiritual energy because it was frigid and my extremities were paralyzed. Finally I was able to move my hands and feet a little, and normal sensation gradually returned.

This happened in less than a year after I began yoga. During the next two years, the vishuddhi and anāhata chakras were awakened. My svādhishthāna, manipūra and sahasrāra chakras, as stated before, became active before the others.

After the sahasrāra chakra was awakened, my astral body was able to leave through the Brahman Gate. This enabled me to see the outside world during meditation, as the following example illustrates.

About ten years ago, while meditating as usual, I was able to "see" a stranger in the shrine, even though my eyes were closed and I was facing away from the other meditators. After meditation, when I greeted the other practitioners, I looked carefully at the old woman whom I had never seen before and saw the following scene extrasensorily.

I saw fields in the foothills of a large and beautiful mountain, which I recognized to be Mount Ōyama. A farmer, whom I realized to be the father of this woman, removed an old tumulus from one of the fields in order to enlarge his farm. The scene shifted and I saw that later one of his descendants and a few of the villagers had gone insane. This brought on the realization that the field was the site of an old battlefield in the war between the Tokugawa and Takeda families about four hundred years ago and that it was in this tumulus that a Takeda warrior who died in the battle was buried. When the farmer removed the tumulus, the warrior's soul had become angry and began to haunt the farmer and his descendants. This caused this woman's eldest son (the farmer's grandson) to become schizophrenic, which fact had induced her to come to the shrine to pray for help.

When I told her what I had seen, she was intensely surprised. Immediately, she went back to her birthplace, the place I had described in my vision, and ascertained that the other facts were true. The next day she came to the shrine and told us that when her son had been in the first year of high school, he had become so mentally unstable that he was unable to attend classes. He had stayed in his room all day long, writing in his diary that he was one of the Takeda warriors. His mother had had absolutely no idea what he meant. For the five years since then he had been in a mental hospital.

The mother implored me to help her son. For the next week, I negotiated intensively with the warrior's soul and finally persuaded him to leave the son. The woman came a week later and told me that the son had left the hospital, was returning to normal, and was already able to help her in the vegetable store.

This experience made it even clearer to me that events in the real world are deeply connected to both past events and to events in the spiritual world. Further, the experience dif-

fered from simple astral projection in that it was not accompanied by coldness and stiffness in the body nor by loss of
consciousness. Although my consciousness did dim somewhat, I was able to observe my surroundings precisely.
Similar experiences have since happened to me many times.

After the awakening of the sahasrāra chakra, the abilities
that had come through the awakening of the lower chakras
became stronger. At the same time, these chakras became active at a higher level and those which had not been completely awake, the vishuddhi and anāhata chakras, awoke steadily
from that point on. Further, as the sahasrāra became increasingly active in higher dimensions, I received the following
abilities:

> the ability to enter and affect the bodies of others;
> the ability to extend my existence and to include others
> within it;
> the ability to work freely, transcending karma and the
> restrictions of the body, and
> the ability to be granted union with Divine power.

The foregoing is a general description of the awakening
and activities of each chakra and the corresponding psi-
abilities derived from my experience over the last thirty
years. In conclusion, there are three points I wish to stress
concerning the awakening of chakras. First, chakra awakening is a process which must be undergone if the soul is to
evolve and if enlightenment is to be reached. One of the
Upanishads says that one cannot reach enlightenment
without awakening and recognizing the chakras, and I
believe this to be true. Second, it seems to me that whichever
chakra awakens first differs from person to person. Because
of one's individual karma and nature, there are characteristic chakras which are more easily activated and more liable
to be awakened by the movement of kundalinī in any given
individual. Finally, I wish to stress that overuse of the
paranormal ability of one chakra is apt to cause abnormality

or disease in the internal organs controlled by that chakra, and may even lead to an early death.

In the second half of this chapter, I would like to discuss the scientific research which I have conducted with the intent of experimentally verifying the truths experienced by myself and many others in spiritual practice. These discussions will hinge on the experimental observations obtained by the AMI and the Chakra Instrument, physiological recording devices which I developed.

The AMI—Apparatus for Measuring the Functional Conditions of Meridians and their Corresponding Internal Organs —is an instrument designed to measure the initial skin current, as well as the steady state current, in response to DC voltage externally applied at special acupuncture points located alongside the base of finger and toe nails. According to acupuncture theory, these special points—called "sei (well) points" are ostensibly the terminal points of meridians where the Ki energy either enters or exits the body. Experiments on some 2000 subjects strongly suggest that the relative magnitudes of such skin current values reflect the functional conditions of Ki energy in the meridians. The data from these experiments have been collated into a set of criteria for the assessment of functional conditions, whether normal or disordered in terms of excess, deficiency, or imbalance of Ki energy. Each of these criteria was established on the basis of statistical analysis and clinical examination. They are stored in the computer memory so that the diagnosis of the functional condition of each meridian can be automatically performed by the computer, which yields columns of numbers to produce a data chart.

The Chakra Instrument was designed to detect the energy generated in the body and then emitted from it in terms of various physical variables. Unlike the electroencephalograph and other instruments of electrophysiology, it is designed to detect minute energy changes (electric,

AMI

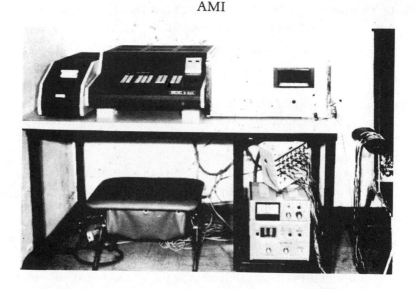

magnetic, optical) in the immediate environment of the subject. The detectors are installed inside a light-proof room which is electrostatically shielded by grounded lead sheeting embedded in the walls. Furthermore, the inside surfaces of the room are completely covered with thin aluminum sheeting, also grounded, so that the electric potential of the room is kept uniform and practically zero. A round disk copper electrode (d = 10cm) and a photo-electric cell as positioned 12-20 cm in front of the subject, level with the supposed location of a given chakra. This location is then monitored for the detection of electrical or optical signals generated by the subject, who is seated still and motionless on a chair. A detector of magnetic field fluctuation is placed on the floor in front or to the side of the subject. The signals are amplified and analyzed by a signal processor, a power spectrum analyzer, and other similar equipment located outside the room and then recorded simultaneously on a multichannel strip chart recorder along with conventional variables such as respiration, ECG, plethysmograph and GSR.

The Chakra Instrument
—Head Amplifier—

The
Chakra Instrument
—Electrode Box—

The Chakra Instrument
—DC Amplifier, Signal Processor—

Before summarizing the research, some more background is necessary. Much of the research begins with the hypothesis that the chakras are each closely connected with certain nervous plexuses and with their corresponding internal organs. This hypothesis is not original, but one that has been advanced and supported by studies of modern medical science as well as by the accounts of personal experiences of yoga practitioners accumulated over thousands of years. The supposed correspondence runs as follows:

Mūlādharā chakra — sacral and coccygeal plexuses
Svādhishthāna chakra — sacral plexus; urogenital
   system
Manipūra chakra — solar plexus; digestive system
Anāhata chakra — cardiac plexus; circulatory system
Vishuddhi chakra — superior, middle, and interior cer-
   vical ganglia; respiratory system
Ājnā chakra — pituitary body, interbrain, autonomic
   nervous system and hormone system
Sahasrāra chakra — cerebral cortex, entire nervous
   system; organs and tissues of the entire body

It is presumably due to this correspondence between chakras and nervous plexuses that yogis are thought to undergo gradual physiological changes which result in an increased range of activities of such internal organs as the heart, stomach, kidney, urinary bladder and sexual organs.

Various studies were carried out in order to investigate possible differences in the functional ranges of said organs between subjects who evidence no chakra activity and of subjects who do. These included a survey on disease susceptibility and an analysis of GSR responses to electrical stimulus at viscero-cutaneous reflex points, both of which are described below.

Members of our yoga society, about 100 in number, were divided into the three following groups.

Group A — comprised of those whose chakras evidenced advanced activity

Group B — comprised of those whose chakras evidenced beginning activity

Group C — comprised of those whose chakras were still dormant

This classification was carried out on the basis of extra-sensory observations made by myself and others with similar abilities, as well as one on the subjects' descriptions of their own experiences.

We first conducted a comparative study of disease susceptibility. Each individual filled out a questionnaire designed to determine to which category of disease he was susceptible. The answers were then scored, category by category. One point was assigned to every category of disease to which the subject was judged susceptible according to pre-set criteria. The scores of individuals were summed up, category by category, for each group and then divided by the number of individuals in the group to obtain the average susceptibility. The chart below shows each group's tendencies thus obtained, multiplied by 100.

In terms of the internal organs that are supposedly connected to a chakra, Group A showed the highest susceptibility to disease, Group B the second highest, and Group C the lowest. This result suggests that in comparison to Group C, Groups A and B are more susceptible to functional troubles in those internal organs connected with the chakras—a fact potentially indicative of the functional excitement and/or instability in those organs concerned.

We next studied the functional conditions of the internal organs by means of electrical stimulation of the head zones.

The viscero-cutaneous reflex points in the sympathetic nervous dermatomes of the heart, stomach, kidneys, and

Statistical Diagram of Susceptibility to Disease

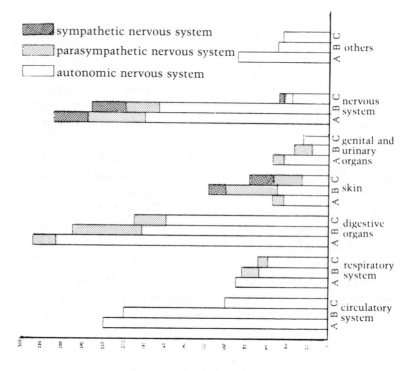

urogential organs (which approximately coincide in the trunk with the spinal dermatome) were chosen for electrical stimulation because these internal organs, again, are presumably closely connected with the anāhata, manipūra, and svādhishthāna chakras respectively. The GSR signals were monitored before and after stimulation as an indicator of the functional condition of the entire sympathetic nervous system as well as of the reactions of the sympathetic nerves controlling each internal organ.

Viscero-cutaneous Reflex Points
(Acupuncture points)

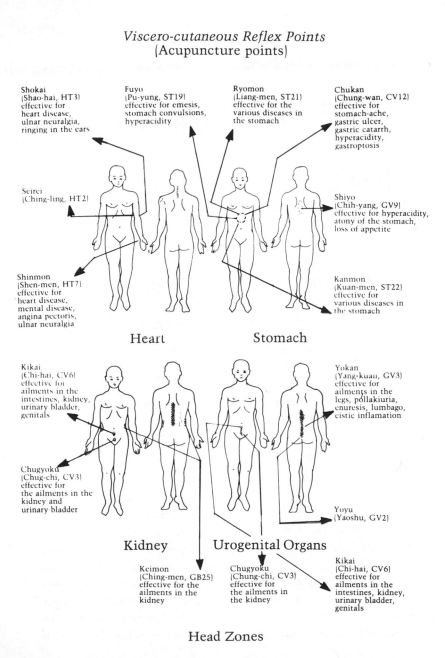

Shokai
(Shao-hai, HT3)
effective for
heart disease,
ulnar neuralgia,
ringing in the ears

Fuyo
(Pu-yung, ST19)
effective for emesis,
stomach convulsions,
hyperacidity

Ryomon
(Liang-men, ST21)
effective for the
various diseases in
the stomach

Chukan
(Chung-wan, CV12)
effective for
stomach-ache,
gastric catarrh,
hyperacidity,
gastroptosis

Seirei
(Ching-ling, HT2)

Shiyo
(Chih-yang, GV9)
effective for hyperacidity,
atony of the stomach,
loss of appetite

Shinmon
(Shen-men, HT7)
effective for
heart disease,
mental disease,
angina pectoris,
ulnar neuralgia

Kanmon
(Kuan-men, ST22)
effective for
various diseases in
the stomach

Heart   Stomach

Kikai
(Chi-hai, CV6)
effective for
ailments in the
intestines, kidney,
urinary bladder,
genitals

Yokan
(Yang-kuan, GV3)
effective for
ailments in the
legs, pollakiuria,
enuresis, lumbago,
cistic inflamation

Chugyoku
(Chug-chi, CV3)
effective for
the ailments in the
kidney and
urinary bladder

Yoyu
(Yaoshu, GV2)

Kidney   Urogenital Organs

Keimon
(Ching-men, GB25)
effective for the
ailments in the
kidney

Chugyoku
(Chung-chi, CV3)
effective for
the ailments in
the kidney

Kikai
(Chi-hai, CV6)
effective for
ailments in the
intestines, kidney,
urinary bladder,
genitals

Head Zones

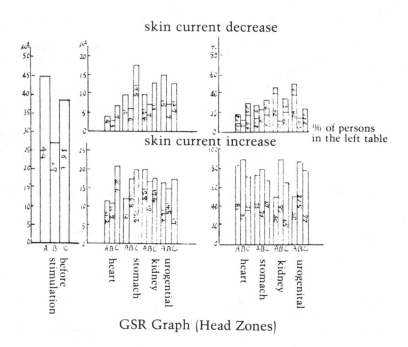

skin current decrease

skin current increase

% of persons in the left table

GSR Graph (Head Zones)

The comparative analysis of the GSR response is shown in the figure above. Group A showed the highest pre-stimulation GSR, Group C the second highest, and Group B the lowest. However, after stimulation, Groups A and B showed smaller GSR current than Group C for such organs as the heart, stomach and urogenital organs. For the kidneys alone the results were different; Group A showing the highest value. This result indicates that for Group A the reaction of the autonomic nervous system to external stimuli is predominantly parasympathetic. It is particularly worthy of note that Group A showed both the highest sympathetic activity before stimulation and the strongest parasympathetic reaction to external stimuli. This fact suggests that Group A subjects possess a wider range of dynamic balance between the two mutually opposing functions of the sympathetic and parasympathetic nervous systems than do the subjects in Group C.

Thus, it might be conjectured that those who have active chakras tend to have wider ranges of related autonomic activity, as revealed through functional excitement and/or instability, than do those whose chakras are not yet active.

In another series of investigations, the ECG and plethysmograph were employed to attempt to clarify any functional dissimilarities in the cardio-vascular systems of yogis and ordinary persons, as they might relate to the anāhata chakra.

The uppermost line in the figure (p. 266) for the ordinary person is the plethysmograph. It shows almost constant amplitudes with very slight base-line fluctuation. The pulse rate is 65.8/minute. In contrast to this, the plethysmograph of a yogi from Kakinanda, India, shows a periodic wavy fluctuation of the base line with 7-10 pulses superimposed on each wave. In many similar studies I found that, for ordinary subjects, the baseline fluctuation is minimal. This indicates that the basal blood flow is constant. In the case of yogis and other long-term spiritual practitioners, however, I have often noted large rhythmical fluctuations in the basal blood flow in addition to the regular pulsations of the heart beat. This implies to me that in cases like that of the Kakinanda yogi the autonomic nerves controlling the cardiovascular system— blood vessels in particular—function somehow in a rhythmic fashion. This, in turn, suggests that the functional range of the autonomic nerves, the range of dynamic balance beween the sympathetic and parasympathetic systems, is almost abnormally wider in yogis than in ordinary persons.

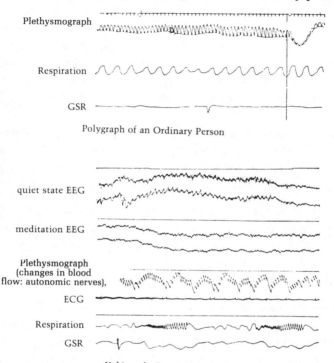

Polygraph of an Ordinary Person

Kakinanda Guru's Polygraph

As another example, here is some information on a yogi who claims to have awakened his anāhata chakra and to have achieved voluntary control over his cardiac functions. He was studied at the Lanaula Yoga Institute located near Bombay, India. The figure below shows the photo of the yogi's ECG recorded by the director of the Institute.

The fourth line of the ECG recording clearly indicates that the yogi's heart beat stopped for about five seconds. This feat was not achieved by the yogi's will power alone, however. The respiration monitored along with the ECG shows that the yogi's breathing also stopped when his heart stopped. Thus, holding the breath seems to facilitate the cardiac arrest, which is understandable from a neuro-physiological stand-point.

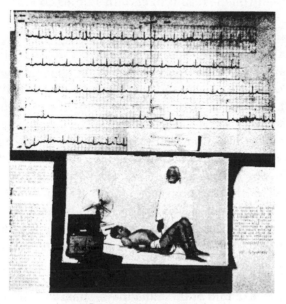

Lanaula Yogi's ECG

On the basis of the scientific observations described above, a proposition may be presented that the functional conditions of the automatic nerves and the internal organs controlled by them are different for yogis than for ordinary persons. It seems that yogis have a much wider range of autonomic activities. I also feel there are indications that this capacity increases as a person develops the chakras until finally he gains voluntary control over those internal organs connected with the chakras. Again, these observations suggest indirect scientific support for the existence of the chakras in that the activation and awakening of the chakras may have led to activation of the autonomic nerves and the organs that are supposedly connected with the chakras.

A variety of studies has been performed at our Institute with the Chakra Instrument and the AMI machine, which has led to some very provocative results. I would like to concentrate here on the results of certain studies conducted with subjects who had clearly displayed various types of chakra activity and psi-abilities.

Basically, we found that the type of psi ability evidenced does seem to be connected to the specific chakras supposedly responsible for them and that such subjects, in turn, do show characteristic patterns of abnormality in their meridian systems.

Further, we have found supportive evidence of the traditional notion that psi abilities can be classified into two types: the powers of reception and the powers of generation. The powers of reception seem to be linked to the lower chakras, the powers of generation to the higher.

To aid in understanding this distinction, let us examine Satyananda's explanation of which psi abilities appear when the lower chakras are awakened:

> The awakening of the mūlādhāra chakra brings complete knowledge of the kundalinī (the source of life forces stored in this chakra) and the power to awaken the kundalinī, thereby giving rise to abilities such as levitation, voluntary control of respiration, thought, emotion, and semen, and the ability to create desired fragrances.
>
> The awakening of the svādhishthāna chakra eliminates the fear of water, sharpens the sense of taste, and brings the power of intuitive perception leading to comprehensive knowledge of the astral body, the energy body, and the nādīs and meridians.
>
> The awakening of the manipūra chakra eliminates the fear of fire, brings the power to discover hidden treasures, the power to know the condition of one's own body, and the power to cure disease and maintain

good health by the use of the prāna of this chakra. Also, the power to absorb energy from the sahasrāra chakra may be obtained.

We can see from the above descriptions that these three chakras have one principle in common. They all function to maintain things as given and established. In other words, they have little potency to independently create something in the outside world. On the other hand, when the anāhata chakra is awakened, it is said that one gains the ability to actualize desires in the outside world. The principle of the anāhata chakra is love, and it is thought to contain the power to create energy and to transmit this energy to others.

The term ESP (extra-sensory perception) basically refers to the ability to perceive beyond the range of the five physical senses. According to our experience, those whose psi-abilities are predominantly of the ESP type, whether congenital or acquired through religious training, normally excel in receiving information both of animate and inanimate origin, e.g., telepathy, clairvoyance, psychometry. etc. However, they usually show little sign of the power to affect external objects or the minds of others and thereby to cause various phenomena to occur. Those with awakened anāhata chakras, on the other hand, strongly manifest such creative abilities as psychokinesis and psychic healing.

It has been found, as a result of repeated AMI testing, that those whose psi-abilities are predominantly of the ESP type tend to show apparent functional disorders — overactivity, underactivity, energy excess or deficiency — in the stomach, spleen (pancreas), triple heater, kidney, and the urinary bladder meridians. Most specifically, energy deficiency in the spleen-pancreas meridian is often noted. (See Fig. p. 270) Theoretically, these meridians are those that supply ki energy to the internal organs indicated by their names, which are, as mentioned earlier, related to the lower chakras.

AMI data – ESP type

Date Feb.20, 1975 ~~AM~~ PM
3 V 14 T(°C) 1010 mb 57 %

No. S-18

Name M. K. M(P) age

Birth Date

History of disease

Chief complaint,
Subjective symptoms

Blood presure
Diagnosis, Treatment

X̄ of Li, Ri	BP	1014.9642
	AP	38.9214
	P	976.0428
D̄ of difference X̄ of Li, Ri	BP	99.2142
	AP	7.6714
	P	97.8571
δ of L%,R%	BP	0.1056
	AP	0.4905
	P	0.0999

-----Lenient ——— regid

L%, R%:
BP.P deteriorated 0.78 | normal 0.85 | overactive 1.11 | 1.21
AP 0.49 | 0.60 | 1.21 | 1.59

D%:
BP.P stable 0.00 | 1.21 | unstable 1.80
AP 0.00 | 1.21 | 1.90

D̄/X̄:
BP.P deteriorated 0.08 | normal | unstable 0.15
AP 0.22 | 0.66

δ of L%,R%:
BP.P overactive 0.10 | stable | unstable 0.26
AP 0.21 | 0.71

meridian		D%	L%	R%	Li , Ri
Lung	BP	1.1288	-1.2601	1.1497	
	AP	0.8733	-2.5590	-2.3868	
	P	1.0760	1.2083	1.1004	0. 1279.
Large Intestine	BP	0.1310	1.0729	1.0601	996. 1.
	AP	1.3296	0.6937	0.9557	1167.
	P	0.2370	1.0880	1.0642	929. 2.
Heart Constrictor	BP	1.3203	1.1497	1.0207	1089. 270.
	AP	-2.3333	1.1458	0.6859	3.
	P	1.1557	1.1499	1.0340	1076. 372.
Diaphragm	BP	1.4917	1.0788	0.9330	4. 1167.
	AP	1.2774	1.1947	0.9429	446. 5.
	P	1.4122	1.0742	0.9326	1036. 267.
Triple Heater	BP	-3.4974	1.1507	0.8088	6. 1095.
	AP	1.5121	1.2949	0.9968	465. 7.
	P	-3.4274	1.1450	0.8013	947. 367.
Heart	BP	0.4132	0.9320	0.8916	8. 1168.
	AP	1.8001	-0.3699	0.7425	504. 9.
	P	0.5671	0.9544	0.8976	821. 388.
Small Intestine	BP	-1.9452	0.9655	-0.7753	10. 946.
	AP	0.3910	0.9043	0.8273	144. 11.
	P	-1.9416	0.9679	-0.7733	905. 289.
Spleen	BP	0.1713	1.0059	1.0226	12. 980.
	AP	0.0651	-0.3622	-0.3751	352. 13.
	P	0.1686	1.0316	1.0485	787. 322.
Liver	BP	0.3729	1.0532	1.0167	14. 1021.
	AP	0.3519	1.3231	1.2538	141. 15.
	P	0.3505	1.0424	1.0073	1038. 146.
Stomach	BP	0.1713	0.9685	0.9852	16. 1069.
	AP	0.8342	1.3026	1.1381	515. 17.
	P	0.2391	0.9551	0.9791	1032. 239.
Stomach Blanch	BP	0.4334	0.8995	0.9419	
	AP	1.7076	0.9943	0.6577	
	P	0.5732	0.8957	0.9532	
Gall Bladder	BP	0.5039	1.0581	1.0089	
	AP	0.5474	0.7990	0.6911	
	P	0.4680	1.0684	1.0215	
Kidney	BP	-1.8948	0.8709	1.0561	
	AP	0.1433	0.9994	1.0277	
	P	-1.9099	0.8658	1.0573	
Urinary Bladder	BP	0.5241	0.9566	0.9054	
	AP	0.7430	0.7605	0.6140	
	P	0.4731	0.9645	0.9170	

Many subjects whose psi-abilities fall predominantly into the PK classification have also been tested on the AMI machine. Their AMI data tend to show energy excess and instability in those meridians—the heart, heart constrictor, and diaphragm meridians—related to the function of the heart and, we think, the anāhata chakra. Besides such apparent functional disorders in the meridian system, those who are predominantly of the PK type often show arrhythmia and patterns characteristic of angina pectoris in their electrocardiograms.

Thus, the empirical knowledge handed down since ancient times and the personal accounts of modern–day yogis do find a degree of scientific support in the results of the AMI tests. In summary, those who have awakened the three lower chakras to some degree and have consequent ESP abilities do tend to show functional disorders in the meridians related to the digestive organs (controlled by the manipūra chakra), and/or urogenital organs (controlled by the mūlādhāra chakra and svādhishthāna chakra). Those who have awakened the anāhata chakra and have consequent psychokinetic abilities do tend to show functional disorders in the heart and the meridians related to the function of the heart, as well as show evidence of the AMI patterns seemingly linked to the three lower chakras.

Chakra instrument studies further clarify this relationship. Dr. A.K. Tebecis, a former professor at Canberra University who has studied yoga throughout Asia, visited our Institute in Tokyo. He is an earnest yogi who claims to have experienced astral projection due to the awakening of the kundalinī. Before being measured he told us that he had a chronic disorder of the digestive system and that he usually concentrated on the anāhata chakra during meditation. Dr. Tebecis was tested by the AMI and the chakra instrument and the following results were obtained.

The AMI test showed instabilities in the heart constrictor and diaphragm meridians, and also in the stomach, stomach

AMI data - A.K.T.

Date Aug. 25, 1975 AM/PM
3 V 28 T(°C) 1007 mb 59 %

No. 3900 S-22

Name A.K.T. (M)F
age

Birth Date 32

History of disease

Nothing major

Chief complaint,
Subjective symptoms

Dysfunction of digestive
system

Blood presure

Diagnosis, Treatment

X̄ of Li, Ri	BP	1103.0357
	AP	18.1178
	P	1084.9178
D̄ of difference / X̄ of Li, Ri	BP	140.2142
	AP	5.4785
	P	139.9928
σ of L%,R%	BP	0.1236
	AP	0.2728
	P	0.1265

-----Lenient ——— regid

L%, R%:

	deteriorated	normal	overactive	
BP.P	0.78	0.85	1.11	1.21
AP	0.49	0.60	1.21	1.59

D%:

	stable		variable function
BP.P	0.00	1.21	1.80
AP	0.00	1.21	1.90

D̄/X̄:

	deteriorated	normal	variable function
BP.P	0.08		0.15
AP	0.22		0.66

σ of L%,R%:

	excessive or ... function	stable	variable function
BP.P		0.10	0.26
AP		0.21	0.71

meridian		D%	L%	R%	Li , Ri
Lung	BP	1.3622	1.1287	0.9555	
	AP	-1.9895	0.9383	1.5399	
	P	1.4422	1.1318	0.9457	0.
Large Intestine	BP	-1.8186	1.1477	0.9165	1245.
	AP	1.3324	0.7285	1.1314	170.
	P	-1.8736	1.1547	0.9129	1.
Heart Constrictor	BP	1.3408	1.0371	0.8666	1054. 279.
	AP	0.6205	1.2418	1.0542	2. 1266.
	P	1.3186	1.0337	0.8635	132. 3.
Diaphragm	BP	1.3265	1.0045	0.8358	1011. 205.
	AP	0.9308	0.9493	1.2308	4. 1144.
	P	1.3650	1.0054	0.8292	225. 0.
Triple Heater	BP	-2.3892	1.0072	-0.7035	5. 956.
	AP	1.0221	1.3688	1.0597	191. 6.
	P	-2.3529	1.0011	-0.6975	1108. 172.
Heart	BP	0.7702	0.9709	0.8730	7. 922.
	AP	0.7483	1.3908	1.1645	223. 8.
	P	0.7421	0.9639	0.8681	1111. 248.
Small Intestine	BP	1.5618	0.9718	-0.7733	9. 776.
	AP	1.2046	0.5629	0.9272	192. 10.
	P	1.6115	0.9786	-0.7707	1071. 252.
Spleen	BP	0.0641	1.1767	1.1849	11. 963.
	AP	0.4928	0.7837	0.9327	211. 12.
	P	0.0450	1.1833	1.1891	1072. 102.
Liver	BP	0.4350	1.1858	1.1305	13. 853.
	AP	0.5658	1.3964	1.2253	168. 14.
	P	0.4135	1.1823	1.1289	1298. 142.
Stomach	BP	1.6260	1.0208	0.8141	15. 1307.
	AP	1.2594	0.6512	1.0321	169. 16.
	P	1.6779	1.0269	0.8104	1308. 1107.
Stomach Blanch	BP	0.5562	1.0253	0.9546	126.
	AP	1.6975	1.3522	0.8389	
	P	0.4907	1.0198	0.9565	
Gall Bladder	BP	0.2781	1.0752	1.0398	
	AP	1.2777	1.0762	0.6899	
	P	0.2285	1.0751	1.0457	
Kidney	BP	0.2852	1.1024	1.0661	
	AP	0.7666	0.7727	0.5409	
	P	0.2557	1.1079	1.0749	
Urinary Bladder	BP	0.1854	1.0271	1.0035	
	AP	0.0912	0.7230	0.6954	
	P	0.1821	1.0322	1.0087	

branch, and large intestine meridians, as well as energy deficiency and instability in the triple heater and small intestine meridians (which are thought to be controlled by the svādhishthāna chakra). This result is consistent with the chronic condition of his digestive system and his yogic practice on the anāhata chakra.

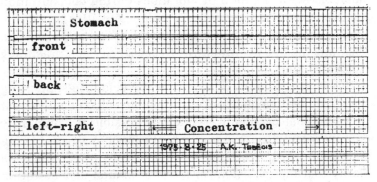

a. Chakra Instrument Data — A.K.T., Stomach

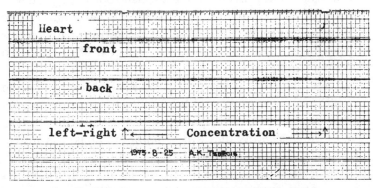

b. Chakra Instrument Data — A.K.T., Heart

In the Chakra Instrument test, his manipūra and ānahata chakras were chosen for measurement. The electric field vibrations in front of these chakras were monitored continuously for a total of three minutes. That is, three different periods — before concentration on the chakra, during concentration, and after concentration — were each monitored for one minute. No substantial change due to concentration was noticed in the test on the manipūra chakra, on which Dr. Tebecis did not usually concentrate in his daily yoga practice. However, the test on the anāhata chakra showed considerable intensification of vibrations during concentration relative to the signals monitored before and after concentration, as shown in Fig. b. It is to be noted here that the anāhata chakra is the one on which Dr. Tebecis had been practicing concentration.

This is one example of experimental evidence supporting the notion that mental concentration on a chakra activates it in a way that eventually renders it possible to voluntarily emit increasingly larger amounts of energy by means of concentration on it. We hope to demonstrate with increasing clarity that the persistent practice of mental concentration on a chakra awakens the chakra and that the psi-abilities associated with it begin to manifest.

As a result of improvements in the electrodes of the Chakra Instrument as well as reduction of the background electric field inside the room, the natures of the various psi energies in the chakras gradually became a bit clearer, as the two following examples will illustrate.

The AMI data of R.B. shows an excess of energy, and large instability between right and left in the stomach and spleen meridians (Pg. 275). The patterns in the data themselves suggest the possibility that R.B.'s manipūra chakra is active.

R.B. was next tested on the chakra instrument with an electrode placed 15-20 cms, in front of the manipūra chakra. When control readings were taken during the relaxed state, positive electric potential was observed around the manipūra chakra. The subject was then instructed to concentrate on the manipūra chakra, just as she usually did in her daily yoga practice. During this period of concentration, each

AMI data — R.B.

Meridian		D ♂	L ♂	R ♂	(L♂+R♂)/2
肺 Lung	BP	0.130	1.164	1.182	1.175
	AP	1.2v4	1.272	0.494	0.963
	P	0.153	1.163	1.184	1.174
大腸 Large Intestine	BP	0.086	0.949	0.937	0.943
	AP	0.519	1.041	0.809	0.925
	P	0.078	0.948	0.938	0.943
心包 Heart Constrictor	BP	0.130	0.868	0.686	0.677
	AP	1.037	1.157	0.694	0.625
	P	0.149	0.806	0.687	0.677
膈兪 Diaphragm	BP	0.275	0.893	0.855	0.874
	AP	1.554	1.272	0.578	0.925
	P	0.248	0.691	0.856	0.874
三焦 Triple Heater	BP	0.289	0.855	0.895	0.875
	AP	1.2v7	1.388	0.804	1.098
	P	0.313	0.852	0.895	0.874
心 Heart	BP	0.221	0.956	0.967	0.971
	AP	1.554	1.388	0.694	1.041
	P	0.252	0.953	0.988	0.971
小腸 Small Intestine	BP	0.313	0.817	-0.773	0.745
	AP	1.037	1.157	0.694	0.925
	P	0.301	0.815	-0.773	0.794
脾 Spleen	BP	-5.424	-1.742	0.994	-1.368
	AP	1.814	1.504	0.694	1.099
	P	-5.410	-1.744	0.995	-1.370
肝 Liver	BP	0.050	0.967	0.994	0.990
	AP	0.259	1.041	0.925	0.983
	P	0.055	0.987	0.994	0.990
胃 Stomach	BP	-3.012	1.069	-1.484	-1.277
	AP	0.517	1.157	1.368	1.273
	P	-3.013	1.06d	-1.485	-1.277
八邪 Stomach Branch	BP	0.724	0.824	0.924	0.874
	AP	0.260	0.925	0.609	0.867
	P	0.731	0.823	0.925	0.874
胆 Gall Bladder	BP	-2.363	-1.220	0.893	1.056
	AP	1.037	1.388	0.925	1.157
	P	-2.357	-1.219	0.893	1.056
腎 Kidney	BP	0.912	1.075	0.949	1.012
	AP	0.777	1.272	0.925	1.099
	P	0.901	1.074	0.949	1.011
膀胱 Urinary Bladder	BP	0.050	0.912	0.905	0.908
	AP	1.037	0.925	-0.462	0.893
	P	0.032	0.912	0.907	0.910

LI, RI:

0. 184.984 10.990 1. 187.842 5.996 2. 150.845 8.994 3. 148.940 6.989 4. 137.984 9.996 5. 140.842 5.996 6. 141.953 10.990 7. 135.919 4.993 8. 135.919 11.992 9. 142.271 6.989 10. 151.957 11. 11. 156.879 5.996 12. 129.886 9.996 13. 122.899 5.996 14. 170.052 10.990 25. 150.845 7.992 26. 144.970 7.992 27. 143.859 3.990 1.100 1.199

time she had a subjective sensation of psi energy ejection, the positive electric potential around the manipūra chakra vanished (Pg. 276).

These data lead to some interesting speculation. One might surmise that the psi energy generated a negative electrical potential which neutralized the positive electrical charge. However, it is also possible to postulate the creation of new physical energy. In fact, it is my opinion that the psi energy emitted from R.B.'s manipūra chakra actually extinguished the surrounding physical energy. I take this stand because the positive potential was precisely neutralized and because there was never any appearance of a negative potential.

276

Two days later the same experiment was repeated, but R.B. felt ill and could feel no psi energy ejection from the manipūra chakra. Concurrently, the positive electrical potential around the manipūra was not altered in any way.

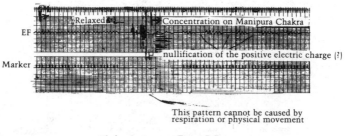

Chakra Instrument Data—R.B.

Let us turn to the next revealing example.

The AMI readings of subject M.Y. show instability and either excess or depletion of energy in the spleen, stomach, stomach branch, and small intestine meridians, following the patterns we have noted in those with active manipūra and svahdhishthāna chakras. Instability and excess of depletion of energy in the heart, heart constrictor, and diaphragm meridians are also noted, suggesting an active anāhata chakra.

Chakra instrument measurements were next taken of this subject with the electrode placed 15-20 cms, in front of the anāhata chakra. Recordings made as a control in the relaxed state showed positive electrical potential generated in the skin corresponding to the supposed location of the anāhata chakra (Fig. a, p. 278). She was then asked to concentrate on her anāhata chakra, and it was arranged that whenever she had the subjective sensation of psi energy being emitted from that chakra, she would press a button which caused a mark to be made on the chart (Fig. b, p. 278). It was found that when this mark appeared, the photoelectric cell signalled the presence of a weak light being generated in the light-proof

AMI data ∟M.Y.

Date June 24, 1977 朴 4:15
0.5 V 21 T(°C) 996 mb 70 %

No.

Name __M. Y.__ M/Ⓕ
age

Birth Date

History of disease

Chief complaint,
Subjective symptoms

Blood presure
Diagnosis, Treatment

X̄ of Li, Ri	BP	134.253
	AP	2.948
	P	131.305
D̄ of difference X̄ of Li, Ri	BP	-0.316
	AP	0.375
	P	-0.319
δ of L%,R%	BP	-0.327
	AP	0.379
	P	-0.330

-----Lenient ——— regid

L%, R%:
BP.P deteriorated / normal / overactive
| 0.78 | 0.85 | 1.11 | 1.21 |
AP
| 0.49 | 0.60 | 1.21 | 1.59 |

D%:
BP.P stable / unstable function
| 0.00 | 1.21 | 1.80 |
AP
| 0.00 | 1.21 | 1.90 |

D̄/X̄:
BP.P deteriorated function / normal / unstable function
| 0.08 | 0.15 |
AP
| 0.22 | 0.66 |

δ of L%,R%:
BP.P overactive or antiphlogistic function / stable / unstable function
| 0.10 | 0.26 |
AP
| 0.21 | 0.71 |

meridian		D%	L%	R%	(L%+R%)/2	Li, Ri
Lung	BP	0.423	0.945	1.079	1.012	0. 126.933
	AP	0.817	1.355	1.050	1.203	39.972
	P	0.450	0.936	1.080	1.008	1. 144.932
Large Intestine	BP	0.120	0.766	0.804	0.785	30.975
	AP	0.182	0.915	0.847	0.881	2. 102.889
	P	0.126	0.763	0.803	0.783	26.992
Heart Constrictor	BP	1.645	-1.250	-0.729	0.989	3. 107.994 24.986
	AP	-2.908	1.491	-0.406	0.949	4. 167.901
	P	1.590	-1.245	-0.736	0.990	43.984
Diaphragm	BP	0.000	-0.722	-0.722	-0.722	5. 97.920 11.977
	AP	0.908	1.152	0.813	0.983	6. 96.979
	P	0.023	-0.712	-0.720	-0.716	33.984
Triple Heater	BP	0.754	-0.632	0.871	-0.751	7. 96.979 23.983
	AP	0.182	1.152	1.084	1.118	8. 84.890
	P	0.769	-0.620	0.866	-0.743	33.984
Heart	BP	0.941	1.027	-0.729	0.878	9. 116.993 31.978
	AP	-2.091	1.491	0.711	1.101	10. 137.947
	P	0.898	1.017	-0.729	0.873	43.904
Small Intestine	BP	0.518	-0.328	-0.692	-0.610	11. 97.920 20.974
	AP	0.273	0.847	0.949	0.898	12. 70.921
	P	0.517	-0.521	-0.686	-0.603	24.986
Spleen	BP	-3.196	-2.122	1.109	-1.615	13. 92.950
	AP	-3.364	-1.933	0.677	1.305	27.995
	P	-3.148 δ	-2.126	1.119	-1.622	133.918 16.992
Liver	BP	0.445 '	0.908	1.049	0.978	24. 160.916
	AP	0.638	0.983	0.745	0.864	18.998
	P	0.467	0.906	1.056	0.981	25. 126.933 19.971
Stomach	BP	-1.999	0.952	-1.585	-1.269	26. 127.873
	AP	1.000	1.389	-1.763	1.576	21.977
	P	-1.998	0.942	-1.581	-1.262	27. 150.976 12.980
Stomach Blanch	BP	-2.305	0.863	-1.593	-1.228	
	AP	0.544	1.152	1.355	1.254	
	P	-2.320	0.856	-1.599	-1.228	
Gall Bladder	BP	0.306	1.094	0.997	1.406	
	AP	0.182	0.644	0.576	0.610	
	P	0.305	1.104	1.006	1.055	
Kidney	BP	0.799	1.198	0.945	1.072	
	AP	0.088	0.644	0.677	0.660	
	P	0.811	1.211	0.951	1.081	
Urinary Bladder	BP	0.543	0.952	1.124	1.038	
	AP	0.817	0.745	-0.440	0.592	
	P	0.571	0.957	1.139	1.048	

room (Figure b, the hump in the bottom line), and the elec-
rodes of the chakra monitor detected electrical energy of
high potential and frequency — 10kc/s to 100kc/s (Figure b,
top line).

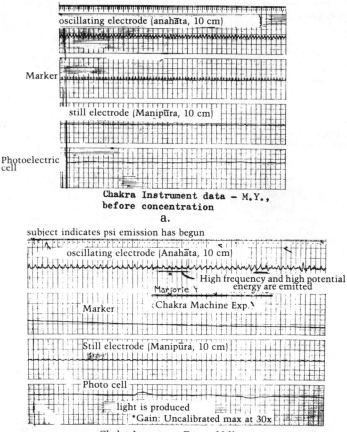

Chakra Instrument data - M.Y.,
before concentration
a.

Chakra Instrument Data —M.Y.,
during concentration

b.

This set of data implies quite profoundly that psi energy working in the anāhata chakra may just be able to create energy in the physical dimension (light, electricity, etc.).

The recordings made with R.B. and M.Y. on the AMI and Chakra Instrument point to the possibility that the psi energy working in the chakras can extinguish or create energy in the physical dimension. These two properties are of great significance and, if they can be further substantiated, would indicate the need for a basic revision of the Law of Conservation of Energy as presently formulated in modern physics.

These results may also hold the clue to understanding the underlying principles of psychic healing, particularly as manifested in as dramatic a form as psychic surgery. If it is true that psi energy can extinguish the energy of the physical dimension, then matter—which is an agglomeration of physical energy—can also be extinguished or "dissolved" by it. Utilizing this mechanism, it might be possible that the psychic surgeon's hands can temporarily dissolve an opening into the patient's body and that the psi energy emitted from the fingers can dissolve diseased areas in the corpus of the patient.

Further, if psi energy can extinguish or create physical energy, traditional religious teachings such as those which assert that the physical world is a manifestation of mind and that mind is able to control matter may possess a degree of truth heretofore unrealized by most of mankind.

I feel that the continuation of research into the nature of psi energies, by many others as well as myself, will lead to considerable change in our views of matter, of mind and body, of human beings, and of the world itself.

Summary

I would like to end, in outline form, with a summary of my views on the chakras and nādīs.

1. The existence of chakras and nādīs
   A. Both my personal experience and experiments lead me to believe that chakras and nādīs exist.
   B. My belief in the existence of the nādīs stems from three sources:
      a. The results obtained with the AMI and the chakra instrument indicate that there are close connections between psi energy, the chakras, and the meridians.
      b. The flows of the nādīs seem to correspond much more closely to those of the meridians than those of the nervous system.
      c. Scientific experimentation has turned up evidence in support of traditional meridian theory.
2. The nature and function of chakras and nādīs
   A. The chakras are the centers of the body's energy systems, which exist in each of the three different dimensions: physical, astral, and causal.
   B. Each chakra has three levels, and each level of the chakra functions in the corresponding dimension. These functions, however, are closely related to each other.

C. The chakras act as intermediaries between the three dimensions, and can convert the energy of one dimension into that of another.

D. The chakras are also intermediaries between the physical body and consciousness, between the astral body and manas, and between the causal body and the karana, that is, between the body and the mind of each dimension. Further, the chakras act to integrate the interrelationship between the three bodies and minds in a holistic manner.

E. Each chakra has its own sounds (nāda and mantra) and geometrical figure (yantra), which can be perceived extrasensorily.

F. The chakras, as the centers of the energy system of the physical dimension, seem to correspond to certain important points of acupuncture, and the energy channels—the nādīs—seem to be essentially the same as the meridians.

G. The aura (wheel of light) of an awakened chakra shines more brightly and is larger than that of a dormant chakra. Even in the same person, an awakened chakra shines more brightly than the others, and the energy ejected from that chakra is stronger.

H. The awakening of a chakra is recognized by the awakening of psi abilities related to that chakra.

3. The Relation Between Karma and the Chakras

A. In each person, one chakra is naturally more active than the others, but which one it is differs from person to person according to the individual's karma and nature.

B. Which chakra is most easily awakened by yoga practice depends again on karma and on the person's nature. The chakra which is working most actively due to these two factors generally awakens first.

4. Spiritual Enlightenment and the Chakras

To awaken the chakras is of extreme importance in spiritual advancement towards enlightenment. It is very difficult to achieve enlightenment without the awakening of the chakras.

5. Dangerous Conduct: Abuse of One Chakra

Overuse of one chakra is dangerous. For example, overuse of the manipūra chakra causes disease in the digestive organs and that of the anahata leads to heart disease. To carry such overuse beyond a certain limit may even lead to death.

Profile of the Author

Dr. Hiroshi Motoyama, the well-known Japanese scholar, was born on Shōdō Island in Kagawa Prefecture, Japan. Now in his late fifties, Dr. Motoyama graduated from the Tokyo University of Education with Ph. D. degrees in philosophy and clinical psychology.

Dr. Motoyama is both a scientist, trained in empirical methodology, and a psychic who has experientially gained deep philosophical knowledge. He is the head priest of Tamamitsu Shrine in Tokyo, and a serious yogi well-versed in the yoga treatises. His scientific endeavors resulted in the establishment of the Institute for Religious Psychology, a research facility, and the International Association for Religion and Parapsychology, an international organization whose members perform research in these and related fields. Dr. Motoyama is the author of over 30 books and numerous monographs and papers, and has traveled widely throughout the world, participating in conferences and presenting his work.

In recognition of his important work in the field, UNESCO selected him in 1974 as one of the world's ten foremost parapsychologists. He has also been honored by several renowned scientific and religious organizations and serves as an advisor to various international associations and institutes in related fields.

Readers who wish to learn more about Dr. Motoyama's work, and those who share his interest in the scientific research of Psi phenomena and the study of religious experience, may contact the International Association for Religion and Parapsychology (IARP) at the following addresses:

IARP (Main Office)
4-11-7 Inokashira
Mitaka-shi
Tokyo 181
Japan
Telephone: (0422) 48-3535

IARP (U.S. Branch)
399 Sunset Drive
Encinitas, Calif. 92024
Telephone: (714) 753-8857

Index

A

abdominal breathing, 78
Absolute, 20, 32
acupuncture, 26, 27, 43, 52
acupuncture meridians, See meridians
agnisar kriyā (fire breathing), 93, 106, 120
ajapa-japa, 123-124
ājnā chakra, 25, 69; aura, 25, 212; awakening of author's, 251-253; diagram, 210; etymology, 210; in Gorakshashatakam, 188; and karma, 253; and karma purification, 36, 110-111, 211; method for awakening, 109-111, 124; and mūlādhāra chakra, 211; Satyananda's description, 210-213; and shambhavi mudrā, 97, 98; in Shat-chakra-nirūpana, 175-178; symbol, 210; in Upanishads, 133
ākāshā (void), 102, 123, 234
ākāshi mudrā (consciousness of inner space), 86, 98
alambushā nādī, 147
amā-kalā (nectar-dripping phase of moon), 180, 181
Amaterasu Okami, 20
ambrosia, 23, 165, 169, 233; See also nectar
AMI (apparatus for measuring meridian and organ functions), 257, 268, 271, 276, 279; and anāhata chakra, 271, 276; and manipūra chakra, 275
anāhata chakra, 28, 65; aura, 25; author's awakening, 246-249; bīja mantra, 184-239; diagram, 232;

etymology, 228; in Gorakshashatakam, 186; and nonattachment, 246, 247; method for awakening, 122-124; and paranormal abilities, 231; preconditions for awakening, 230, 231; and psychic healing, 231, 248; and purification, 36; Satyananda's description, 227-232; in Shat-chakra-nirūpana, 172, 173; in Upanishads, 133; yantra, 232
animal centers (chakras), 206, 218
ankle bending, 45
ankle cranking, 46
ankle rotation, 46
antaranga kumbhaka (internal breath retention), 81
antaranga (inner) trātaka, 119
Antaratma (the True Self), 175
apana vayu, 92, 116, 157, 162, 225, 226
apas (water element), 223
ardha matsyendrāsana (half spinal twist), 68, 69
āsanas, 32, 40-41, 109: defined, 40-41; general instructions, 41-43
ashvini (horse) mudrā, 92, 99-100
astral body, 22, 23, 25, 33, 77, 102, 126, 191, 202; appearance, 212
astral centers (chakras), 201-203
astral projection, 204
Ātmā, 175, 177, 180, 183, 187,188
Atman, 30, 230
auras (of chakras), 24-25
autonomic nervous system, and chakra activity, 264, 265-268
Avalokiteshvāra (Kannon), 20, 224
Avalon, Arthur, See Sir John Woodroffe
Ayurveda, 43, 152

287

288

B

Baddha yoni āsana, 74
bahiranga kumbhaka (external breath retention), 82
bahiranga trātaka (gazing at external object), 119
bandha (psychic lock), 33, 40, 88-94
Benzaiten (Sarasvati), 223
bhakti yoga, 203
bhastrika (bellows) prānāyāma, 82-84, 127
bhu namanāsana (spinal twist prostration pose), 69-70
bhujangani mudrā (snake breathing), 99
bhujangāsana (cobra pose), 60-61
Bihar School of Yoga, 209
bīja (seed) mantra, 165, 170, 183, 184
Blavatsky, Mme. H. P., 190
Brahma, 21, 131, 175, 222
Brahma granthi (Knot of Brahma), 143, 216
Brahma nādī, 164, 219
Brahman, 30, 131, 173, 175, 180, 181, 183, 186, 230
Brahman gate, 25, 26, 106, 128, 133, 141, 162, 179, 241, 254
breath retention, See kumbhaka
Brhandaranyaka Upanishad, 158
brow chakra, 196
Buddha, 20
buddhi (intelligence), 177, 179

C

cardiac plexus, 197
cardiovascular system (of yogis), 266
causal body, 22, 25, 131, 211
celibacy, 73, 92
chaitanyā (fully awakened consciousness), 212
chakra, 22-25; abuse of, 256, 285; author's description of location and functions, 24-25; causal, 283; and Christian mythology, 197; Leadbeater's description, 192-197; and moral development, 193-194; and nerve plexuses, 197; physical, 283; Satyananda's definition,

209-210; scientific evidence of existence, 257-281, 283
chakra awakening, 27-29, 54; effects of, 128; methods for, 109-118
Chakra Instrument, 257-258, 273, 281; anāhata chakra data, 278; manipūra chakra data, 275-278
The Chakras, 184, 189, 190
chest breathing, 78
chin mudrā, 72, 73, 96-97
chitra nādī, 153, 155, 218-219
chītrinī nādī, 155, 164-165, 176
"circulation of light" (shōshūten), 143, 253
clairaudience, 135, 217
clairvoyance, 217, 269
conception vessel meridian, 25, 147
contentment, 37
continence, 35, 36
coronary plexus, 197
crow-walking, 49
crown chakra, 196-197
Cūdamini Upanishad, 131, 133, 147

D

Dākinī, 166
dakshina nauli, 121
devadatta vāyu, 159
dhanamjaya vāyu, 159
dhanurāsana (bow pose), 61-62, 114
dhārāna (concentration), 32
dhyāna (meditation), 32, 167, 176
Dhyānabindu Upanishad, 193
digestive fire (of manipūra chakra), 224
disease susceptibility study of yoga practitioners, 261
dynamic spinal twist, 67

E

earth element, 214
ECG (electrocardiogram), 258, 266, 271
enlightenment (and chakra awakening), 284, 285
esotericism, 19-21
ESP (extra-sensory perception), 27; type (of PSI ability), 269; and meridian dysfunction, 269, 271